APPLES
of
NORTH
AMERICA

TOM BURFORD

Apples

OF NORTH AMERICA

*192 Exceptional Varieties
for Gardeners,
Growers, and Cooks*

Timber Press

PORTLAND | LONDON

Photography credits appear on page 284.

Published in 2013 by Timber Press, Inc.

The Haseltine Building
133 S.W. Second Avenue, Suite 450
Portland, Oregon 97204-3527
timberpress.com

2 The Quadrant
135 Salusbury Road
London NW6 6RJ
timberpress.co.uk

Printed in China
Book design by Patrick Barber

Library of Congress Cataloging-in-Publication Data

Burford, Tom.
    Apples of North America: 192 exceptional varieties for gardeners, growers, and
cooks/Tom Burford.—1st ed.
        p. cm.
    Includes bibliographical references and index.
    ISBN 978-1-60469-249-5
    1. Apples—Varieties—North America. 2. Apples—North America. I. Title.
    SB363.3.A1B87 2013
    634′.11—dc23   2012045130

*To the memories
of my parents and brother*
Thomas Russell Burford
Frances Antoinette Whitehead
and
Walter Russell Burford

Contents

An Introduction and Brief History

MY INTRODUCTION TO the table of delight and plenty began on a very hot late August day in 1935 when my mother and grandmother set off with a white oak woven basket designated for apple picking. They headed to the nearby orchard to harvest Smokehouse apples, a nineteenth-century Pennsylvania fruit which ripen over a long period in late summer and early fall and are noted for becoming caramelized and high-flavored when fried. On arrival my mother exclaimed they must hurry back to the house with no apples for supper. Ten minutes later I entered the world, barely escaping drawing my first earthly breath in the shade of an apple tree.

I've spent most of my life among apples trees in the Blue Ridge Mountains of Virginia, an apple-growing region since the early eighteenth century.

That orchard, in the foothills of the Blue Ridge Mountains of Virginia, contained about one hundred varieties and reflected the history of the apple in America. The trees in the orchard included varieties intended for dessert, cooking, cider, drying, applesauce, apple butter, and even livestock food. The apples ripened from June until November and came from storage until the crop was ready the next year.

In these isolated mountains with limited communications one became naïve, unaware that but few had access to the hundreds of varieties readily available that could be grafted, grown, and eaten. I was later to learn that not many people had the necessary skill or inclination to make an apple tree or explore a different variety. It became the classic negative axiom "let someone else do it" and indeed the wrong ones did, destroying the apple culture of America in the process.

For fifty years I painfully watched the disappearance of the apple culture and the emergence of so-called beautiful apples, a source of malnourishment that even posed a consumption risk from chemical contamination. Eating with our eyes brought this tasteless object to the fruit bowls of America. And the diversity of available varieties dropped to a few dozen. One look at the apple display in a supermarket should bring tears and an exclamation of "what have we done to you?"

The response from apple connoisseurs, some fanatical like I, and organizations like the North American Fruit Explorers (founded in 1965 out of a round-robin correspondence group on uncommon fruits) was to begin distributing lesser-known apple varieties and teach grafting classes. These efforts would launch the unending search, once again, for apples of flavor instead of beauty and market value. Now, varieties that are left are not only retrieved from our rich American heritage, perhaps the greatest apple diversity in the modern world, but science has intervened to provide modern varieties that meet the challenge of the onslaught of pests and diseases that have emerged. The apple is zooming to the forefront as a food commodity in a new American agriculture. I am in the misunderstood but enviable position of having experienced a production and richness of the food world that today we are struggling to recapture. I am optimistic, however, that we can again make eating and the ritual of eating a joy for all. This is epitomized by what is happening to the apple.

I have presented 192 North American apple varieties in this book, but this is just a handful of the thousands that deserve recognition and adulation. As you

A crate of Wickson Crab, a super sweet variety developed in California by plant breeder Albert Etter.

explore this world, be aware and understanding that every apple has its moment when it expresses itself at the zenith of flavor. Seldom, however, do we have this sensory experience. Most often, the apple is trying to define itself and will be less sweet or tart or crisp or melting than it holds the potential to be, but it will still satisfy our longing for the apple-taste experience. In the hundreds of apple tastings I have conducted, the same apple variety can bring the countenance of pleasure to one ("the best apple I ever ate") and distaste to another ("are you sure this isn't a green persimmon?"). Think of each apple as distinctive and strive to escape the ones that all taste and look the same, as most from the supermarket do. It is an adventure.

This book is intended to be practical instructions, history lessons, folklore, and particularly, inspiration and motivation—not necessarily to grow your own apples, but as an apple consumer to demand what has been denied. Above all, it is to encourage and support others to produce apples in great abundance. Then apples can, once again, be bartered, shared, and bestowed as gifts to nourish the mind, body, and soul: an unending, joyful adventure.

A Brief History of the Apple

THE STORY OF the apple begins in Asia Minor in the region of Kazakhstan, where wild apple orchards still exist today with broad varietal diversity. From here a genetic explosion would evolve into one of the major food commodities of the world. Along and beyond the fabled maritime and overland silk routes of the East, seeds were dispersed to the temperate zones of the world by both humans and beasts and the culture of the apple began. By 2500 B.C. apples were growing throughout Mesopotamia and Persia and varieties were dispersed, intentionally planted, and named to become part of the food cultures of the world.

The classical Greek period of the fifth to fourth centuries B.C. contained considerable horticultural knowledge, particularly regarding the act of grafting in which specific apples of merit are deliberately joined to a separate root system. The Greek writer Theophrastus was aware that apple seeds would not produce the same apple when planted and wrote, "Seedlings of . . . apples produce an inferior kind which is acid instead of sweet . . . and this is why men graft." Armed with information gained from the Greek horticultural experience, the Roman Empire of the first century B.C. further advanced the art and science of fruit growing. The Roman writer Pliny the Elder in 77–79 A.D. described more than twenty named varieties in his *Natural History*. As the Romans migrated abroad to extend their empire, orchards were established throughout continental Europe and into the British Isles.

Beginning in the early 1600s, sacks of seeds and named apple trees of European heritage were brought across a treacherous Atlantic Ocean and mingled with the new apple varieties of America to make orchards of a magnitude the world had never seen. *Malus pumila*, the domestic apple we know today on supermarket shelves, is not a native fruit of America. A few native crabapples, notably *Malus angustifolia*, *Malus ioensis*, and *Malus coronaria*, were found on arrival by the colonists but were not a significant food commodity. Seeds, buds, and small trees of the apples from the British Isles and Europe trickled into the temperate zones of the New World to establish the apple as a new food commodity. By the 1650s, apple orchards with thousands of trees had been planted specifically for cider production, a replacement for the water that so often was unfit to drink.

Production was so successful that by 1820 cider was not only the national beverage but cider became a currency, a major commodity for barter. From the great cider orchards of America with tens of thousands of trees planted from the random seeds collected from the ubiquitous cider presses, a tree occasionally would produce a fruit with desirable eating qualities. Cider seedling orchards became the natural breeding laboratories for the selection of apples that were suitable for eating out of hand. Every seed in every apple is a new variety; so, planting the seeds of named varieties from abroad in the rich soil of the colonies produced many different varieties. Trueness to name was unimportant because the purpose of the apple in new America was focused on producing juice for cider.

With buds from the acclimated varieties grafted to any seedling stock and grown out for a few years in the first American fruit tree nurseries, orchards with named apple selections were planted for the first time in America. After the establishment of orchards along the Eastern seaboard, the second wave of new American varieties began with the distribution of seedling trees by nurserymen like John Chapman (better known as Johnny Appleseed) along the routes of westward migration spurred on by the Homestead acts beginning in 1862 and by manifest destiny. These "Joe" Appleseed seedling trees added hundreds, even thousands, of new American varieties to central and western America.

By 1850 uncounted named apple varieties for fresh eating, cooking, cider making, apple butter, applesauce, drying, pickling, vinegar, wine, and even livestock food were listed in nursery catalogs. There was remarkable acclimated diversity of varieties in New England, the mid-Atlantic, the upper Midwest, and the Northwest—and even some varieties adapted to the Deep South. In 1905, W. H. Ragan's *Nomenclature of the Apple: Catalogue of Known Varieties Referred to in American Publications from 1804–1904* listed 17,000 cultivars.

At a time of such abundance, the future state of the apple would have been almost unthinkable. But the enactment of Prohibition in 1919—as well as the later rejection of natural apple juice (both sweet and fermented) in favor of soft drinks—greatly damaged the cider industry. After World War ii, with flight from farm and orchard, grafting by orchardists of regional varieties was seldom practiced and even the great agricultural skill of grafting was generationally interrupted and forgotten. By the middle of the twentieth century, large conglomerate nurseries would have gained control of varietal diversity and the number of offerings in the enticing color catalogs would drop to only a few dozen.

Happily, in the early decades of the twenty-first century we are now striving to return to the dynamic and richness of the apple culture that was abandoned. The apple future is full of promise.

Part One
APPLE
VARIETIES
A TO Z

E ACH OF THE nearly 200 varieties portrayed in this section was selected for a variety of reasons including flavor, interesting historical context, or the sheer remarkability of existence after being lost for a period to the world of cultivation, as has been the fate of many heirloom apples. The apples photographed were deliberately selected not as stereotypical specimens—the perfect fruit of the supermarket ilk— but rather as apples that would be found on the tree sometimes with less color, splashes of sooty blotch, fly speck, or even an insect bite or scab deformity. These are apples of the real world.

Choosing which varieties to include in this book was difficult because so many loomed with merit. It is important to note that selection was made from what was available in the 2011 and 2012 crops and some desirable candidates were biennial and thus unavailable. Others did not survive the transport to the photo studio and were substituted. Apples were chosen to express geographic diversity. Finally, taste being subjective, many of those represented may not be preferred by some, but others will praise their merits.

For each apple, general comments are followed by an array of categories, which combined reveal the intimate details of the apple. I offer here a short explanation on how to interpret these descriptions.

OTHER NAMES Some apples have dozens of names, most arising from the fruit's shape, taste, or place of origin. Original names were often unintentionally corrupted when called a like-sounding name by others or confused with a look-alike variety. There was an intentional corruption around 1897 when the American Pomological Society assigned a single name to apple varieties with multiple words in their name.

HISTORY Documents that tell the story of an apple, especially those of the past, can be accurately detailed, sketchy, fabricated, embellished, and often, apocryphal. Sometimes little is known about the fruit and occasionally another will leave an elaborate trail. Many of the history descriptions of varieties in this book express my personal experience with the apple.

EXTERIOR AND INTERIOR DESCRIPTIONS AND TREE CHARACTERISTICS The first two of these categories summarize the typical size, shape, and coloring (skin and flesh) of the apple, along with flavor, aroma, and other distinguishing elements. The third offers an overview of the tree's growth habit and vigor, along with its known tendency to bear early or slowly, annually or biennially, or to produce light or heavy crops; other tree features such as bloom time or pollination prowess are included when applicable.

DISEASE RESISTANCE The apple's resistance or susceptibility to the major apple diseases (apple scab, cedar apple rust, and fireblight) is recorded. When the apple is known to be particularly affected by a specific pest or disease, more details are included.

SEASON OF RIPENING A general season of ripening, early summer through late winter, is assigned to each apple but it must be noted that ripening times given, in this book as well as in catalog descriptions, are not always accurate. Summer-ripening apples can run into early fall, and winter apples may never fully ripen if planted in a region so cold that the maturity time is cut short. We can only approximate the season of ripening to offer a guideline for watching and testing. Global warming has also played a role in changing the ripening time and chilling hours of apples. The time to harvest will be learned by doing.

USES This synopsis of the best use or uses of the variety is culled from historical knowledge and personal experience. The uses range in complexity from simply eating the apple as dessert; baking, frying, or drying the slices; or transforming the apple into cider, vinegar, butter, sauce, or jelly.

STORAGE QUALITY The rating of each apple on a scale from excellent to poor roughly corresponds to how long the apple will keep in common storage before degrading. These ratings—excellent (keeps for up to one year); very good (keeps for up to six months), good (keeps for two months), fair (keeps for one month), and poor (only keeps for a few weeks)—are approximations dependent upon the condition of the apple when harvested, the cultivar, and how the apple is stored. See page 245 for more information on harvesting and storing apples.

American Beauty

I ONCE INCLUDED American Beauty on a list of my favorite dessert apples compiled for the Pennsylvania-based Backyard Fruit Growers organization. My appreciation for the sweet and slightly floral quality of this variety hasn't waned, but since that time I've added a few hundred more apples with merit to my mental catalog. My "favorite" apple is often the last one I ate.

OTHER NAMES Beauty of America, Sterling, Sterling Beauty. The 1897 name change to Sterling reflected the American Pomological Society's erstwhile effort to assign a single name to every apple variety.

HISTORY The origin date of this variety is unknown; it was found at the site of an old orchard near Sterling, Massachusetts. It was occasionally grown in the mid-Atlantic region during the early twentieth century and old trees bearing uncommonly large fruit are still found in Virginia and Maryland.

EXTERIOR DESCRIPTION This apple grows large and round and has a faint ribbing. The yellowish-green background is covered by a maroon-red blush (sometimes streaked) and a rough-textured russet dotted with light-colored lenticels.

INTERIOR DESCRIPTION The cream-colored flesh is dense, juicy, and sweet with a vinous overtone. It has a very small core.

TREE CHARACTERISTICS It is a productive annual bearer.

DISEASE RESISTANCE Moderately resistant to the major apple diseases

SEASON OF RIPENING Early fall

USES Primarily dessert, but also for baking

STORAGE QUALITY Good

American Summer Pearmain

LIKE PUMPKIN SWEET, this apple often bursts when fully ripe on the tree, splattering upon contact with the ground and immediately attracting varmints and insects. The taste when mature is very sweet rather than tart, a factor which contributed to its prominence for dessert and cider making before granulated sugar was readily available.

OTHER NAMES American Pearmain, Early Summer Pearmain, Summer Pearmain, Watkins Early. In the mid-Atlantic region, it was simply called Pearmain.

HISTORY Date and place of origin are not known. In his 1817 work, *A View of the Cultivation of Fruit Trees*, William Coxe refers to it as Early Summer Pearmain and states that the apple was "frequently preferred to a fine pear."

EXTERIOR DESCRIPTION Fruit is moderately sized, slightly oblong, and deeply indented on both the blossom and stem ends. When exposed to the sun, the apple develops occasionally striped bright purple-red skin and profuse lenticels. In the shade, the skin is dull red with faint dots.

INTERIOR DESCRIPTION The yellowish flesh is juicy, tender, and aromatic with large cells.

TREE CHARACTERISTICS The growth is moderate and upright. In his 1867 book, *Apples*, the American pomologist John Warder describes the tree as hardy in New England.

DISEASE RESISTANCE Susceptible to fireblight; moderately resistant to other major apple diseases.

SEASON OF RIPENING Midsummer. It ripens over two to three weeks.

USES Dessert, baking, and frying

STORAGE QUALITY Fair

Arkansas Black

As a boy my father warned me never to hit anyone in the head with this very hard apple: it would kill. This durability along with its excellent keeping quality—a few months in storage will turn the flesh a rich yellow color and enhance the flavor—contributed to the rise of Arkansas Black as a major popular variety sold nationally by fruit tree nurseries.

OTHER NAMES Ark Black. It is sometimes confused with the dissimilar Black Twig. I once told a white lie to an octogenarian who came to the nursery to get another tree of Arkansas Black but held a Black Twig apple in his hand. His daughter agreed the truth should not be spoken.

HISTORY It is recognized by early sources as having been first produced in 1870 in the orchard of a Mr. Brathwaite, approximately one and a half miles northwest of Bentonville, Arkansas. The exact parentage is unknown but it is speculated to be a Winesap seedling. Seedling apple orchards had been first planted in the Ozarks (some by the Cherokee) as early as 1822, and by 1900 Benton County had forty thousand acres of production orchards with fresh fruit, apple drying, brandy, and vinegar making as major industries.

EXTERIOR DESCRIPTION A medium-sized, regularly round apple. The lively red skin deepens to purplish red or nearly black on the sun-exposed side of the fruit. Skin is smooth with a waxy or greasy finish, especially after storage.

INTERIOR DESCRIPTION Yellowish flesh is very hard and crisp with a distinctive aromatic flavor.

TREE CHARACTERISTICS The tree is moderately vigorous in growth with long slender branches. It has dark reddish-olive bark and dark green leaves that are somewhat folded and waved. In the past this pollen-sterile tree was pollinated with Ben Davis, Winter Banana, Yates, or Grimes Golden; now it is more often pollinated with Golden Delicious and Red Delicious or fruitless crabapples.

DISEASE RESISTANCE Susceptible to apple scab and fireblight; generally resistant to the other major apple diseases. It appears to be less susceptible to codling moth larvae damage because of its thick tough skin.

SEASON OF RIPENING Late fall

USES Dessert, pie making, frying, apple butter, and cider

STORAGE QUALITY Excellent

Bailey Sweet

IN HIS 1905 book, *Apples of New York*, S. A. Beach describes Bailey Sweet as "a very beautiful red apple, distinctly sweet and of very good quality" but he goes on to criticize its keeping quality, hardiness, and disease resistance. Indeed, I have found this early description to be quite apt; it needs a good spray program in order to be productive.

OTHER NAMES Bailey's Golden Sweet, Bailey's Sweet, Edgerly Sweet, Howard's Sweet, Paterson's Sweet, Patterson Sweet. It is also erroneously called Sweet Winesap, a distinct variety.

HISTORY Bailey Sweet appeared around 1840 in Perry, New York (Wyoming County). The variety was likely brought to Perry from another location.

EXTERIOR DESCRIPTION Fruit is medium to large and roundish. The smooth bright yellow skin is nearly covered by a deep red flush. It also has darker red stripes and is sometimes netted with russeting.

INTERIOR DESCRIPTION The yellowish flesh is somewhat coarse, juicy, and tender with a sweet flavor.

TREE CHARACTERISTICS Upright, spreading, and open in framework, the tree is slow growing and frequently has a weak root system, even on seedling stock. The bark is dark red; leaves are often sparse, medium in size, shiny, and somewhat folded.

DISEASE RESISTANCE Susceptible to the major apple diseases

SEASON OF RIPENING Early fall

USES Dessert and applesauce

STORAGE QUALITY Poor. It will only last for a few weeks in common storage.

Baldwin

Despite a tendency to produce a full crop one year and a light crop the following year, Baldwin became a classic variety in nineteenth-century New England thanks to notable flavor and keeping quality. But after suffering severe damage during the harsh winters of 1934 and 1935, the Baldwin orchards were replanted with the more promising annual-bearing McIntosh.

OTHER NAMES Butters Apple, Flech, Pecker, Steel's Red Winter, Woodpecker. A number of cultivars have been developed and the earlier ones have more intense flavor.

HISTORY Baldwin was found around 1750 in Wilmington, Massachusetts (near Boston). In the 1847 edition of *The Horticulturist and Journal of Rural Art and Rural Taste*, edited by Henry T. Williams, it was praised and described as growing on the farm of Mr. Butters, for whom it was originally named. Over time it became referred to it as the Woodpecker apple because of the bird's frequent visits to the tree, which was shortened by some to Pecker. Eventually, Colonel Baldwin promoted the fruit and his name was attached. The original tree died at some point between 1817 and 1832 and the location is now marked by a monument to the Baldwin apple.

EXTERIOR DESCRIPTION Fruit is large and roundish, narrowing just a little toward the blossom end. The yellow skin is nearly covered with crimson stripes on the sun-exposed side (cultivars will vary with the stripes and amount of crimson) and white star-shaped flecks. The thick skin protects it from bruising and possibly from some insect damage.

INTERIOR DESCRIPTION The yellowish-white flesh is crisp, tender, sprightly, subacid, and aromatic. Seeds are ovate to pyriform. The fruit contains 13.64 percent sugar that ferments to at least 6 percent alcohol.

TREE CHARACTERISTICS It is slow to begin bearing and tends toward biennial or even triennial production. It is also a poor pollinator for other varieties. The tree is long-lived, growing large even on a size-controlling rootstock. The broad leaves are folded near the edge rather than toward the midrib and have fairly sharp serrations that curve toward the leaf tips. It has reddish-olive bark.

DISEASE RESISTANCE It is susceptible to apple scab and Baldwin spot, a physiological condition of brown flecks in the flesh just under the skin.

SEASON OF RIPENING Late fall

USES All-purpose, but especially pie making, cider, and dessert

STORAGE QUALITY Good, except for those with Baldwin spot

Ben Davis

IN THE MIDWEST, this durable apple was once known as a "mortgage lifter" for the income it generated by the shipment of barge loads on the Mississippi River to New Orleans for export. Even after its export popularity faded, nurseries continued to propagate Ben Davis as a pollinator for the dominating Winesap orchards until the middle of the twentieth century.

OTHER NAMES Baltimore Pippin, Baltimore Red, Black Ben Davis, Carolina Red Streak, Funkhouse, Hutchinson Pippin, Joe Allen, Kentucky Pippin, New York Pippin, Red Pippin, Red Streak, Victoria Pippin, Virginia Pippin. Gano is sometimes said to be the same as Ben Davis, a sport of Ben Davis, or a parent of Ben Davis.

HISTORY Some say that it appeared around 1880 in Washington County, Arkansas, but others claim that it originated in Tennessee, Kentucky, or Virginia. This dependable tree was widely planted after the Civil War for cider making.

EXTERIOR DESCRIPTION Fruit is medium to large and oblate with obscure ribbing. Very firm and bruise resistant, the skin is waxy, smooth, and glossy. It has red stripes over a red background.

INTERIOR DESCRIPTION The deprecating nickname "cotton apple" was given to Ben Davis based on the apple's dense, coarse, fairly dry, white flesh.

TREE CHARACTERISTICS This medium-sized vigorous tree grows upright and begins to bear at an early age, producing heavy crops annually. It has waxed leaves which become narrow at the base and apex. Older bark is purplish. The center of the tree should be opened by pruning to permit air and sun penetration, thus reducing disease. It tends to bloom late and escape late frosts.

DISEASE RESISTANCE Susceptible to cedar apple rust; only moderately susceptible to the other major diseases.

SEASON OF RIPENING Late fall

USES Dessert (when more favorable varieties are depleted), cider, and drying

STORAGE QUALITY Excellent

Benham

During the late nineteenth century Benham trees were found in every backyard orchard in Appalachia, partly due to its useful tendency to ripen over several weeks. Even now, very old trees are still found in that area bearing small but usable fruit. The dried apples were prized for making stack cakes, a boldly layered traditional holiday treat in the region.

OTHER NAMES Benam, Brown, Clairborne (the Tennessee county where it was once extensively grown), Nat Ewing, Yearry. There is another apple named Benham from Michigan thought to be a seedling of Baldwin.

HISTORY Benham was offered in a Virginia nursery catalog in 1887; it is thought to have originated in Tennessee but the exact location is unknown. It gained distinction as a cooking and drying apple throughout the Appalachian region and was grown commercially in Lee County, Virginia, at the end of the nineteenth century.

EXTERIOR DESCRIPTION Fruit is medium in size, roundish, and sometimes ribbed. The greenish-yellow skin is blushed on the sun-exposed side and has russet dots haloed with green over most of the surface. The stem is thick and short and often there is a fleshy protuberance in the cavity.

INTERIOR DESCRIPTION Whitish flesh is juicy, tender, fine-grained, and oxidizes slowly. The sweetish flavor is sometimes described as nutty.

TREE CHARACTERISTICS The medium-sized tree is moderately vigorous and bears annual crops.

DISEASE RESISTANCE Moderately resistant to the major apple diseases

SEASON OF RIPENING Midsummer

USES Dessert, drying, and frying

STORAGE QUALITY Poor

Benoni

THIS HIGH-FLAVORED New England apple was widespread in the mid-Atlantic during the early twentieth century and was available in many southern nurseries. In *Apples of New York* (1905) Beach praised it as a fine dessert apple, attractive in appearance but too small to be a good market apple. Like many apples of similarly petite stature, Benoni was cast aside and eventually disappeared from commerce.

OTHER NAMES Fail-Me-Never

HISTORY Benoni was introduced before 1832 by E.M. Richards in Dedham, Massachusetts.

EXTERIOR DESCRIPTION Fruit is small and roundish, narrowing toward the calyx. The thin orange-yellow skin is blushed red and covered by carmine stripes and whitish flecks. It has a short, slender stem.

INTERIOR DESCRIPTION Flesh is yellow, crisp, and juicy with a vinous taste. The seeds are pale brown.

TREE CHARACTERISTICS The upright-growing tree remains small even on standard rootstock. It begins to bear at an early age. It produces heavy crops and needs to be thinned to minimize its biennial habit.

DISEASE RESISTANCE Susceptible to cedar apple rust; moderately resistant to the other major diseases.

SEASON OF RIPENING Midsummer. It ripens over two to three weeks.

USES Primarily dessert

STORAGE QUALITY Poor

Bentley

THIS VARIETY WAS greatly valued during the nineteenth century because the trees begin to bear fruit early and the sugary apples store well. I was told by a local old-timer apple connoisseur with a particular fondness for very sweet apples—and a way with words—that Bentley was the Rolls-Royce of apples.

OTHER NAMES Bentley's Sweet

HISTORY Virginia is considered its place of origin. It was listed in a catalog from 1845, but some sources place it in the early 1800s.

EXTERIOR DESCRIPTION Medium to large and roundish with flattened ends. It has smooth yellow skin blushed and striped dull red, as well as inconspicuous dark brown dots. In *Apples of New York* (1905) Beach states that the stem is short to medium, but apples that I've fruited have long stems.

INTERIOR DESCRIPTION The creamy-yellow flesh is fine-grained, crisp, juicy, and sweet.

TREE CHARACTERISTICS This medium-sized, slow-growing tree is productive and hardy. It begins to bear fruit when young.

DISEASE RESISTANCE Susceptible to bitter rot; moderately resistant to the other major diseases.

SEASON OF RIPENING Late fall

USES Dessert and cider

STORAGE QUALITY Excellent

Bethel

THIS MILD-FLAVORED Pearmain-type apple from New England was once widely planted near the area of Virginia where I grew up because of the coincidental existence of a nineteenth-century planned river community called Bethel. It's no surprise that the townspeople were drawn to the apple for this superficial reason, but by the middle of the twentieth century most of the trees had disappeared from neglect.

OTHER NAMES None. Historically, Bethel has been confused with the variety Stone, but it is now considered to be a distinct variety.

HISTORY The apple was found in Bethel, Vermont, and it was noted in the U.S. Agricultural Report of 1886. It was dispersed throughout New England and Canada during the 1890s.

EXTERIOR DESCRIPTION A large fruit, roundish and slightly conical. Skin is tough, described by Beach in *Apples of New York* as "deep yellow washed and mottled with red and striped with purplish carmine, becoming very dark red in highly colored specimens." The apples bruise easily.

INTERIOR DESCRIPTION The yellowish flesh is crisp, moderately tender, and juicy.

TREE CHARACTERISTICS This moderately vigorous, round, spreading tree has a tendency to grow large and produce rather small buds. It is subject to pre-harvest drop. Planting is recommended only for home and local market use.

DISEASE RESISTANCE Moderately susceptible to the major apple diseases

SEASON OF RIPENING Late fall

USES Dessert

STORAGE QUALITY Excellent

Bevan's Favorite

In 1985 APPLE HISTORIAN and author Lee Calhoun found an old Bevan's Favorite tree growing in Alamance County, North Carolina. He went on to return this tasty summer-ripening variety to commerce, an effort for which all apple lovers should be quite grateful.

OTHER NAMES Bivins, Early Bevans, Striped June

HISTORY It appeared at some point 1849 in the vicinity of Salem, New Jersey.

EXTERIOR DESCRIPTION Fruit is small to medium and round with flattened ends. It has yellow skin with some bright red stripes.

INTERIOR DESCRIPTION The flesh is crisp, firm, juicy and sprightly when harvested just at maturity. If the fruit is left on the tree too long the flesh becomes soft and drier.

TREE CHARACTERISTICS The tree is vigorous and heavy bearing. It must be properly pruned and the fruit thinned in order to produce apples large enough for marketing.

DISEASE RESISTANCE Moderately susceptible to the major apple diseases

SEASON OF RIPENING Midsummer

USES Dessert, baking, and frying

STORAGE QUALITY Fair

Black Gilliflower

THE SHEEP-NOSE shape is the most memorable feature of the Black Gilliflower apple. When presenting it at apple tastings, I hold it to my nose and say the word "sheep" and the tasters immediately make the association. It has an acquired taste for eating out-of-hand. I sometimes refer to it as an "olive apple" in the sense that it is either loved or loathed.

OTHER NAMES Black Sheepnose, Black Spitzenburg, Red Gilliflower, Sheepnose

HISTORY Considered to have come from Connecticut in the late eighteenth century, this apple was cited by Manning in 1841 under the name Red Gilliflower, and by Hovey in 1850 under the same name with Black Gilliflower as a synonym. This variety and Yellow Bellflower are speculated to be the parents of Red Delicious.

EXTERIOR DESCRIPTION Fruit is medium to large and oblong. It has dry dark red skin that deepens to black and the finish is often dull.

INTERIOR DESCRIPTION The greenish-white flesh is dry, coarse, and tender. It has a distinctive aroma and flavor.

TREE CHARACTERISTICS Grows large and upright. For dessert or culinary use, fruit must be picked before becoming too ripe on the tree. After ripening, the fruit will hang on the tree into winter so the tree is sometimes planted specifically for wildlife food.

DISEASE RESISTANCE Moderately resistant to the major apple diseases

SEASON OF RIPENING Mid-fall

USES Primarily drying, also baking and sometimes dessert

STORAGE QUALITY Fair

Black Oxford

THE DARK-COLORED Black Oxford apple is the New England similitude of the newer southern Arkansas Black. The equally balanced sweet-tart taste is enhanced by long storage. In late winter the apples will be at the zenith of flavor.

OTHER NAMES None

HISTORY It is reported the seedling was found around 1790 by Nathaniel Haskell on the farm of a nail maker named Valentine in Paris, Maine (Oxford County). Records exist that the original tree was still producing in 1907.

EXTERIOR DESCRIPTION Fruit is medium in size and roundish. The deep purple skin is covered with a bloom that is nearly black.

INTERIOR DESCRIPTION The whitish-green flesh sometimes displays a bit of red color just under the skin.

TREE CHARACTERISTICS It is considered to be a shy biennial bearer that produces very heavy crops in the year of bearing. The tree can live to be more than one hundred years old.

DISEASE RESISTANCE Moderately resistant to the major apple diseases

SEASON OF RIPENING Late fall

USES All-purpose, especially cider and drying

STORAGE QUALITY Excellent

Black Twig

BLACK TWIG is recognized as the state apple of Tennessee, likely because it was reputed to be the favorite apple of native son and president, Andrew Jackson. This noted keeper develops a very heavy coating of wax in storage. One touch and you will appreciate its nickname: greasy apple.

OTHER NAMES Big Black Twig, Pamplin's Eclipse, Paragon, Thorpe's Blacktwig, Twitty's Paragon. It is confused with Arkansas Black, Arkansaw, and Mammoth Black Twig. There is a modern cultivar of the same name that is more medium red in color, but with similar taste.

HISTORY It was found as a seedling around 1830 on the farm of Major Rankin Toole in Fayetteville, Tennessee. A local nurseryman named Twitty propagated and distributed the variety.

EXTERIOR DESCRIPTION Fruit is medium to large and roundish. The skin coloration varies but it is generally green to yellow and covered with dark red stripes. Sometimes it appears mostly red, other times some of the background will show through the overlay colors. The skin develops a waxy finish in storage.

INTERIOR DESCRIPTION Yellow flesh is juicy, breaking, and aromatic.

TREE CHARACTERISTICS Growth is dense, drooping, and vigorous with annual bearing. It requires a pollinator to be fruitful. The commercial orchards of central Virginia used Grimes Golden, Winter Banana, and Virginia (Hewes) Crab to make fruitful the pollen-sterile Black Twig, Arkansas Black, and Winesap.

DISEASE RESISTANCE It is moderately susceptible to the major diseases but adaptable century-old trees have been found still bearing fruit.

SEASON OF RIPENING Late fall

USES Dessert, apple butter, and cider

STORAGE QUALITY Excellent

Blue Pearmain

During tours of my orchard in which hundreds of varieties were growing, I frequently heard exclamations of "look at those blue apples!" upon the collective sighting of Blue Pearmain. It is the bloom, the heavy coating on the skin surface, which reflects the bluish cast. The appearance is more striking than the mild-flavored taste, an attribute typical of all apples in the Pearmain group.

OTHER NAMES None

HISTORY The exact date and place of origin are unknown. In 1833 the pomologist William Kenrick wrote in the *New American Orchardist* that Blue Pearmain had probably been in cultivation for a century or more and was prevalent in the vicinity of Boston in the early part of the nineteenth century.

EXTERIOR DESCRIPTION Fruit is large and oblate. The pale red background is splashed and striped with purplish red and the entire surface is covered by a pale blue bloom.

INTERIOR DESCRIPTION The coarse yellowish flesh is mildly sweet and aromatic.

TREE CHARACTERISTICS The spreading tree is moderately large in size and vigor. It is a slow grower in the nursery.

DISEASE RESISTANCE Moderately resistant to the major apple diseases

SEASON OF RIPENING Late fall

USES Primarily dessert, but also frying and baking

STORAGE QUALITY Fair. It will shrivel in storage.

Bottle Greening

THIS APPLE NAME derives from the tradition of farm workmen hiding their liquor bottles in a hollow of the tree for convenient nipping during the day. Bottle Greening apples have more of a pinkish blush on their green skin than Rhode Island Greening apples, but otherwise the varieties are quite similar in appearance.

OTHER NAMES None

HISTORY The seedling is speculated to have originated early in the nineteenth century on a farm bordering New York and Vermont. The original tree was still standing in the 1850s.

EXTERIOR DESCRIPTION Fruit is medium to large and oblate to ovate with a short stem. The smooth grass-green skin has a dull pinkish blush.

INTERIOR DESCRIPTION The whitish flesh is firm and tender and very juicy and aromatic.

TREE CHARACTERISTICS Hardy and moderately vigorous, the tree has a round top and is open in form. It produces crops annually.

DISEASE RESISTANCE Moderately resistant to the major apple diseases

SEASON OF RIPENING Late fall

USES Primarily dessert, but also frying and pie making

STORAGE QUALITY Fair. It will shrivel in storage.

Brushy Mountain Limbertwig

THIS VARIETY STANDS out among the more than forty recognized Limbertwigs for its noted dependability to provide an annual crop. The taste has to be personally experienced but I liken it to the complex flavor of a Winesap without the vinous influence. A cultural parallel can be drawn between all Appalachian Limbertwigs and the potatoes in Ireland. Both were survival foods, so imbued in the people who grew them that they could not imagine life without.

OTHER NAMES None

HISTORY It likely originated around the Brushy Mountain area of Alexander County, North Carolina; the apple is still available in this region.

EXTERIOR DESCRIPTION The medium-sized fruit is round, becoming slightly conical at the blossom end. It has reddish and clear yellow skin with brownish lenticels regularly spaced over the entire surface.

INTERIOR DESCRIPTION The yellow flesh is very juicy with a strong aroma.

TREE CHARACTERISTICS The tree has a pronounced weeping branch configuration that is characteristic of most Limbertwig varieties. It demands proper pruning to bear full crops.

DISEASE RESISTANCE Good resistance to the major diseases

SEASON OF RIPENING Late fall

USES All-purpose

STORAGE QUALITY Good

Buckingham

A LONGTIME FAVORITE in the South and mid-Atlantic during the nineteenth century, Buckingham was able to be successfully planted in warmer regions due to its low chill hour requirement. Root suckers were often transplanted to establish orchards and stock was distributed widely by wagon during the westward migration.

OTHER NAMES Bachelor, Blackburn, Byer's, Byer's Red, Equinetely, Frankfort Queen, Henshaw, Kentucky Fall Queen, Lexington Queen, Merit, Ne Plus Ultra, Queen, Red Horse

HISTORY It was first cited by pomologist William Coxe in 1817. It is thought to have originated in Louisa County, Virginia, rather than nearby Buckingham County for which it is named.

EXTERIOR DESCRIPTION Fruit is large and somewhat irregularly oblate with a short stalk. The pale yellow skin is flushed and mottled red; striped and blushed bright carmine; and covered with white dots.

INTERIOR DESCRIPTION The flesh is juicy, yellow, and crisp with a sprightly subacid flavor. It has a small core.

TREE CHARACTERISTICS This moderately twiggy grower bears full crops annually.

DISEASE RESISTANCE Moderately resistant to the major apple diseases

SEASON OF RIPENING Late summer to early fall

USES All-purpose, particularly baking

STORAGE QUALITY Fair

Burford Redflesh

THE BURFORD BROTHERS Nursery propagated and marketed this red-fleshed variety from the 1970s until the late 1990s. It was used by my family as a color additive to cider and it is now being used again for that purpose by a commercial cider maker in Virginia. The bright red flesh also makes for a dramatic presentation during apple tastings: it can be cut in half, fitted together again, and suddenly flashed at the audience.

OTHER NAMES Watermelon Apple

HISTORY Burford Redflesh is possibly a seedling of Red Siberian Crab which was used as a rootstock and occasionally produced fruit in the nursery. The oldest tree, now gone, was found at the estate of the mother of American patriot Patrick Henry in Amherst County, Virginia.

EXTERIOR DESCRIPTION Fruit is medium to large in size and round-oblate. The deep yellow background is mottled red.

INTERIOR DESCRIPTION The coarse flesh is watermelon red and very tart.

TREE CHARACTERISTICS The tree is moderate in size and round in shape. The foliage is deep purple in color and the shape is reminiscent of potato leaves. Landscape architects appreciate the unique foliage.

DISEASE RESISTANCE Resistant to the major apple diseases

SEASON OF RIPENING Mid-fall

USES Cider and ornamental design

STORAGE QUALITY Good

Cameo

AFTER BEING HIGHLY promoted, Cameo has become a minor mainstream variety often found in the produce departments of supermarkets. The conical fruit is reminiscent of Red Delicious but with less-pronounced knobs on the blossom end.

OTHER NAMES American Cameo, Carousel (its original name)

HISTORY It was discovered in 1987 by the Caudle family in Dryden, Washington. Cameo may be a cross of Red Delicious and Golden Delicious, which were both present in the orchard.

EXTERIOR DESCRIPTION Fruit is medium in size and conical. The creamy orange background is layered with bright red stripes.

INTERIOR DESCRIPTION Flesh is firm and crisp with an aromatic flavor.

TREE CHARACTERISTICS This is a semi-spur variety with moderate vigor. It begins to bear at an early age and produces full crops annually.

DISEASE RESISTANCE Moderately resistant to the major apple diseases

SEASON OF RIPENING Fall

USES Dessert, applesauce, and pie making. It is also good for salad making because the flesh does not oxidize rapidly.

STORAGE QUALITY Good

Caney Fork Limbertwig

THIS APPALACHIAN Limbertwig was among the many varieties collected by the late Reverend Henry Morton of Gatlinburg, Tennessee. We began corresponding in the 1970s, sharing scionwood and apple stories. In those days, the significance of the rich and diverse Limbertwigs was not yet fully recognized, but now they have become increasingly celebrated and planted.

OTHER NAMES Caney, Caney Limbertwig

HISTORY The date of origin is unknown but it originated in the Caney Fork region of the Cumberland Mountains in Kentucky.

EXTERIOR DESCRIPTION Fruit is medium to large and oblate. A heavy russeting appears in the stem cavity and sometimes irregularly covers the shoulder of the fruit. The yellow background is overlaid with a medium-red color and prominent whitish lenticels that are evenly spaced over the surface. The stem is medium in length but robust in girth.

INTERIOR DESCRIPTION The yellowish-white flesh is crisp, crunchy, and juicy. It has the distinctive Limbertwig taste.

TREE CHARACTERISTICS The limbs droop moderately, although not quite as much as some other Limbertwig varieties.

DISEASE RESISTANCE Moderately resistant to the major apple diseases

SEASON OF RIPENING Early winter

USES Dessert and baking

STORAGE QUALITY Good

Cannon Pearmain

In Virginia, Cannon Pearmain was planted at Thomas Jefferson's summer home, Poplar Forest (near Lynchburg), but not at his Monticello estate near Charlottesville. In 1998 I worked with the archeologist at Poplar Forest to take scionwood from the last survivor and propagate new trees. Just in time too, as the survivor tree died in 2000. The next year, with our newly grafted trees, a small commercial planting was made again in Bedford County, Virginia.

OTHER NAMES Alpain, Anderson, Cannon, Green Cannon, Red Cannon

HISTORY Speculated to be from Bedford County, Virginia, in the vicinity of Thomas Jefferson's Poplar Forest, it was offered for sale by the Bailey Nursery in the 1804 *Virginia Argus* newspaper, but likely was available in the late eighteenth century as well. Beach references all date after 1851, dismissing it as a southern variety that does not grow well in the North. In the early twentieth century Cannon Pearmain was produced commercially in central Virginia, but nearly disappeared from cultivation by 1950.

EXTERIOR DESCRIPTION The medium to large, ovate fruit has a greenish-yellow skin flushed with brick red and striped with carmine. It is usually covered with yellow dots. A long stem projects obliquely from the fruit.

INTERIOR DESCRIPTION Creamy yellow flesh is, crisp, juicy, and coarse. It has a subacid flavor.

TREE CHARACTERISTICS This very vigorous tree was noted to become extremely large. It is severely biennial in production and has tough limbs which seldom break. The tree grows best in rich soil and at higher elevations, more than 1,000 feet above sea level.

DISEASE RESISTANCE Good resistance to the major diseases

SEASON OF RIPENING Late fall

USES All-purpose

STORAGE QUALITY Excellent. The harvested apples were often piled on beds of straw beneath the tree and then covered with straw for long winter storage.

Carter's Blue

AFTER MANY YEARS of unavailability in the United States, author and fruit historian Lee Calhoun (of Pittsboro, North Carolina) was responsible for locating Carter's Blue at the National Fruit Trust in Kent, England, and returning it to commerce in America. The tree is prized for vigorous growth and the high flavor of apples produced.

OTHER NAMES Lady Fitzpatrick, Patton

HISTORY Carter's Blue is thought to have originated around the middle of the nineteenth century. It was found and promoted by Colonel Carter of Mount Meigs, Alabama (near Montgomery).

EXTERIOR DESCRIPTION Fruit is medium to large and round to oblate. The greenish-yellow background is nearly covered with layers of red and irregular dark red stripes. A purplish-blue bloom covers the skin surface and white lenticels are prominent.

INTERIOR DESCRIPTION The white flesh is crisp, juicy, and aromatic.

TREE CHARACTERISTICS This vigorous grower bears heavy crops annually. It has greenish-blue foliage.

DISEASE RESISTANCE Susceptible to cedar apple rust; moderately resistant to the other major diseases.

SEASON OF RIPENING Late fall

USES Dessert

STORAGE QUALITY Poor

Cauley

It can be hard to know if apple flavor will be increased or decreased by the dehydrating process, but it's always worth experimentation. With Cauley apples grown in Virginia, I've found that their mild fresh flavor becomes significantly more pronounced when dried. Sometimes, too, the apple will weigh more than a pound—another reason to give it a shot in your drying trays.

OTHER NAMES Cally. An apple called Colley was noted but not described by the 1860 American Pomological Society meeting in Philadelphia; this is thought to be the same as Cauley.

HISTORY In the 1920s, three trees of this Deep South variety were planted at the Delta Branch Agricultural Experiment Station in Stoneville, Mississippi. The scionwood came from a tree found in 1919 in the yard of a John Cauley from Grenada, Mississippi. Only one of the three trees survived the 1927 Mississippi River flood.

EXTERIOR DESCRIPTION The apple is large to very large, roundish, and slightly lopsided. The greenish-yellow skin is overlaid with a reddish blush and darker reddish stripes. Prominent brownish dots are scattered unevenly over the surface.

INTERIOR DESCRIPTION The mild-flavored whitish flesh has a hint of yellow when fully mature.

TREE CHARACTERISTICS This vigorous tree bears heavily on limbs that are resilient and do not break with large fruit loads. It blooms late.

DISEASE RESISTANCE Moderate. There are conflicting reports on the tree's susceptibility to fireblight.

SEASON OF RIPENING Late summer

USES Baking, drying, and dessert

STORAGE QUALITY Good for a late-summer variety

Cheese Apple

I ONCE PLANTED seeds from numerous specimens of Cheese Apple, desperately hoping for a lookalike, but alas, they were all green and bitter. The apple's name arose from its oblate shape, which is reminiscent of a classic wheel of cheddar.

OTHER NAMES Carolina Greening, Crank, Green, Green Cheese, Green Crank, Greening, Southern Greening, Southern Pippin, Turner's Cheese, Winter Cheese, Winter Greening

HISTORY It is considered to be an eighteenth-century variety from North Carolina or Georgia but no documentation exists to confirm the exact place of origin.

EXTERIOR DESCRIPTION This medium to large apple is generally oblate although some variation in shape does occur. The deep green skin ripens to pale yellow with a reddish-bronze blush on the side facing the sun.

INTERIOR DESCRIPTION The whitish-ivory flesh is crisp, tender, and fairly juicy.

TREE CHARACTERISTICS The moderately vigorous tree is a late bloomer like Ralls and produces full crops annually.

DISEASE RESISTANCE Good resistance to the major diseases

SEASON OF RIPENING Fall

USES All-purpose

STORAGE QUALITY Good

Chehalis

A SELF-POLLINATOR ARMED with some disease resistance, Chehalis is a variety of choice for the low-spray and organic fruit grower. Keep in mind when planning that the tree is slow to begin producing fruit and can be a shy bearer; however, picking before it is fully ripe will extend the season of ripening.

OTHER NAMES None

HISTORY Chehalis originated in 1937 in Oakville, Washington.

EXTERIOR DESCRIPTION This large, round apple is slightly more elongated than Golden Delicious but otherwise is similar in appearance. The yellow skin occasionally has a reddish blush on the sun-exposed side and may be somewhat russeted near the blossom end. When fully ripe, the skin feels greasy like Black Twig and other apples in the Winesap family.

INTERIOR DESCRIPTION The cream-colored flesh is crisp and juicy with a medium to fine texture. It has a low acid content. When grown in the hot and humid mid-Atlantic, the flavor is less pronounced.

TREE CHARACTERISTICS It is a brushy tree that requires careful pruning. Branches are stiff and upright.

DISEASE RESISTANCE Resistant to apple scab (sometimes called scab immune); generally resistant to powdery mildew.

SEASON OF RIPENING Late summer

USES Dessert, baking, and pie making

STORAGE QUALITY Poor

Chenango Strawberry

This BEAUTIFUL SUMMER apple is a great choice for the home orchard. It ripens over two to three weeks so multiple pickings are required in order to get mature fruit with high flavor. Apples should be harvested just as the skin turns a milky color and then consumed or processed in a timely fashion; fruit quality and color begin to degrade after only a few weeks in storage.

OTHER NAMES Buckley, Chenango, Early Sugar Loaf, Frank, Jackson, Sherwood's Favorite, Smyrna

HISTORY It was noted in 1854 as having originated in Lebanon, New York (Madison County), but other sources report that it was brought by settlers from Connecticut to Chenango County, New York.

EXTERIOR DESCRIPTION The medium to large fruit is long and conical. Skin is smooth, shiny, aromatic, and slightly translucent. The background is generally greenish or yellowish white with red stripes and a bright pink blush on the sun-exposed side. The fruit will have increased red stripes or sometimes an all-over red skin in colder climates and at higher elevations; the red color is diminished when grown in warmer regions.

INTERIOR DESCRIPTION The tender, juicy flesh is very aromatic. Unless overripe, even poorly colored fruit will have good flavor.

TREE CHARACTERISTICS The tree is hardy, long-lived, and begins to bear early. It is a regular bearer, alternating between light and heavy crops. It has yellowish-green bark; the similarly colored leaves are large and flattish with sharp, shallow serrations.

DISEASE RESISTANCE Susceptible to fireblight; moderately resistant to the other major diseases.

SEASON OF RIPENING Midsummer to late summer

USES Dessert and applesauce

STORAGE QUALITY Poor

Chestnut Crab

With its large and aromatic blossoms, Chestnut Crab trees are desirable candidates for edible landscaping. The trees also make an attractive screen when covered with foliage or fruit. The apples can be cooked or eaten right out of hand, although I once overheard a boy remark that they were so little you would have to eat a peck to get a bellyache.

OTHER NAMES MN 240

HISTORY It was introduced in 1946. Chestnut Crab is a cross of Malinda and a crabapple developed at the Minnesota Agricultural Experiment Station.

EXTERIOR DESCRIPTION This round apple is small (about 2 inches in diameter) and has a yellow background overlaid with light red coloring and some russeting. The skin color is sometimes described as reddish bronze.

INTERIOR DESCRIPTION The white-yellowish flesh is crisp, juicy, and sweetish. The flavor is often called nutty and is occasionally described as having a hint of vanilla.

TREE CHARACTERISTICS The moderately vigorous tree takes a compact form and produces full crops annually. The fruit hangs long on the tree after ripening.

DISEASE RESISTANCE Somewhat resistant to cedar apple rust; moderately susceptible to apple scab and fireblight.

SEASON OF RIPENING Late summer to early fall. It ripens over several weeks.

USES Dessert, cider, pickling, applesauce, and ornamental landscaping

STORAGE QUALITY Fair

Cole's Quince

THIS APPLE WAS raised in Maine by Captain Henry Cole, and later described by his son, S. W. Cole, in *The American Fruit Book* (1849) as juicy and pleasantly mild with a high quince flavor and aroma. A few Cole's Quince apples combined with a tart variety and a sweet variety will make an exceptional apple pie.

OTHER NAMES Pear Apple, Quince, Quince Apple, Seneca Favorite, Seneca Spice

HISTORY It originated in Cornish, Maine, and was first described in 1806.

EXTERIOR DESCRIPTION Fruit size is medium to large and the shape is intermediate to flat, convex, and ribbed at the eye and on the body. It has yellow skin flushed with red on the sun-exposed side.

INTERIOR DESCRIPTION The yellowish-white flesh is coarse, crisp, juicy, and tender with a light acidic flavor.

TREE CHARACTERISTICS It is moderate in vigor as grown in Virginia. It produces some fruit each year but often the tree is a shy bearer. Weather conditions affect the fruiting and soil conditions affect the intensity of the flavor.

DISEASE RESISTANCE Moderately resistant to the major diseases

SEASON OF RIPENING Late summer

USES Baking, frying, and dessert

STORAGE QUALITY Fair

Criterion

This seedling was found by chance growing among Red Delicious, Golden Delicious, and Winter Banana trees. It takes the Red Delicious shape and the Golden Delicious taste quality. I do not recommend growing this West Coast variety in the mid-Atlantic and South because of the inferior production.

OTHER NAMES None

HISTORY It originated during the late 1960s in Parker, Washington, and was introduced commercially in 1973.

EXTERIOR DESCRIPTION Fruit is medium to large and elongated, appearing dramatically different depending on where it is grown. In the Northwest, the yellowish-green skin has a reddish-pink blush but in warmer regions, such as the mid-Atlantic, the apple fails to develop the customary brightness. It also has brownish dots over most of the surface, and russeting around the stem.

INTERIOR DESCRIPTION Flesh is crisp and juicy and the mild flavor is mostly sweet with just a hint of tartness.

TREE CHARACTERISTICS This upright, spreading tree produces heavy crops annually. It must be pruned every year for good fruit production.

DISEASE RESISTANCE It is particularly susceptible to the late-summer diseases (sooty blotch and fly speck) in the mid-Atlantic and other warm regions; elsewhere it is moderately susceptible to the major diseases.

SEASON OF RIPENING Late fall

USES Dessert, drying, and particularly for salads because it is slow to oxidize when sliced

STORAGE QUALITY Good

Crow Egg

IT'S POSSIBLE THAT this variety was among the many southern apples that were taken by sailing ship from the ports of New Orleans and Charleston to Australia when the British developed a penal colony there after the American Revolution. Although the American and Australian Crow Egg apples look quite dissimilar, the differences may be attributed to climate rather than genetic variation.

OTHER NAMES Crow's Egg. In the South and mid-Atlantic, it is mistakenly called Black Gilliflower; when grown in New England this variety has a dramatically different appearance and taste.

HISTORY The origin is unknown but it was first noted by pomologist William Kenrick in 1832. Before the end of the nineteenth century it had come to be seldom planted—it is remarkable that it has survived.

EXTERIOR DESCRIPTION The medium-sized apple has a round to ovate shape that is not at all like an actual crow's egg. The yellowish-green background is mostly covered by a dull reddish blush and small but prominent russet dots are scattered irregularly over the surface. The apple is lightly ribbed and the stem is long and slender.

INTERIOR DESCRIPTION The white crisp flesh is juicy and sweet. It has a large core.

TREE CHARACTERISTICS Upright and spreading, the tree is productive even when old. The branches are long, slender, and crooked.

DISEASE RESISTANCE Moderately resistant to most apple diseases, thus the occasional discovery of old abandoned trees.

SEASON OF RIPENING Fall

USES Dessert

STORAGE QUALITY Good

Davey

In 1945, Davey (named for its finder, S. Lothrop Davenport, and pronounced to rhyme with savvy) was awarded a first-class certificate by the Massachusetts Horticultural Society based on its attractive coloration and long, fat stem. The apple has a pleasant aftertaste with a memorable hint of astringency. Davey is considered to be a seedling of McIntosh and was introduced commercially in 1950.

OTHER NAMES None

HISTORY It was discovered in 1928 by S. Lothrop Davenport in an old orchard near North Grafton, Massachusetts. While serving as secretary of the Worcester County Horticultural Society in the 1940s, Davenport began collecting heirloom varieties and later founded the preservation orchard at Old Sturbridge Village in Massachusetts.

EXTERIOR DESCRIPTION The medium-sized apple has a truncate-conic shape and is ribbed on the body. It has pale green skin that is flushed and striped carmine.

INTERIOR DESCRIPTION The white flesh is tinged green. It is firm, somewhat coarse, and slightly sweet and

aromatic. The distinctive flavor is similar to Westfield Seek-No-Further.

TREE CHARACTERISTICS The fruit hangs well on the tree with little pre-harvest drop.

DISEASE RESISTANCE Resistant to apple scab; susceptible to the other major diseases.

SEASON OF RIPENING Mid-fall

USES Mainly dessert and sometimes baking and frying

STORAGE QUALITY Good

Early Harvest

EARLY HARVEST—a widely planted home variety in eighteenth- and nineteenth-century America—is making a comeback in contemporary backyard orchards. It ripens over two to three weeks early in the season, offering a splendidly flavored fruit to those starved for freshness.

OTHER NAMES Bracken, Canada, Early French Reinette, Early July Pippin, Early June, Glass Apple, July Pippin, Prince's Early Harvest, Prince's Harvest, Sinclair's Yellow, Tart Bough

HISTORY The exact place of origin is unknown. It was listed by McMahon in 1805 as Early Harvest, and described by Coxe in 1817 under the names Prince's Harvest and Early French Reinette.

EXTERIOR DESCRIPTION This medium-sized, round apple has a delicate, slender stem (sometimes about 1½ inches long) and bruises readily. When fully ripe, the skin is straw yellow in color sometimes with an orange blush and whitish specks that turn brown.

INTERIOR DESCRIPTION Very white flesh is crisp and juicy with a sprightly flavor. The core is small and the abundant seeds are light brown and ovate. The flavor is nicely balanced between sweet and tart.

TREE CHARACTERISTICS Upright and slow-growing, the tree bears early and heavily. It has a tendency to produce considerable undersized fruit which makes it unsuitable for commercial production; fruit quality is increased if the tree is grown in rich soil. It has reddish-brown wood with small white specks.

DISEASE RESISTANCE Moderately susceptible to the major diseases

SEASON OF RIPENING Midsummer

USES Baking, applesauce, frying, and sometimes for dessert

STORAGE QUALITY Fair

Early Joe

THE USUAL PROCESS is that thousands of seeds must be planted and fruited in order to create a single variety of merit. But Early Joe, remarkably, came out of the same seedling orchard that produced two other significant varieties: Northern Spy and Melon. This crispy apple is perfect for out-of-hand eating, but is also useful for processing into all sorts of products.

OTHER NAMES None

HISTORY It came from an orchard grown from seeds that were brought around 1800 from Salisbury, Connecticut, to East Bloomfield, New York. In 1843 it was exhibited by Judge Jonathan Buel at the New York State Agricultural Society in Rochester.

EXTERIOR DESCRIPTION Fruit is small to medium and oblate to conical. The pale greenish-yellow skin has irregular stripes and splashes of dull dark red. Russet dots cover most of the surface.

INTERIOR DESCRIPTION The fine-grained yellowish flesh is very tender and crisp. It has a spicy, vinous flavor which has also been described as pear-like.

TREE CHARACTERISTICS The tree is small to medium in size and slow growing; it begins to bear young but is biennial in production. There is little pre-harvest drop but it has a predominance of undersized fruit so heavy thinning is important. Young grafted trees are difficult to grow in the nursery and need optimum conditions to produce good fruit.

DISEASE RESISTANCE Susceptible to apple scab; somewhat susceptible to cedar apple rust.

SEASON OF RIPENING Midsummer

USES All-purpose, but mostly for dessert

STORAGE QUALITY Fair

Empire

THE APPROPRIATELY NAMED Empire is the seedling of two dominating parents: McIntosh and Red Delicious. An outstanding dessert apple, the creamy white flesh has the satisfying tendency to break off in crisp chunks when bitten. The variety is a dependable choice for the home orchard, ripening about two weeks after McIntosh in late fall, and has been increasingly valued as a cider maker during the early years of the twenty-first century.

OTHER NAMES NY 45500-5. Cultivars include Crown Empire, Royal Empire, and Thome Empire.

HISTORY This cross of McIntosh and Red Delicious was developed in the late 1940s and first fruited in 1954. It was released in 1966 by the New York State Agricultural Experiment Station in Geneva.

EXTERIOR DESCRIPTION This round apple is usually medium in size when the tree is thinned. It has waxy skin which is dark red on the sun-exposed side and yellow on the underside.

INTERIOR DESCRIPTION The creamy white flesh is very crisp, juicy, and more sweet than tart in flavor.

TREE CHARACTERISTICS This vigorous, early-bearing tree develops wide crotch angles and tends to have a spur growth habit.

DISEASE RESISTANCE Highly susceptible to apple scab; somewhat resistant to fireblight and powdery mildew.

SEASON OF RIPENING Late fall

USES Dessert, pie making, and cider

STORAGE QUALITY Good

Esopus Spitzenburg

IT IS TOLD that Thomas Jefferson repeatedly planted Esopus Spitzenburg at his Monticello fruitery but never succeeded with making it a productive variety. This however, didn't stop it from becoming his favorite apple—or so the story goes. Personally, I suspect he liked many other apples as well.

OTHER NAMES Spitz, Spitzenburg. It is sometimes spelled Spitzenberg.

HISTORY It was known around 1790, originating in Esopus, New York (Ulster County), and was planted commercially in the nineteenth and twentieth centuries. Considered to be one of the classic dessert apples of the world, Esopus Spitzenburg has ranked in the top five for more than twenty years at the annual Monticello apple tasting that I conduct. It is likely a parent of Jonathan and is classified in the Baldwin apple group.

EXTERIOR DESCRIPTION Fruit is medium to large and roundish to conical with a tough and sometimes waxy skin. The rich orange-yellow color is often completely covered with bright red and darker red stripes; in full sun it occasionally darkens to a purplish blush. The surface is irregularly dotted with russeting.

INTERIOR DESCRIPTION The yellowish flesh is crisp, juicy, and fine-grained. It has a spicy, complex flavor often described as aromatic and sprightly.

TREE CHARACTERISTICS Open and spreading, the slow-growing tree has wide-angled crotches of slender and drooping branches. The foliage can be sparse. Esopus Spitzenburg tends toward biennial bearing; a pollinator variety planted nearby will increase production.

DISEASE RESISTANCE In warmer regions, it is highly susceptible to fireblight and moderately susceptible to apple scab, collar rot, and canker. Apples left on the tree too long will develop Jonathan spot, a condition which causes brown skin-deep marks that detract from its appearance; trees planted at elevations over 1,000 feet will have reduced susceptibility.

SEASON OF RIPENING Mid-fall to late fall

USES Dessert and cider

STORAGE QUALITY Good. Harvesting just as fruit matures extends the shelf life.

Fallawater

THIS APPLE HAS two enclaves of reverence: the Pennsylvania area where it originated and the mountains of West Virginia. Due to climate and soil conditions varying greatly between the northern and southern locales, a Pennsylvania Fallawater would be tart and covered with red stripes while the same apple grown in West Virginia (such as the one pictured) would be greener in color and milder in flavor.

OTHER NAMES Brubaker, Formwalder, Green Mountain Pippin, Kelly, Molly Whopper, Mountain Pippin, Pine's Beauty of the West, Pound, Prim's Beauty of the West, Talpahawkins, Tulpehocken, Winter Blush

HISTORY Originating before 1842 in Bucks County, Pennsylvania, this variety remained in limited commercial production until its popularity increased in the middle of the twentieth century. It continues to be a common variety for backyard planting in West Virginia.

EXTERIOR DESCRIPTION The round apple is large to very large (it can grow to 6 inches in diameter) with a very short stem. In New England it tends to have dull red to bright red skin with russet dots. In Appalachia the color of the skin is grass-green, ripening to yellow-green.

INTERIOR DESCRIPTION The white flesh has a green tinge; it is firm, coarse, and crisp.

TREE CHARACTERISTICS A triploid, Fallawater is slow to develop roots in the nursery, but it becomes a large, vigorous, upright tree in the orchard.

DISEASE RESISTANCE Susceptible to cedar apple rust; only moderately susceptible to the other diseases.

SEASON OF RIPENING Late fall. It ripens over a few weeks.

USES Baking, applesauce, and dessert

STORAGE QUALITY Poor

Fall Pippin

THIS VERY OLD variety was an essential backyard and kitchen orchard variety in the nineteenth century, primarily due to its habit of ripening irregularly over three weeks. One-hundred-year-old trees are still occasionally found bearing useable fruit.

OTHER NAMES American Fall, Autumn Pippin, Cobbet's Fall, Episcopal, Golden Pippin, Philadelphia Pippin, Prince's Large Pippin, Sudlow's Fall Pippin, Summer Pippin, York Pippin. It is incorrectly known as Cat Head and Holland Pippin. It may be the same as Camuesar, the national apple of Spain.

HISTORY It was first recorded in 1806 although the exact place of origin is unknown. It is likely an American variety that is a seedling of White Spanish Reinette or Holland Pippin, both of which it resembles.

EXTERIOR DESCRIPTION The fruit is large, round, slightly elongated, and moderately russeted in the stem cavity. Skin is green, ripening to clear yellow, sometimes with a reddish blush on the sun-exposed side.

INTERIOR DESCRIPTION The yellowish-white flesh is tender and juicy. The core is fairly small and the seeds are brownish and ovate.

TREE CHARACTERISTICS The vigorously growing, hardy, upright, spreading tree will live for a long time. Wood is dark brown in color. The large, shiny leaves are folded, reflexed, and sharply and irregularly serrated.

DISEASE RESISTANCE Susceptible to apple scab; somewhat resistant to the other major diseases.

SEASON OF RIPENING Early to late fall

USES Baking and dessert

STORAGE QUALITY Fair for an early-ripening apple

Fall Russet

LIKE FRESH APPLES, dried apples express a diversity of taste, texture, and color. Although the small size of Fall Russet apples means that slicing them for drying can be tedious, it is more than worth the effort for the intensity of rich flavor, sometimes described as pear-like, retained in the finished product.

OTHER NAMES Autumn Pomme Gris, as described in Downing's 1859 book, *The Fruit and Fruit Trees of America.*

HISTORY This apple originated in 1859 in Franklin, Michigan. It shares a name with a number of other russeted apples and the identity of the variety remains uncertain.

EXTERIOR DESCRIPTION A small, round apple covered with a yellowish green or golden russet. It is often irregularly webbed with gray and dark green and flushed with orange.

INTERIOR DESCRIPTION The creamy yellow flesh is crisp with a sweet-tart flavor.

TREE CHARACTERISTICS This moderately growing tree has drooping branches and bears fruit in clusters, like many crabapples.

DISEASE RESISTANCE Good. It is suitable for planting in organic orchards.

SEASON OF RIPENING Fall

USES Dessert, applesauce, apple butter, drying, and cider

STORAGE QUALITY Fair

Fall Wine

ALTHOUGH THIS VARIETY originated in New England, it was much more prevalent in the mid-Atlantic. I've occasionally come across a Fall Wine apple tree that is past fifty years old and still bearing fruit with particularly intense vinous flavor. At a Virginia estate with such an ancient tree, the juice is especially treasured during their yearly cider making event.

OTHER NAMES Hawer, House, Hower, Musk Spice, Ohio Wine, Sharpe's Spice, Sweet Wine, Uncle Sam's Best, Wine, Wine of Cole

HISTORY It probably originated around 1832 in the garden of Judge Jonathan Buel in Albany, New York. For many years, it was thought to have been lost to cultivation until it was rediscovered in the 1950s by Fred Ashworth of Heuvelton, New York.

EXTERIOR DESCRIPTION Fruit is medium in size with a roundish-oblate shape. The skin is rich red marbled over clear yellow with brownish-red spots and specks. It is sometimes faintly striped. The apples bruise easily.

INTERIOR DESCRIPTION Juicy and mild, the yellow flesh is sweet and tender with a vinous and subacid flavor. It has a small core.

TREE CHARACTERISTICS The moderately productive tree has a biennial tendency and will mature to be average in size with drooping branches. It is particularly subject to pre-harvest drop of immature apples.

DISEASE RESISTANCE Moderately resistant to the major apple diseases

SEASON OF RIPENING Fall

USES Dessert and cider

STORAGE QUALITY Poor

Fanny

A DEPENDABLE APPLE with Pennsylvania origins, Fanny became popular in the South during the last quarter of the nineteenth century and first quarter of the twentieth century. The variety's tendency to ripen in late June, when few other fresh apples are available, solidified it as a good selection for the home orchard.

OTHER NAMES None

HISTORY Fanny originated before 1869 on the property of Dr. John Eshelman of Lancaster, Pennsylvania.

EXTERIOR DESCRIPTION This medium-sized, round-oblate apple has a slender stem that is medium to long. The smooth, clear yellow skin is overlaid with a bright red color and carmine stripes that follow the slight ribbing of the apple. Small yellowish dots also appear on the surface.

INTERIOR DESCRIPTION Tender and juicy, the white flesh may be tinged with yellow and is sometimes stained with red.

TREE CHARACTERISTICS The vigorous tree bears heavy crops annually.

DISEASE RESISTANCE Moderately resistant to the major apple diseases

SEASON OF RIPENING Midsummer

USES Dessert and sometimes for baking and frying

STORAGE QUALITY Fair

Fortune

This large, high-colored, spicy apple is counted among the many crosses made by eminent plant breeder and Cornell professor Roger Way. In time Fortune was overshadowed by Empire, one of its parents, which possesses the more favorable tendency to bear annually instead of biennially.

OTHER NAMES NY429A

HISTORY This cross of Schoharie Spy and Empire was developed in 1962 at Cornell University's New York State Agricultural Experiment Station in Geneva. A patent was applied for in 1995.

EXTERIOR DESCRIPTION Fruit is large to very large and round to oblong. The greenish background is mostly covered with an attractive burgundy red.

INTERIOR DESCRIPTION The crisp, cream-colored flesh is spicy with a tart-sweet balance of flavor.

TREE CHARACTERISTICS Growth is vigorous but it tends toward biennial bearing if allowed to crop heavily.

DISEASE RESISTANCE It is susceptible to apple scab, fireblight, and bitter pit (spray protection should be considered to combat this disease).

SEASON OF RIPENING Late fall. It ripens about two weeks after McIntosh and around the same time as Empire.

USES Dessert, baking, and in salads

STORAGE QUALITY Very good

Freedom

FREEDOM HAS BEEN called the ugly duckling of disease-resistant apple varieties. But that shouldn't detract from its many merits. These include the freedom from apple scab infection for which it was named, a high rate of productivity, and an ability to serve as a good pollinator for its more attractive sibling, Liberty.

OTHER NAMES None

HISTORY The sister apple of Liberty, Freedom was developed from crosses of Macoun, Antonovka, Golden Delicious, and a named cross of Rome in 1959 at the New York State Agricultural Experiment Station in Geneva. It was distributed for field testing in 1970 and introduced as a patented variety in 1983.

EXTERIOR DESCRIPTION A medium-sized round apple with bright red skin on a faint yellow background.

INTERIOR DESCRIPTION The yellowish flesh is crisp and very juicy.

TREE CHARACTERISTICS The vigorous, spreading tree requires careful pruning to maintain its shape and produce quality fruit.

DISEASE RESISTANCE Quite resistant to apple scab; moderately resistant to cedar apple rust, powdery mildew, and fireblight.

SEASON OF RIPENING Fall

USES Dessert, applesauce, and cider

STORAGE QUALITY Good

Gano

AT LEAST HALF of the "Gano" apples sent to me for identification are not Gano at all. It's always important not to rush to judgment during the identification process—even if that frustrates the person seeking confirmation. I start by examining the physical characteristics of the exterior, particularly the stem size and extensiveness of russeting and lenticels, before moving on to the interior (core and seed shape) and then to the generally most conclusive (and enjoyable) act of tasting. It is often easier for me to say what the apple is not rather than what it is.

OTHER NAMES Black Ben Davis, Jacks Red, Mesa Red, Ozark, Payton, Reagan, Red Ben Davis

HISTORY This apple is thought to have originated in Kentucky or Missouri around 1880. It is speculated to be a seedling of Ben Davis and is historically considered to be the same as Black Ben Davis (which was named for a Mr. Black not the apple's skin color). The true identity has been a controversial subject since the end of the Civil War when Arkansas was establishing new orchards with nursery stock from Stark Bro's Nursery in Missouri.

EXTERIOR DESCRIPTION Fruit is medium in size and round. The light yellow background is flushed and striped light red which ripens to purplish red; in the shade, the skin retains more yellow color. Yellow dots irregularly cover the surface.

INTERIOR DESCRIPTION The whitish flesh is tinged with yellow. It is firm, coarse, crisp, and juicy with a subacid flavor.

TREE CHARACTERISTICS Like Ben Davis, this medium-sized tree is a vigorous upright grower with narrow waxy leaves and purplish older bark. The tree center should be opened by pruning to permit air and sunlight penetration. It begins to bear early and produces heavy crops annually. It also blooms late, escaping frosts.

DISEASE RESISTANCE Moderately susceptible to the major apple diseases

SEASON OF RIPENING Late fall

USES Dessert, baking, pie making, and frying

STORAGE QUALITY Good

Garden Royal

FOR MANY DECADES this small apple was pushed aside into obscurity until around 1980 when the Michigan apple connoisseur Robert Nitschke rediscovered its rich and aromatic flavor and sent it to me for propagation. In Virginia it is more prone to disease and exhibits less of a melting pear quality as when it is grown in Michigan or other cooler regions.

OTHER NAMES None

HISTORY Garden Royal was found in 1847 on the Bowker Farm in Sudbury, Massachusetts.

EXTERIOR DESCRIPTION The fruit is small and round with some faint ribbing. The thin greenish-yellow skin is nearly flushed red with stripes and splashes of carmine. Distinct russet dots are also scattered over the surface.

INTERIOR DESCRIPTION The yellowish flesh is juicy and aromatic. It can be almost melting in tenderness, like a mature pear.

TREE CHARACTERISTICS This vigorous grower is very upright and begins to bear early. It produces heavy crops and tends toward biennial bearing.

DISEASE RESISTANCE It is susceptible to the major apple diseases, especially in warmer regions.

SEASON OF RIPENING Late summer

USES Dessert

STORAGE QUALITY Poor

Gilpin

GILPIN'S SMALL SIZE is not indicative of the magnitude of beauty and flavor it possesses. Traditionally known as a cider maker, this is also an excellent dessert fruit—especially after spending a little time in storage. Gilpin is counted among the varieties that bloom late (Northern Spy and Rome Beauty are others) which means it can be planted in areas where late frosts are a problem.

OTHER NAMES Barker's Liner, Carthouse, Dollars and Cents, Little Red Romanite, Romanite, Roman Knight

HISTORY It was known in the early 1800s, likely originating in Virginia before being taken to New England. William Coxe wrote in 1817 that it was named for a Delaware family.

EXTERIOR DESCRIPTION Fruit is medium in size and round to oblong with a long stem. The smooth, polished skin has a yellow background with dark red and rich yellow streaks.

INTERIOR DESCRIPTION The yellowish flesh is initially coarse and very firm; it does not develop its juicy, tender flesh until stored for a few months. It has a complex sweet flavor.

TREE CHARACTERISTICS The tree is hardy, open, spreading, and vigorous. The fruit hangs on the tree late in the season.

DISEASE RESISTANCE Moderately resistant to the major diseases

SEASON OF RIPENING Late fall

USES Cider and dessert

STORAGE QUALITY Good

Ginger Gold

THIS APPLE WAS first brought to notice after the seedling appeared in the orchard of Clyde and Ginger Harvey in Nelson County, Virginia. I personally know the Harvey family and watched the emergence of this important commercial variety. When it first entered the market, I received dozens of requests from orchardists and nurseries for samples.

OTHER NAMES None. Ginger Gold is a registered trade name of Adams County Nursery, Inc., which tested the apple for genetic stability before releasing it for commercial production; there is also a trademarked cultivar called Mountain Cove.

HISTORY The seedling was discovered in 1980 in the Harvey orchard near Lovingston, Virginia. It was reported to have appeared among a replanted block of Winesap trees that were washed out during the devastating 1969 Hurricane Camille flood. It is speculated that Golden Delicious and Newtown Pippin (which were growing in the vicinity) are parents, although this claim is not scientifically supported.

EXTERIOR DESCRIPTION Fruit is medium to large and round to oblate. The greenish-gold skin turns yellow when fully ripe and the flavor is more sweet than tart.

INTERIOR DESCRIPTION The cream-colored flesh is crisp and juicy. The flesh is slow to oxidize when cut and the slices hold their shape when cooked.

TREE CHARACTERISTICS The tree grows vigorously, developing desirable wide-angle crotches.

DISEASE RESISTANCE Susceptible to fireblight and powdery mildew; moderately resistant to other major diseases.

USES Dessert, salads, and pie making

STORAGE QUALITY Poor in common storage; in commercial controlled atmosphere storage, however, it will keep for about six months.

Gloria Mundi

In 1860, a specimen was recorded that measured 18 inches in circumference and weighed three pounds. Although the Gloria Mundi apples in my orchard may have never reached such impressive proportions, the fruiting tree was always a show stopper.

OTHER NAMES American Gloria Mundi, American Mammoth, Baltimore, Baltimore Pippin, Belle Debois, Belle Josephine, Copp's Mammoth, Glazenwood, Kinderhook Pippin, Melon, Monstrous Pippin, Mountain Flora, Ox Apple, Pound, Vandyne Apple

HISTORY Some reports claim that Gloria Mundi originated on the farm of a Mr. Crooks near Red Hook, New York, but this has been disputed. Writing in 1817, pomologist William Coxe placed its origin around 1804 on Long Island, New York. There is also an unsubstantiated claim that the apple came from Germany.

EXTERIOR DESCRIPTION Fruit is large to very large and irregularly shaped. The silvery-green skin ripens to golden yellow with somewhat of a purplish-brown flush, but it does not have stripes. Prominent white or gray lenticels appear on the surface and a conspicuous deep brown russet often covers the stem end and over the shoulders. The smooth skin becomes greasy in storage.

INTERIOR DESCRIPTION The creamy-white flesh sometimes has a greenish-yellow tinge. It is coarse and dry and has an acid flavor.

TREE CHARACTERISTICS This large, hardy tree is vigorous and spreading in form. It is a shy bearer but attention to pollination will increase the yield.

DISEASE RESISTANCE Moderately resistant to the major diseases

SEASON OF RIPENING Early fall

USES Baking and dessert

STORAGE QUALITY Poor

Golden Delicious

THIS VARIETY EXEMPLIFIES the compromise of loss of taste in favor of "attractive" appearance in apple breeding programs. Considered to be self-fertile, it is an excellent pollinator for other varieties because it blooms multiple times in midseason. Some local orchardists in the foothills of the Blue Ridge Mountains called it Rooster Tree for its pollination prowess.

OTHER NAMES Annit, Mullins Yellow Seedling, Yellow Delicious. There are many strains, sports, and cultivars. A few nurseries still market it under the name Yellow Delicious, originally a ruse to avoid paying the royalty that Stark Bro's Nursery in Missouri imposed after receiving a patent around 1915.

HISTORY It appeared around 1912 on the farm of Anderson Mullins in Clay County, West Virginia. It is speculated to be a seedling of a Grimes Golden tree; the pollination parent is unverified but Golden Reinette trees were growing nearby. In 1914 Mullins sold the tree for five thousand dollars to Stark Bro's Nursery. A steel cage was erected around the tree to prevent theft of scionwood for propagation, but scionwood had already been cut.

EXTERIOR DESCRIPTION The medium to large, conical apple has a dry golden-yellow skin that bruises easily. Early cultivars had some russeting on the skin surface and an effort was made to breed it out.

INTERIOR DESCRIPTION Flesh is firm, crisp, and juicy with a mild sweet flavor.

TREE CHARACTERISTICS This self-fertile tree bears crops at a young age and annually. The tree has a round-headed habit with wide-angle crotches and thinning is necessary to achieve large fruit size. It has yellowish-olive bark and folded, waved leaves with sharp serrations.

DISEASE RESISTANCE Susceptible to the major apple diseases

SEASON OF RIPENING Fall

USES All purpose, especially for dessert, and pie making. It is also a high-sugar variety for cider making.

STORAGE QUALITY Fair. It will shrivel in storage.

Golden Nugget

This apple was originally developed as a specific pollinator for pollen-sterile varieties, like Winesap, and triploids, like Rhode Island Greening. The complex sugary-sweet flavor launched it as a dessert apple of merit, but commercial success was hindered by the apple's small size. It is particularly suitable for fall cider making.

OTHER NAMES None

HISTORY This 1932 cross of Golden Russet and Cox's Orange Pippin was made for a pollination investigation by the Canadian Department of Agriculture at the Atlantic Food and Horticulture Research Centre in Kentville, Nova Scotia. It was selected for release in 1964 by Dr. C. J. Bishop.

EXTERIOR DESCRIPTION It is small to medium in size and broadly conical with a long stem of medium thickness. The yellow skin is streaked and splashed orange and scattered with russet.

INTERIOR DESCRIPTION The ivory flesh is juicy, crisp, and sweetly flavored.

TREE CHARACTERISTICS This vigorous tree is an early and heavy bearer, remaining small even on standard rootstock. The branches are thin with many slender fruit spurs.

DISEASE RESISTANCE Moderately susceptible to the major apple diseases

SEASON OF RIPENING Fall

USES Dessert, baking, frying, and cider

STORAGE QUALITY Fair

Golden Russet

I ONCE MADE a list of more than twenty apples that have been referred to as Golden Russet. This one in particular was described by Downing in his 1859 book, *The Fruits and Fruit Trees of America*, and appeared soon after Roxbury Russet, a vintage American apple which Golden Russet resembles in all ways except for shape. It is well-known as a cider maker, embodying all aspects of a quality product: acid, sugar, tannin, and aroma.

OTHER NAMES Bullet Pippin, English Golden Russet, Fox Apple, Long Tom, Russet Golden, Rusty Coat. There are many strains and cultivars.

HISTORY It was known in the 1700s and likely came from New York.

EXTERIOR DESCRIPTION This medium-sized apple has russeted skin which varies in color from gray-green to golden-bronze and has a bright coppery-orange cheek. Under favorable conditions, the skin is smooth and the shape uniformly round, unlike Roxbury Russet which is flat at both ends.

INTERIOR DESCRIPTION The fine-grained, yellowish flesh is crisp with an exceptionally sugary juice.

TREE CHARACTERISTICS It is a tip bearer with a tendency toward biennial bearing; cross-pollination is necessary to produce heavy crops. It has dark reddish-olive bark with prominent whitish lenticels and dull dark green leaves that are sharply serrated. Fruit will hang on the tree after leaf fall.

DISEASE RESISTANCE Resistant to apple scab and cedar apple rust; only moderately resistant to the other major diseases.

SEASON OF RIPENING Late fall

USES Dessert, cooking, cider, and drying

STORAGE QUALITY Good

Goldrush

An outstanding keeper that will retain its sprightly flavor and crisp texture in storage, Goldrush is also gaining respect as a paramount modern variety for cider making. This promising apple truly has few shortcomings except that it is heavily spurred with buds and must be well thinned to produce quality fruit and prevent breakage and biennial bearing.

OTHER NAMES Co-op 38

HISTORY This cross of Golden Delicious and Co-op 17 was developed in 1972 at Purdue University in West Lafayette, Indiana.

EXTERIOR DESCRIPTION The medium-sized apple is round to conical with yellowish-green skin. It often has a faint reddish blush although in the mid-Atlantic the blush is sometimes significant.

INTERIOR DESCRIPTION The flesh has a rich, spicy flavor high in acid and sugar, which meld after a few months of storage.

TREE CHARACTERISTICS This slightly upright and moderately vigorous tree has limited branching but wide crotch angles.

DISEASE RESISTANCE Very resistant to apple scab and powdery mildew (as publicized by the developers); moderately resistant to fireblight; susceptible to cedar apple rust.

SEASON OF RIPENING Fall

USES Dessert, pie making, drying, and increasingly for cider

STORAGE QUALITY Very good

Granite Beauty

I WAS INTRODUCED to this distinctively spicy apple in 1994 by my longtime friend and colleague Ben Watson. We were collaborating on the Ark of Taste for the international organization Slow Food. This project consisted of identifying worthy varieties that were at risk of becoming extinct, and Granite Beauty was among the selections. Spearheaded by Watson, the Monadnock Heritage Nursery is now focused on recovering this variety of merit and returning it to commerce.

OTHER NAMES None

HISTORY It appeared around 1815 on the farm of Zephaniah Breed in Weare, New Hampshire, and gained admiration in New England as a fruit for the backyard as well as the commercial market. In 1860 Breed reported selling Granite Beauty apples for one dollar per bushel at a time when a full barrel of other varieties brought the same price.

EXTERIOR DESCRIPTION This large, round fruit becomes slightly oblique at the ends. The bronze-yellow background is splashed, striped, and nearly covered by a vermillion red. The skin feels greasy or waxy to the touch. It shares its slightly hammered (or "peened") look with early strains of Granny Smith.

INTERIOR DESCRIPTION The yellowish-white flesh is crisp, tender, and juicy with a balance of sugar and acid. A spiciness which has been compared to coriander or cardamom dominates the flavor.

TREE CHARACTERISTICS This cold-hardy, early-bearing tree produces annual quality crops.

DISEASE RESISTANCE Moderately resistant to the major diseases

SEASON OF RIPENING Late fall

USES Dessert and baking

STORAGE QUALITY Good. The spicy taste intensifies after a period of storage.

Gray Pearmain

For the North-South Apple Shootout at the 2011 CiderDays in Massachusetts, I presented the southern varieties and John Bunker—apple historian, author, friend, and Maine native—presented the northern varieties. The pear-like Gray Pearmain was one of his choices and it ranked second in a field of fourteen for best flavor.

OTHER NAMES None

HISTORY It was noted in the 1885 Maine Pomological Society proceedings but it was likely available much earlier. Documents indicate that it was grown in the nineteenth century in the mid-Atlantic and upper Midwest.

EXTERIOR DESCRIPTION A medium-sized, oblate apple with a pale yellow skin that sometimes has a faint rosy blush.

INTERIOR DESCRIPTION The white flesh is crisp and dense with a sweet-tart balance, ripening on the sweet side.

TREE CHARACTERISTICS This moderately vigorous tree is slow growing but produces crops annually, even on very old trees.

DISEASE RESISTANCE Moderately resistant to the major apple diseases

SEASON OF RIPENING Late fall

USES Dessert

STORAGE QUALITY Good

Green Pippin

ALTHOUGH THE NAME is generic, this apple, propagated for generations, is not just another chance green apple seedling. It has great merit including wonderful taste that tends to be tart, sweetening up a bit in storage. I regularly design this variety into organic and low-spray orchards because it is disease resistant and dependable. Green Pippin apples are an especially good choice for making pies when combined with a very sweet variety.

OTHER NAMES None. There are possibly a number of apples named Green Pippin and some may be the seedling of the one described here.

HISTORY It was known before 1867. One source claims that it originated in Indiana but very old trees have been found in Virginia as well.

EXTERIOR DESCRIPTION Fruit is medium in size and round. The deep green skin ripens to yellow and a short, thick stem protrudes from a heavily russeted cavity.

INTERIOR DESCRIPTION The white flesh is crisp, juicy, and aromatic with an acidic bite.

TREE CHARACTERISTICS The vigorous trees have brushy limbs, requiring heavy annual pruning to produce quality fruit.

DISEASE RESISTANCE Resistant to the major apple diseases; somewhat susceptible to the late-summer diseases fly speck and sooty blotch.

SEASON OF RIPENING Mid-fall to late fall. It ripens over a number of weeks.

USES Frying, dessert, apple butter, and pie making

STORAGE QUALITY Good

Grimes Golden

My mother, who likely had tasted a few hundred apple varieties, when asked to name her favorite three replied: "Grimes, Grimes, and Grimes." This classic American apple is used for a broad spectrum of purposes, including making hard cider and brandy, and was quite prevalent in early homesteads orchards. Trees have been found in abandoned Virginian orchards still bearing small, sooty-blotched fruit of extraordinary flavor, even after fifty years of neglect.

OTHER NAMES Grimes, Grimes Golden Pippin

HISTORY It was found in 1804 by Thomas Grimes in Brooke County, West Virginia, near where John Chapman—better known as Johnny Appleseed—and his brother established a cider mill and nursery. Grimes Golden is believed to be a parent of Golden Delicious.

EXTERIOR DESCRIPTION The small to medium fruit is roundish to slightly oblong. It has greenish-yellow skin which ripens to clear yellow and is sometimes roughened with yellow or russet dots.

INTERIOR DESCRIPTION The yellowish flesh is crisp and tender with a spicy, sweet flavor. It contains 18.81 percent sugar that ferments to 9 percent alcohol.

TREE CHARACTERISTICS It tends to over crop and must be heavily thinned to produce larger fruit. The leaves are shiny, smooth, dark green, and heavily folded with fine serrations. Knobs at the base of its branches make the limbs more resistant to breakage. Grimes Golden is self-fertile and is an excellent pollinator for other varieties.

DISEASE RESISTANCE Susceptible to collar rot; somewhat resistant to fireblight and cedar apple rust. Century-old trees have learned to tolerate the diseases year after year and are sometimes found bearing small but delectable fruit.

SEASON OF RIPENING Mid-fall to late fall

USES All-purpose, particularly for frying and apple butter. In Virginia's Blue Ridge Mountains it was especially cherished for making hard cider and brandy. Old still sites are often surrounded by Grimes Golden trees.

STORAGE QUALITY Fair. It has been my experience that Grimes Golden will store longer than modern cultivars of its child, Golden Delicious.

Haralson

HARALSON IS a progeny of Malinda, a variety that was widely planted for its cold hardiness in the northern states. It is a good example of selecting a certain variety for climate, soil, or other environmental reasons. It will retain good flavor for a few months in storage and will hold its shape and texture when baked.

OTHER NAMES None. A sport called Red Haralson with a solid red blush dominates the market for this variety.

HISTORY This open-pollinated cross of Malinda and what was considered to be Ben Davis was developed in 1913 and released commercially in 1923 by the University of Minnesota. It is named for Charles Haralson, superintendent of the University of Minnesota Fruit Breeding Farm. DNA testing indicates that Wealthy is the likely pollen parent.

EXTERIOR DESCRIPTION The medium-sized, round-oblate apple has deep red skin with red stripes and a long, slender stem.

INTERIOR DESCRIPTION White flesh is crisp, firm, juicy, and tender with a mild tart flavor.

TREE CHARACTERISTICS This vigorous tree tends toward biennial bearing. Young trees are very precocious and begin to bear the second year after planting; the grower must guard against the tree producing fruit before it is developed enough to hang the crop. As a late-blooming variety, it is suitable for areas prone to late frosts.

DISEASE RESISTANCE Susceptible to apple scab; resistant to fireblight and cedar apple rust.

SEASON OF RIPENING Late fall

USES Dessert, baking, and cider

STORAGE QUALITY Good

Harrison

It is remarkable that a cider maker of this merit disappeared from cultivation and was on the brink of extinction. The juice from Harrison apples makes an extremely dark, rich cider with an exceptional mouth-feel. Harrison is also economically valuable because when the apple is pressed the juice flows like from an open faucet. I have measured the volume as approximately 18 percent greater than Winesap, another renowned cider variety.

OTHER NAMES None

HISTORY It appeared in the early nineteenth century (likely in Essex County, New Jersey) and was grown extensively throughout the mid-Atlantic and eastern United States. It was a leading variety for cider production, often blended with juice from Campfield or Graniwinkle apples, from the early 1800s until the early 1900s; documentation from this period indicates that it was highly regarded for cider taste and profitability. In his 1817 publication, William Coxe states that Harrison commanded the highest price on the New York market as a single-variety cider: "frequently ten dollars and upwards per barrel when fined for bottling." It was rediscovered by Paul Gidez in New Jersey in 1976. Since then, other single ancient trees have been found elsewhere in New Jersey, Maryland, and Virginia.

EXTERIOR DESCRIPTION This small, round apple has a stem that is at least an inch long. The skin is yellow and sometimes has a light pink blush when grown in the mid-Atlantic. It is covered by tiny black spots which give the surface a rough texture.

INTERIOR DESCRIPTION The dense yellow flesh looks dry but it yields an extraordinary volume of juice when pressed.

TREE CHARACTERISTICS It is a heavy annual bearer—a single tree on standard rootstock can produce close to one hundred bushels of apples.

DISEASE RESISTANCE Resistant to apple scab and free of rots

SEASON OF RIPENING Late fall

USES Primarily cider, but occasionally dessert

STORAGE QUALITY Good

Hauer Pippin

Once again, small commercial plantings of a few hundred Hauer Pippin trees are being made in California and elsewhere to meet local demand. The renewed interest in this apple, promoted by the Monterey Bay chapter of Slow Food, is an example of the pivotal swing by consumers from appearance back to taste. The apple's defined sweetness and clove-like flavor make it an obvious comeback candidate.

OTHER NAMES Christmas Apple, so-called for its late November ripening and subsequent availability as a fresh apple during the Christmas season.

HISTORY Around 1890 in Aptos, California (Santa Cruz County), Peter Hauer discovered a chance seedling growing along the road next to the summer home of a man named Claus Speckles. It is believed that the Hauer Pippin apple is a seedling of two varieties growing within Speckles' garden: Yellow Bellflower and the famous English apple variety, Cox Orange Pippin. The Hauer Pippin apples that Peter Hauer shipped to England were received in March and sold at a premium price.

EXTERIOR DESCRIPTION The medium to large apple is round to flat-round. It has a thick green skin that develops a rich red blush when fully mature. Prominent white lenticels, some with brownish centers, cover the surface of the apple.

INTERIOR DESCRIPTION Flesh is yellowish white. It is juicy with a very high sugar content and relatively low acidity even after several weeks of storage.

TREE CHARACTERISTICS The moderately vigorous tree bears full crops annually and the fruit will hang on the tree late in the season. It requires a long growing season to fully mature.

DISEASE RESISTANCE Resistant to the major apple diseases; it is suitable for organic or low-spray production commercially.

SEASON OF RIPENING Late fall

USES Dessert

STORAGE QUALITY Good

IN MY VIRGINIA orchard visitors would marvel at the big clear yellow apples with anticipation for an exotic tropical taste. But Hawaii apples grown in the east do not take on the same sweetness or pineapple intensity as those produced in California and other western regions. In the right setting, however, this variety is capable of convincing any apple-eating neophyte of the abundance of flavors in the apple world.

OTHER NAMES None

HISTORY This cross of Golden Delicious and Gravenstein was introduced by William Silva around 1945 in Sebastopol, California.

EXTERIOR DESCRIPTION This large and roundish apple is waxy to the touch. It has clear yellow skin and sometimes light pinkish-orange stripes which give the fruit an orange color.

INTERIOR DESCRIPTION The crisp-textured flesh has a distinctive pineapple flavor and is exceptionally sweet when grown in western regions.

TREE CHARACTERISTICS Tree growth is moderate and it must be properly pruned to discourage its biennial tendency. It does produce wide-angle crotches.

DISEASE RESISTANCE Susceptible to apple scab and bitter pit; somewhat resistant to cedar apple rust.

SEASON OF RIPENING Late fall

USES Dessert and sometimes baking

STORAGE QUALITY Fair

Hawkeye

THE SWEET, FLORAL aroma of Hawkeye is one of my earliest olfactory memories. From humble Iowa beginnings in the later part of the nineteenth century, Hawkeye has been bred for more than one hundred years to be redder, larger, and more elongated. The revelatory joke emerged that the bigger and redder, the less the flavor. One would never equate the Red Delicious in today's marketplace—the most stereotypical and widely grown apple in the world—with the original apple from which it came.

OTHER NAMES Delicious Hiatt Original, Delicious Standard, Hawkeye Delicious, Original Delicious, Red Delicious, Stark Delicious. There are more than 300 named variations or cultivars.

HISTORY Around 1880 Jesse Hiatt, a farmer from Peru, Iowa, noticed a chance seedling growing in his orchard. It is told that Hiatt deliberately chopped the unwanted seedling down twice before permitting it to grow and fruit. In 1892 Hiatt entered the Hawkeye (so-called for his state's nickname) into a competition held by Stark Bro's Nursery to find an apple to replace Ben Davis, which was lagging in sales. Hawkeye won the competition and in 1895 Stark Bro's bought the rights and renamed it Delicious. In 1912 Stark bought the rights to a yellow apple from West Virginia which they named Golden Delicious; at that point the original Delicious became Red Delicious.

EXTERIOR DESCRIPTION Fruit is large and elongated with five points or knobs on the blossom end. The green background is coated and striped red with patches of yellow shining through. Hawkeye has more stripes and less of a pointed nose than modern cultivars.

INTERIOR DESCRIPTION The white flesh is tender, fine-grained, crisp, and juicy with a mild flavor and a distinctive, memorable aroma.

TREE CHARACTERISTICS The vigorous tree produces wide crotch angles. It is slow to begin bearing; if properly thinned, it will bear full crops annually once established. It is adapted to many types of soil and climate conditions for apple production.

DISEASE RESISTANCE Somewhat resistant to fireblight and cedar apple rust

SEASON OF RIPENING Mid-fall

USES Dessert. It is not suitable for cooking or making cider.

STORAGE QUALITY Fair

Hawley

FOR MANY YEARS I attempted to grow this tree in the hot and humid Virginia weather but the relentless apple scab destruction was unsustainable without a full spray schedule. I have since become resigned to saving my enjoyment of Hawley apples for New England visits, which as a region is significantly less prone to scab.

OTHER NAMES Douse, Dows, Dowse, Howley

HISTORY It was first recognized around 1750 in New Canaan, New York. The fruit came from seeds brought from Milford, Connecticut.

EXTERIOR DESCRIPTION Fruit is large and globular with a stem that is approximately ¾ of an inch long. The smooth, waxy skin is greenish yellow with an inconspicuous brown blush. Russet dots and flecks cover most of the surface, especially toward the wide, deep cavity.

INTERIOR DESCRIPTION The yellowish-white flesh is fine-grained, soft, juicy, and subacid.

TREE CHARACTERISTICS It is slow to begin bearing, but once established it will produce moderate crops annually.

DISEASE RESISTANCE Susceptible to apple scab; moderately resistant to the other major diseases.

SEASON OF RIPENING Mid-fall

USES Dessert and apple butter

STORAGE QUALITY Fair

Hidden Rose

My Michigan apple explorer friend, Robert Nitschke, suggested around 1975 that I try growing this rosy-fleshed variety, but with Virginia heat and humidity the resulting apple was of unremarkable flavor and washed-out appearance. The tree is much more likely to thrive in cooler regions and to produce a juicy, crisp fruit with a good flavor balance between sweet and tart.

OTHER NAMES Airlie Red Flesh

HISTORY It was found before 1960 as a young tree growing on the farm property of Lucky and Audrey Newell near Airlie, Oregon. This land was later sold to Louis Kimzey, who discovered it again and promoted it. There is another claim that it was found by William Schulz of Philomath, Oregon, who named it Airlie Red Flesh for the nearby town of Airlie.

EXTERIOR DESCRIPTION Fruit is medium in size and elongated. The yellow skin has a reddish blush when exposed to full sunlight (understory fruit will have little red coloration) and it has whitish dots on the surface.

INTERIOR DESCRIPTION The flesh color varies from deep red to pale pink. It is juicy, crisp, sugary and richly flavored.

TREE CHARACTERISTICS Tree growth is very slow in the mid-Atlantic, but in other locations the growth rate is moderate and it produces moderate to light crops annually. Trees should be pruned every year to open it up to air circulation and sun penetration.

DISEASE RESISTANCE Moderately resistant to the major diseases

SEASON OF RIPENING Fall

USES Dessert

STORAGE QUALITY Good

Hog Sweet

THROUGHOUT HISTORY THIS variety has been primarily known by two names—Hog Sweet (in the mid-Atlantic and South) and Hog Island Sweet (in New England)—and in fact may potentially be two distinct varieties that share many of the same characteristics. In the South it is speculated that the apple was fed to pigs and other livestock, but in the North it was solely consumed for dessert and never used to feed animals.

OTHER NAMES Hog Apple, Hog Island Sweet, Hog Sweeting, Sweet Pippin, Van Kleck's Sweet

HISTORY The northern origin of the apple was recorded in 1857, although it likely appeared earlier, on Hog Island (now known as Syosset Island) near Long Island, New York; the southern origin of the apple is unknown.

EXTERIOR DESCRIPTION The medium to large, roundish-conical apple has pale greenish-yellow skin. The background is sometimes mottled with red and covered by patches of russet and small russet dots.

INTERIOR DESCRIPTION The yellowish flesh is coarse, crisp, and juicy with a very sweet flavor.

TREE CHARACTERISTICS This vigorous grower bears heavy crops annually. Pruning will improve the size and quality of the apples.

DISEASE RESISTANCE Resistant to the major diseases; it will perform well under organic and low-spray programs.

SEASON OF RIPENING Late fall

USES Dessert, baking, and apple butter

STORAGE QUALITY Good

Honey Cider

THIS VARIETY OF murky provenance was historically valued for dessert and especially for cider making, despite a high susceptibility to fireblight. In the late nineteenth and early twentieth centuries fireblight was not as aggressively rampant as it is now; however, even modern orchards continue to plant it in the face of fireblight because it has such a good reputation as a cider maker. The trees have a better chance of survival at higher elevations and with a good fireblight control program in place.

OTHER NAMES Honey Sweet

HISTORY The exact location of its origin is not known, but it was noted in 1869. It was returned to commerce when Professor Elwood Fisher, a fruit explorer and collector in Harrisonburg, Virginia, found a Honey Cider around 1960 in the Shenandoah Valley of Virginia—a hotbed of apple production for centuries.

EXTERIOR DESCRIPTION This medium-sized, round apple is slightly flattened on the ends. The yellow skin is streaked and mottled with red and pink.

INTERIOR DESCRIPTION The yellowish flesh is very sweet, juicy, and firm.

DISEASE RESISTANCE Highly susceptible to fireblight in warmer low-elevation areas; moderately resistant to the other major apple diseases.

SEASON OF RIPENING Late summer to early fall

USES Dessert and cider

STORAGE QUALITY Fair

Honeycrisp

DURING THE LATE twentieth and early twenty-first centuries, Honeycrisp has become established as one of the darlings of the apple world. Developed in Minnesota, this winter hardy, high-quality apple is difficult to produce outside of cooler regions and the celebrated flavor and crispness will be lost.

OTHER NAMES None

HISTORY This 1960 cross of Macoun and Honeygold was produced in the University of Minnesota's apple breeding program. The original seedling was planted in 1962 at the University of Minnesota Horticultural Research Center, which is located in the east-central part of the state near Excelsior. Honeycrisp was selected in 1974 and released commercially in 1991.

EXTERIOR DESCRIPTION Fruit is medium to large and oblate to roundly oblate. It has yellow skin that becomes almost entirely red when exposed to the sun. The surface is dotted with small lenticels and the stem end displays some green russeting.

INTERIOR DESCRIPTION The cream-colored flesh is coarse and exceptionally crisp and juicy. It has a subacid flavor that can vary from mild and well-balanced to strongly aromatic depending on the tree's locale and maturity as well as the particular growing season.

DISEASE RESISTANCE Moderately susceptible to the major apple diseases

SEASON OF RIPENING Fall

USES Dessert, pie making, and cider

STORAGE QUALITY Excellent. It retains high flavor in storage.

Hoople's Antique Gold

THIS IS THE beauty queen of the russet apple world. Robert Nitschke of Southmeadow Fruit Gardens in Michigan sent me this highly defined russet and I was impressed not only by its good looks, but also by the remarkably intense and complex flavor which surpasses that of Golden Russet and Roxbury Russet.

OTHER NAMES None

HISTORY It appeared around 1960 in Otway, Ohio. It was a bud mutation from a Golden Delicious tree found in the Hoople Fruit Farm orchard by the owner, Harry Hoople, who sent it for propagation to Southmeadow Fruit Gardens in Baroda, Michigan.

EXTERIOR DESCRIPTION This medium-sized, oblate apple tapers from the stem end to the blossom end. It has a burnished golden skin on a rich yellow background and the surface is evenly russeted.

INTERIOR DESCRIPTION The crisp, juicy, yellow flesh is very flavorful.

TREE CHARACTERISTICS The tree is round and spreading and not as brushy as the Roxbury Russet. It has a moderate growth rate.

DISEASE RESISTANCE Good resistance to the major diseases

SEASON OF RIPENING Mid-fall to late fall

USES Dessert and ornamental landscaping

STORAGE QUALITY Good

Hoover

LIKE ARKANSAS BLACK, Hoover can be a showstopper, especially at higher elevations when the skin becomes such a deep red that it appears nearly black. A low chill requirement of less than 800 hours has historically made this a prime variety for warmer regions. But I have found that, likely because of global warming and the accompanying drop in chill hours, Hoover is not producing as well in southern locations as it previously did.

OTHER NAMES Baltimore Red, Black Coal, Guver, Thunderbolt, Wattangah, Welcome

HISTORY It was known around 1850 and first mentioned in an 1856 nursery catalog that identified it as a seedling from Edisto, South Carolina; in 1857 a horticulture magazine described it in detail. Jim Lawson of Ball Ground, Georgia—a veteran grower of southern apple varieties—offered it in his nursery catalog for many years.

EXTERIOR DESCRIPTION This large roundish-oblate apple generally has a long, slender stem. The yellowish skin is nearly covered with varying shades of red stripes and splashes as well as light-colored dots and russet patches. The coloration can vary from season to season and location to location.

INTERIOR DESCRIPTION The yellowish flesh is firm, juicy, and tender with a brisk acid flavor.

TREE CHARACTERISTICS Upright and spreading, the tree is a vigorous grower and a late bloomer that will miss the late frosts. It is one of the last varieties to shed its leaves and many hang on into winter.

DISEASE RESISTANCE Moderately resistant to the major diseases, especially fireblight

SEASON OF RIPENING Late fall

USES Dessert, baking, and particularly for apple butter

STORAGE QUALITY Good

Horse

FOR GENERATIONS, the Burfords used this eighteenth-century variety for drying and vinegar making. The distinctive flavor once caused a family member to exclaim: "this Horse is tarter than an unripe persimmon!"

OTHER NAMES Green Horse, Hoss, Mammoth Horse, Old Fashion Horse, Oldfield Horse, Summer Horse, Yellow Horse. The variety Haas is distinct and was grown by Gabriel Cerre around 1872 in St. Louis, Missouri.

HISTORY An 1869 USDA publication listed this apple as originating in Nash County, North Carolina. But it is also known to have been offered for sale in 1763 in the *Virginia Gazette*, published in Williamsburg, Virginia.

EXTERIOR DESCRIPTION Fruit is roundish and is typically large. It has a thick, bright yellow skin that is occasionally blushed red.

INTERIOR DESCRIPTION The yellow flesh is coarse, tender, and acidic. Flavor is tart until fully ripe; even then, it is still not sweet.

TREE CHARACTERISTICS The tree is vigorous, long living, spreading in shape. It blooms late in the season and dependably bears good-sized fruit even when thinning is neglected.

DISEASE RESISTANCE Good; it is suitable as a processing apple for organic and low-spray orchards.

SEASON OF RIPENING Midsummer to late summer

USES Apple butter, drying, jelly, vinegar, and livestock food

STORAGE QUALITY Fair for a summer apple

Hubbardston Nonesuch

Ripening between the fall and winter varieties, Hubbardston Nonesuch is a good choice for the home orchard that aims to provide fresh apples throughout the full season of ripening. This apple always ranked high when I presented it during tastings at Old Sturbridge Village in Massachusetts.

OTHER NAMES American Blush, American Nonpareil, Farmer's Profit, Hubbardston's Pippin, John May, Old Town Pippin, Orleans, Van Fleet

HISTORY It was noted in 1832 but probably was known in the late eighteenth century. It was named for the town where it was found: Hubbardston, Massachusetts.

EXTERIOR DESCRIPTION Fruit is large and roundish-conical. The smooth, glossy skin has a rich yellow background that is nearly covered with a deep red and indistinct crimson stripes. It is russeted around the stem base and large russeted specks appear on the surface.

INTERIOR DESCRIPTION The yellowish flesh is juicy, crisp, tender, and subacid. It contains 12.02 percent sugar that ferments to 6 percent alcohol. Sprightly at harvest, the taste is more sweet than tart after storage. It has a small core.

TREE CHARACTERISTICS The tree bears heavy crops early and has a slightly biennial tendency. It has brownish-chestnut wood with whitish specks, and dark green, shiny leaves that are heavily folded and waved. Soil and climate conditions affect the tree and fruit characteristics remarkably, which often makes identification difficult.

DISEASE RESISTANCE Moderately resistant to the major diseases

SEASON OF RIPENING Late fall

USES Primarily dessert, but sometimes for baking and frying

STORAGE QUALITY Good. The smaller fruit will store longer than large ones.

Hudson's Golden Gem

THIS VARIETY HELPED to foster an acceptance of russet or brown-skinned apples. I believe this can be attributed to the pronounced flavor that to some suggests a Bosc pear. It and Zabergau Reinette are probably the largest high-quality russet apples.

OTHER NAMES None

HISTORY It was discovered in a fencerow thicket in Oregon and introduced in 1931 by the Hudson Wholesale Nurseries of Tangent, Oregon.

EXTERIOR DESCRIPTION Fruit is large and conical (shape is irregular in some climates) with a long stem. The uniformly dull russet skin is smooth.

INTERIOR DESCRIPTION Light yellow flesh is sugary, juicy, and crisp. In taste tests it has been described as pear-like and nutty.

TREE CHARACTERISTICS A vigorous, productive annual bearer. The tree remains small regardless of the rootstock and the fruit will hang on the tree long into winter. Cross-pollination will increase fruitfulness.

DISEASE RESISTANCE Somewhat resistant to apple scab; only moderately resistant to the other major apple diseases.

SEASON OF RIPENING Late fall

USES Dessert, baking, drying, and cider. Dried apples taste good but the slices will be dark because the flesh oxides quickly.

Hunt Russet

In the early twentieth century, a government program with the mission to destroy all neglected fruit trees in Massachusetts resulted in the disappearance from cultivation of many heirloom varieties. The fate of Hunt Russet was at risk but it was saved from extinction, likely because of the Davenport preservation collection. It was later planted in 1973 at Old Sturbridge Village in Massachusetts and I am always delighted to present it during apple tastings at that historic site.

OTHER NAMES American Golden Russet of New England, Fay's Russet, Golden Russet of Massachusetts, New England Golden Russet, Russet Pearmain

HISTORY It originated around 1750 about a mile north of Concord, Massachusetts, on the Hunt Farm which is on the south side of Punkatasset Hill, overlooking the Old North Bridge from the Revolutionary War.

EXTERIOR DESCRIPTION Fruit is medium in size, truncate-conical to conical, convex, and slightly ribbed at the eye. The yellow skin is flushed bright red and has russet dots over most of the surface.

INTERIOR DESCRIPTION The whitish flesh is tinged yellow; it is fine-grained, juicy, and tender with a subacid, pear-like flavor.

TREE CHARACTERISTICS Upright and spreading, the tree is a slow grower in the nursery but once moved to the orchard it will grow rapidly and live for a long time.

DISEASE RESISTANCE Susceptible to fireblight; only moderately susceptible to the other diseases.

SEASON OF RIPENING Late fall

USES Dessert

STORAGE QUALITY Very good

Huntsman

Huntsman was one of the hundreds of new apple varieties that came out of the seedling orchards planted in the Midwest for cider making during the nineteenth century. Trees of this era were often distributed widely by Stark Bro's Nursery, which was founded in 1816 in Missouri.

OTHER NAMES Huntsman's Favorite

HISTORY It was found around 1873 on the farm of John Huntsman in Fayette, Missouri.

EXTERIOR DESCRIPTION The large, oblate apple has smooth greenish-yellow skin with an orange-red blush.

INTERIOR DESCRIPTION The firm white flesh is tinged with yellow and has a distinctive aromatic flavor. It is not very crisp but it is juicy and tender.

TREE CHARACTERISTICS The tree is a vigorous grower and has long, slender branches. It does not begin to bear early but is a heavy producer when it does.

DISEASE RESISTANCE Susceptible to apple scab, bitter rot, and (in some regions) sunburn. I've also noticed that it is sometimes severely affected by fireblight as the disease becomes increasingly prevalent in cooler and less humid regions.

SEASON OF RIPENING Mid-fall

USES Dessert

STORAGE QUALITY Fair

Hyslop

EVEN IN HER nineties, my mother would always remind me to set aside a few bushels of Hyslop for apple pickle making. After pricking the apples with a darning needle to prevent bursting, they were lightly cooked in a wide granite pan, packed in quart jars, covered with low-sugar syrup, and processed. The syrup would turn brilliant red from the peel of these brightly colored crabapples.

OTHER NAMES Hislop, Hyslop Crabapple

HISTORY It was first noted in 1869 but the place of origin is unknown.

EXTERIOR DESCRIPTION Fruit is large and round with a long, slender stem. It has dark red or purplish skin which is overspread by a thick bluish-gray bloom.

INTERIOR DESCRIPTION The very firm yellow flesh is sometimes tinged red next to the skin. It is juicy when first ripe but it quickly becomes dry and mealy. It is subacid and astringent and contains 11.84 percent sugar that ferments to about 5 percent alcohol.

TREE CHARACTERISTICS The tree is a good grower, very hardy, and a reliable biennial cropper. Olive-green bark takes on an orange hue when wet. Is has shiny, waved, sharply serrated leaves. Shoots grow in a zigzag manner and fruit is borne in clusters.

DISEASE RESISTANCE Moderately susceptible to the major diseases

SEASON OF RIPENING Midsummer

USES Jelly, cider (for blending with other varieties), pickling, and ornamental landscaping. I often recommend this variety to landscape architects for design because of the configuration of the tree and its interesting bark.

STORAGE QUALITY Poor

Idared

I CAN RECALL times during the May apple storage cleaning when a few boxes of Idared were discovered and quickly devoured with relish. For the Burfords, this was also an imperative variety for apple butter making—often one-third of the kettle was Idared.

OTHER NAMES None

HISTORY This cross of Jonathan and Wagener was made in 1930 at the Idaho Agricultural Experiment Station in Moscow and selected in 1935. The variety increased in popularity after World War II, and sometime later it was widely planted in northern Europe as well.

EXTERIOR DESCRIPTION This apple is medium to large and shape is round to round-conic. Skin color varies from nearly solid red to light red over a greenish background; the longer the apple remains on the tree, the brighter the color.

INTERIOR DESCRIPTION Flesh is crisp, white, and juicy. The flavor is intense at the time of ripening, but diminishes after long storage.

TREE CHARACTERISTICS The tree is small to average in size. It bears when young and produces heavy yields annually. It is one of the few varieties that blooms early and ripens late. Adequate potassium in the soil is necessary for Idared to color well. It is an excellent pollinator for Gravenstein. There is little pre-harvest drop.

DISEASE RESISTANCE Resistant to apple scab; susceptible to fireblight and powdery mildew.

SEASON OF RIPENING Late fall

USES Dessert, cider, baking, pie making, applesauce, and apple butter

STORAGE QUALITY Good

Ingram

This "apple child" of Ralls shares many characteristics with its parent, except for Ingram's pink to crimson skin color. It came about during the second wave of planting seedling cider orchards, in the mid-nineteenth century Midwest, which was essentially the heyday of the apple when thousands of varieties were available. With supply fast outpacing demand in this era, many worthy apples such as Ingram remained relatively unknown.

OTHER NAMES None

HISTORY Around 1850 it came from a seed of a Ralls apple on the farm of Martin Ingram in Springfield, Missouri.

EXTERIOR DESCRIPTION Fruit is medium to large with a truncate-conic shape. It has smooth, thick, tough skin; gray-pink scarfskin is often present. The clear yellow background is dotted and streaked pink to crimson and the surface is covered with numerous conspicuous whitish lenticels.

INTERIOR DESCRIPTION The creamy white flesh (sometimes with a yellow tinge) is firm, crisp, and mildly subacid. It is not quite as juicy as Ralls.

TREE CHARACTERISTICS Vigorous with upright growth, the tree has long, straight branches and brownish-gray bark. The leaves are dark, glossy, and small to medium in size. It bears heavy crops biennially; thinning is essential to prevent limb breakage. Ingram resembles Ralls in its growth habit and very late bloom time (full bloom in central Virginia is around the first week of May).

DISEASE RESISTANCE Moderately susceptible to the major diseases. Like Ralls, the blossoms are subject to fireblight, but there always seems to be enough unaffected blossoms to produce full crops.

SEASON OF RIPENING Late fall

USES Dessert, and sometimes pie making

STORAGE QUALITY Good. It does not shrivel in storage.

Jefferis

THE STRIKINGLY COLORED Jefferis was recognized as the year's best seedling by the Pennsylvania Horticultural Society in 1848. The apple's pear-like flavor, dependable bearing, resistance to some of the major diseases, and long ripening period gave it a competitive edge.

OTHER NAMES Everbearing, Grantham. It is sometimes spelled Jefferies.

HISTORY It originated around 1830 with Isaac Jefferies of Chester County, Pennsylvania. The apple was named by the Pennsylvania Horticultural Society.

EXTERIOR DESCRIPTION Fruit is medium in size and round with flattened ends. The light red skin is covered with darker red (and sometimes orange-red) stripes and the surface has some russet dots. The skin is thin which causes the apple to bruise easily and perhaps to have more susceptibility to insect damage.

INTERIOR DESCRIPTION The yellowish-white flesh is crisp, firm, and tender with a subacid to slightly sweet flavor.

TREE CHARACTERISTICS The tree is hardy and bears heavy crops; it must be thinned attentively to produce sizable fruit.

DISEASE RESISTANCE Resistant to apple scab and powdery mildew

SEASON OF RIPENING Mid-fall. It ripens over a number of weeks which increases its value as a backyard variety.

USES Dessert

STORAGE QUALITY Fair

Johnson's Fine Winter

THIS APPLE, the primordial York, has such a notably different, more intense taste than the modern York and all of the cultivars that have come forth, that it could be classified as a distinct variety. Very old trees are still found thriving in the East and bearing clusters of small but delectable apples. It brings joy to my eyes when I see an old tree, especially when I can pluck the fruit from the branch and enjoy.

OTHER NAMES Jonathan's Fine Winter, Original York

HISTORY It was found around 1820 near Hellam, Pennsylvania. It is reported that John Kline discovered the apple under the leaves and took them to Jonathan Jessop (Jessup), who promoted the apple and carried it to the Friends' annual meeting in Baltimore, where it was first distributed to Virginia. The apple was originally known as Jonathan's Fine Winter after Jonathan Jessop; the name was later corrupted to Johnson's Fine Winter after William Johnson, who lived near York, Pennsylvania.

EXTERIOR DESCRIPTION This small oblique apple has greenish-yellow skin flushed with red.

INTERIOR DESCRIPTION The yellowish flesh is aromatic, crisp, tender, and juicy.

TREE CHARACTERISTICS This vigorous and fast-growing tree bears heavy crops annually.

DISEASE RESISTANCE Moderately resistant to the major diseases

SEASON OF RIPENING Fall

USES Dessert, baking, pie making, apple butter, and cider

STORAGE QUALITY Good

Jonafree

THE JONAFREE APPLE was made in an effort to overcome some of the production weakness of Jonathan, which is recognized as a major market variety. Notably, Jonafree does not develop Jonathan spot, a condition of rots which has been a commercial problem for Jonathan, and it has been called field immune to apple scab. New apples with characteristics similar to varieties well established in the marketplace are seldom competitors, so after a brief time in the market, interest in Jonafree faded.

OTHER NAMES Co-op 22

HISTORY This cross of Jonathan, Red Spy, Golden Delicious, and Rome Beauty was developed in 1965 by the Illinois Agricultural Experiment Station in Urbana.

EXTERIOR DESCRIPTION The medium-sized apple has a round to roundish-oblate shape. The skin is thick and tough (similar to Jonathan) and smooth. It has a yellow-green background which is mostly covered with a medium red color and some light tan dots.

INTERIOR DESCRIPTION Pale yellow flesh is fine-grained, juicy, and crisp. Less acidic than Jonathan, it has a rich flavor and slight aroma.

TREE CHARACTERISTICS The vigorous tree is moderately spreading in form and bears heavy crops annually. Thinning is necessary to produce quality fruit and prevent limb breakage.

DISEASE RESISTANCE Susceptible to powdery mildew; resistant to apple scab and Jonathan spot.

SEASON OF RIPENING Fall. It ripens around the same time as Jonathan.

USES Dessert

STORAGE QUALITY Good

Jonagold

JONAGOLD HAS GARNERED worldwide attention for its broad market appeal. Orchardists appreciate the variety's tendency to bear crops on dwarf stock just three or four years after planting. It is also a good choice for backyard growers, ripening unevenly over two to three weeks and generally necessitating several pickings.

OTHER NAMES None. There are a number of cultivars and strains, such as Nicobel, Jonagored, Jonica, and Red Jonagold, as well as a red sport from Belgium.

HISTORY This cross of Jonathan and Golden Delicious was developed in 1943 at the New York State Agricultural Experiment Station in Geneva. It was named and introduced in 1968.

EXTERIOR DESCRIPTION The large fruit is round to conical and has a long stem that curves to one side. Skin is dry, bumpy, and somewhat tough with little aroma. It is generally yellow with an orange-red blush and a hint of stripes; some strains, like Red Jonagold from Japan, will show about 75 percent red coloration.

INTERIOR DESCRIPTION Juicy and crisp, the creamy-yellow flesh has a balanced sweet-tart flavor that usually ranks high in taste tests.

TREE CHARACTERISTICS The tree is open, spreading, cold hardy, and very precocious, often cropping heavily on the third leaf. Unlike most apple varieties, Jonagold is a triploid (it has 3 sets of 17 chromosomes) and thus needs specific pollinators to ensure heavy fruit set. Avoid using Golden Delicious as a pollen source for Jonagold; good options include Melrose, Akane, Winter Banana, Newtown Pippin, Virginia (Hewes) Crab, or the Snowdrift crabapple. Some winter injury can occur when excessive growth takes place.

DISEASE RESISTANCE Susceptible to powdery mildew, apple scab, and sunburn

SEASON OF RIPENING Fall

USES Dessert, pie making, frying, and cider

STORAGE QUALITY Good

Jonathan

The older strains of Jonathan have a more pronounced flavor than newer ones. I have often proclaimed that Jonathan is a lightning rod for fireblight, but after many years of observation I have witnessed it unaffected by fireblight while so-called resistant varieties nearby were infected. Fireblight is fickle!

OTHER NAMES King Phillip, New Spitzenburg, Phillip Rick, Ulster Seedling. Numerous sports and strains exist including Red Jonathan and Double Red.

HISTORY It originated on the farm of Philip Rick in Woodstock, New York (Ulster County), and was first described by Judge Jonathan Buel, who named it for the finder, Jonathan Hasbrouck. When it was introduced around 1826, its similarity to Esopus Spitzenburg (of which it is considered to be a seedling) prompted it to be called New Spitzenburg.

EXTERIOR DESCRIPTION The medium-sized fruit is round but tapering toward the blossom end. Skin is tough yet thin and smooth and dry to the touch. The yellow background is almost completely blushed and striped bright red.

INTERIOR DESCRIPTION The white flesh is firm, tender, and juicy with a sprightly subacid flavor.

TREE CHARACTERISTICS One of the few self-fruitful apple trees, Jonathan is moderately vigorous and bears early, annually, and heavily. The tree will remain fairly small with slender, delicate growth. Leaves are dull, somewhat coarse, pubescent, and irregularly serrated.

DISEASE RESISTANCE Susceptible to fireblight (especially when young), powdery mildew, and cedar apple rust; somewhat resistant to apple scab.

SEASON OF RIPENING Fall

USES Dessert, applesauce, baking, pie making (when combined with a sweet variety), frying, and cider

STORAGE QUALITY Good

Kearsarge

I WAS INTRODUCED to Kearsarge at Gould Hill Orchard in New Hampshire by my apple-explorer friend, Ben Watson. He found that the thin, tender skin peels easily away from the flesh when cooked, which makes it good for baking whole. The apple has a nice balance of sweetness and acidity that has been described as tasting like pure "fruit drops."

OTHER NAMES None

HISTORY The date of origin is not known but it comes from Gould Hill Orchard in Hopkinton, New Hampshire. It is named for nearby Mount Kearsarge.

EXTERIOR DESCRIPTION This large, blocky-round apple is covered with a reddish blush and darker red streaks on about one-third of the skin's surface. The thin skin does not toughen up. Inconspicuous green dots can be detected in the darker areas and light ribbing appears in the basin.

INTERIOR DESCRIPTION The creamy-yellow flesh is crisp, breaking, juicy, and slightly acidic.

TREE CHARACTERISTICS It grows slower than the moderately vigorous McIntosh and produces full crops annually.

DISEASE RESISTANCE Somewhat resistant to apple scab; moderately susceptible to the other major apple diseases.

SEASON OF RIPENING Late fall

USES Dessert

STORAGE QUALITY Good

Keener Seedling

THE APPLE CATEGORY "rusty coat" has always served as a dumping ground for apples that have any tinge of russeting. But Keener Seedling is the essence of the category: the surface is completely brown with just a few whitish lenticels peeping through. The apple is recognized for excellent keeping quality and a sweet-tart flavor that becomes sweeter and more pronounced after storage.

OTHER NAMES Rusty Coat

HISTORY It was found around 1880 in Lincoln County, North Carolina. According to a report given to Lee Calhoun (North Carolina author and world authority on southern apple varieties), the Keener family had a land grant along Leeper's Creek in Lincoln County; it was there that a family member propagated and distributed the variety.

EXTERIOR DESCRIPTION The medium-sized apple is round with a flattened end. The totally russeted skin is dotted with a few whitish lenticels and occasionally has a slight reddish blush.

INTERIOR DESCRIPTION The white flesh is juicy and fine-grained.

TREE CHARACTERISTICS Although the tree is an early bloomer, the fruit ripen very late in the season and will hang on the tree during early winter.

DISEASE RESISTANCE Highly resistant to the major diseases; this variety is suitable for organic and low-spray production.

SEASON OF RIPENING Late fall to early winter

USES Dessert, jelly, and drying

STORAGE QUALITY Excellent

Keepsake

THIS APPLE EXEMPLIFIES the trend of rejecting varieties due to their small size and "unattractive" appearance, even when furnished with a long list of desirable characteristics: aromatic flavor, crispness, hardiness, tree friendliness, resistance to two major diseases, and remarkably long storage. It is a shame that Keepsake's only accepted claim to fame is as one of the parents of Honeycrisp, a variety that is becoming mainstream in commerce.

OTHER NAMES None

HISTORY This cross of MN 447 and Northern Spy was made in 1978 at the University of Minnesota. It was developed (and thus named) for its keeping quality.

EXTERIOR DESCRIPTION Small to medium in size, this apple is often described as unattractive and irregularly shaped. It has a mostly red skin, depending on the climate in which it is grown and the season of production.

INTERIOR DESCRIPTION The crisp yellow flesh is sweet, spicy, and strongly aromatic.

TREE CHARACTERISTICS The moderately vigorous tree bears heavy crops annually. It responds well to pruning and is generally easy to manage.

DISEASE RESISTANCE Resistant to fireblight and cedar apple rust; only moderately susceptible to the other diseases.

SEASON OF RIPENING Late fall

USES Dessert, baking, and applesauce

STORAGE QUALITY Excellent

Kentucky Limbertwig

THIS MAY BE a variation of Red Limbertwig which is speculated to be one of the earliest, if not the first, named Limbertwigs. The seedling variations from the orchards of Virginia and the Great Smoky Mountains moved westward during the nineteenth century.

OTHER NAMES None

HISTORY This variety appeared in the 1800s in Kentucky, but the exact location of origin is not known.

EXTERIOR DESCRIPTION Fruit is medium to large and round-oblate. The yellow skin is covered with red stripes in varying hues.

INTERIOR DESCRIPTION Flesh is white, juicy, and crisp with a sweet, mild flavor.

TREE CHARACTERISTICS This vigorous tree has the typical Limbertwig willow-like branches. It is an annual bearer but the fruit will be small unless the tree is heavily thinned.

DISEASE RESISTANCE Moderately resistant to the major diseases

SEASON OF RIPENING Late fall

USES Dessert, drying, baking, and frying

STORAGE QUALITY Very good

King David

FOR THE HIGHEST flavor, King David apples should be harvested when fully colored on the tree. It's a delicate balance, however, as fruit that become overripe on the tree will water core, producing translucent cells in the flesh. Some people consider its wine-like flavor and crunchiness to be greater than Winesap. In tastings it always ranks in the top ten even when it is not at optimum flavor.

OTHER NAMES None

HISTORY In 1893 it was found in a fencerow on the farm of Ben Frost in Durham, Arkansas (Washington County). It is speculated to be a cross of Jonathan and Arkansas Black or a cross of Jonathan and Winesap. It was introduced by Stark Bro's Nursery in 1902.

EXTERIOR DESCRIPTION Fruit is small to medium and round. The skin is usually a solid deep red although occasionally it has a pale greenish-yellow background overlaid with dark red; the color varies depending on the growing region and the elevation.

INTERIOR DESCRIPTION The whitish-yellow flesh is sub-acid and slightly sweet in flavor.

TREE CHARACTERISTICS The vigorously growing tree is spreading and tends to be very bushy. It has reddish-olive bark, and dull, coarse leaves with sharp serrations. Fruit hangs on the tree long after ripening and the red color will brighten. Good pollination is necessary for heavy production.

DISEASE RESISTANCE Good resistance to the major apple diseases

SEASON OF RIPENING Late fall

USES Dessert, baking, pie making, applesauce, and cider. The cooked fruit has a rich yellow color.

STORAGE QUALITY Very good

Kinnaird's Choice

WHEN AN early-twentieth-century fruit storage warehouse was being torn down in Lynchburg, Virginia, I rescued handwritten records which chronicled the popularity of Kinnaird's Choice during the Great Depression. Growers of this era recognized the need for flavorful, dependable, late-blooming varieties like this one to assure an annual cash crop.

OTHER NAMES Kinnard, Kinnard's Choice, Red Winter Cluster

HISTORY Noted in 1872, it was found on the farm of Michael Kinnaird in Franklin County, Tennessee. The parentage is unknown but it is speculated to be a cross of Winesap and a Limbertwig variety.

EXTERIOR DESCRIPTION Fruit is medium to large and round with a thick, tough, smooth skin. The yellow background is covered with mottled red (deepening to purple red) and small whitish dots.

INTERIOR DESCRIPTION The white flesh is sometimes tinged yellow. It is crisp, coarse, aromatic, and subacid. The core is small and the seeds are short and plump.

TREE CHARACTERISTICS The tree is vigorous, upright, and brushy. It bears young and yields moderate crops with some tendency toward biennial production. It blooms late, escaping frosts.

DISEASE RESISTANCE Moderately resistant to the major diseases

SEASON OF RIPENING Fall. It ripens between Stayman and Winesap.

USES Dessert, cooking, frying, and cider

STORAGE QUALITY Good

Liberty

TOUTED TO BE the greatest disease-free variety ever developed, Liberty became a popular choice for homeowners beginning in the 1970s, particularly because of its high resistance to apple scab. Even unsprayed, Liberty will prominently display clean foliage in backyard plantings while the leaves, buds, and fruits of nearby scab-susceptible varieties become covered with dull black or grey-brown lesions.

OTHER NAMES NY 55140-19

HISTORY This cross of Macoun with Perdue 54-12 was made in 1955 at the New York State Agricultural Experiment Station in Geneva and was released to the public in 1974. The name "Liberty" was suggested by Bernadine Aldwinckle of the Experiment Station's Entomology and Plant Pathology departments to denote freedom from disease. The pollen was supplied by Dr. Ralph Shay of Purdue University, Indiana. The disease resistance comes from *Malus floribunda*.

EXTERIOR DESCRIPTION This large, round-oblate apple has a short stem. The yellow skin usually has a red blush over most of the surface but coloration will vary depending on the growing region.

INTERIOR DESCRIPTION The creamy white flesh is slightly coarse, crisp, juicy, and sweet.

TREE CHARACTERISTICS A vigorous grower with a round-spreading form, the tree bears heavy crops annually but must be thinned to produce large fruit.

DISEASE RESISTANCE Highly resistant to apple scab (sometimes expressed as immune); resistant to cedar apple rust, powdery mildew, and fireblight.

SEASON OF RIPENING Mid-fall

USES Dessert and cider

STORAGE QUALITY Fair. The flavor is enhanced by a storage period.

Lodi

ALTHOUGH LODI DOES not have the high flavor or culinary quality of other summer cooking apples like Yellow Transparent, Gravenstein, or Early Harvest, its large size was attractive to commercial producers. When overripe, the skin becomes a translucent white and the fruit will attract swarms of bees and Japanese beetles.

OTHER NAMES Early Golden, Golden Lodi, Improved Yellow Transparent, Large Transparent

HISTORY This cross of Yellow Transparent and Montgomery was released in 1924 by the New York State Agricultural Experiment Station in Geneva.

EXTERIOR DESCRIPTION The round-elongated fruit is larger, firmer, and will store longer than its parent, Yellow Transparent. The green skin ripens to clear yellow and sometimes has a brownish-yellow flush. Prominent white or greenish lenticels also appear on the surface.

INTERIOR DESCRIPTION Flesh is white, crisp, juicy, and mildly subacid. It bruises easily but not as readily as Yellow Transparent.

TREE CHARACTERISTICS This vigorous, spreading, productive tree is resistant to cold temperatures. It has yellowish-olive bark and large leaves that are dull and coarse. It bears early (fruit set occurs on two- and three-year-old growth) and requires cross-pollination. When crops are heavy, the tree must be thinned in order to produce large fruit.

DISEASE RESISTANCE Resistant to powdery mildew; somewhat resistant to apple scab; susceptible to fireblight.

SEASON OF RIPENING Early summer. It ripens nearly a week after Yellow Transparent.

USES Applesauce and apple butter

STORAGE QUALITY Poor

Lowry

THIS VARIETY IS often difficult to identify with certainty and apparently a number of seedlings known as "Lowry" are in circulation displaying different characteristics. The real Lowry can be recognized by its crunch and relatively good keeping quality—the flesh will remain hard for weeks even in common storage whereas look-alikes become mealy in a week.

OTHER NAMES Dixie, Lowrey, Mosby's Best, Red Winter. There is a sport called Red Lowry.

HISTORY It appeared around 1850 on the farm of John Lowry near Afton, Virginia. It was first marketed in the early 1900s by Virginian nurseries.

EXTERIOR DESCRIPTION The medium-sized fruit is round, tapering toward the blossom end. Skin is greenish yellow, striped and flushed with varying shades of red, and covered with medium-sized irregularly shaped yellow dots. In central Virginia and the Valley of Virginia it is found with slight variations that can be attributed to environmental rather than varietal differences.

INTERIOR DESCRIPTION Flesh is firm, juicy, and sweet at the peak of ripening. The flavor is more intense when grown at elevations over 1,000 feet.

TREE CHARACTERISTICS The wide-spreading tree is vigorous but growth slows after it has matured for fifteen years. However, trees that are more than fifty years old still bear light annual crops.

DISEASE RESISTANCE Moderately resistant to the major diseases

SEASON OF RIPENING Fall

USES Dessert, apple butter, and cider

STORAGE QUALITY Fair

Lyman's Large Summer

The pomologist Charles Downing, along with many of his mid-nineteenth-century colleagues, considered Lyman's Large Summer to be the best summer dessert apple. Once feared lost to cultivation, it was rediscovered in 1941 as a tree that was first thought to be Cole's Quince (which bears fruit that is more irregularly shaped and acidic than Lyman's Large Summer) but when the tree fruited the true identity was realized.

OTHER NAMES Large Yellow Summer Apple, Lyman's Large

HISTORY According to one source it originated in the town of Amherstburg in Ontario, Canada, with James Dougall, who later exhibited it in Detroit at the Exhibition of the First Horticultural Society of Michigan in 1847. But Downing claims it as an American variety introduced by a man named Lyman of Manchester, Connecticut.

EXTERIOR DESCRIPTION This large apple is flattened at the ends. The smooth skin is green, ripening to clear yellow, and white lenticels cover the surface.

INTERIOR DESCRIPTION The creamy-white flesh is crisp and juicy with a balanced sweet-tart flavor.

TREE CHARACTERISTICS The hardy tree is a tip bearer with long, drooping branches. Production is light until the tree matures.

DISEASE RESISTANCE Moderately resistant to the major diseases

SEASON OF RIPENING Late summer

USES Dessert and cooking

STORAGE QUALITY Fair

Macoun

In the hot and humid mid-Atlantic and South, Macoun will become mealy the day it is harvested. A fruit grower friend in New England once brought me a box of Macoun apples and rightfully teased me that I could not grow them successfully in Virginia. I had no retort and kept my mouth shut— except while chewing and thoroughly enjoying this premium dessert apple.

OTHER NAMES Mekaun

HISTORY This cross of McIntosh and Jersey Black was made in 1909 at the New York State Agricultural Experiment Station in Geneva. It was introduced in 1923 and named for the Canadian fruit grower W. T. Macoun.

EXTERIOR DESCRIPTION This medium-sized, conical to oblate apple has a waxy, smooth, tough skin. The green background is covered with purplish-red blushes and stripes. It also has a bluish bloom and small white dots over the surface.

INTERIOR DESCRIPTION The greenish-white flesh is crisp, juicy, and easily bruised.

TREE CHARACTERISTICS The tree does not grow tall. To develop a spreading top, extra branch thinning is necessary. It has stout, curved branches with roundish, coarse, dark green leaves folded near the edge with sharp, regular serrations; a cluster of drooping leaves often forms at the base of the trunk. Macoun is difficult to thin to increase fruit size and is subject to pre-harvest drop. It blooms late, therefore escaping late frosts.

DISEASE RESISTANCE Resistant to fireblight; susceptible to apple scab and powdery mildew. Some reports indicate that in hot, humid regions it is also susceptible to frogeye leaf spot, a fungus that causes small circular brown spots to form on the leaves.

SEASON OF RIPENING Late fall

USES Dessert and cider

STORAGE QUALITY Good

Magnum Bonum

AFTER EATING PIE made from Magnum Bonum apples, I guarantee that your taste standards will be elevated and the memory engraved. This was also my family's variety of choice for making apple puffs (jokingly called apple poofs in my household). I can still recall those delectable treats being pulled from the wood burning stove's warming closet to greet us after chores.

OTHER NAMES Bona, Bonum, Maggie Bowman, Magna Bonum, Red Bonum

HISTORY Magnum Bonum was grown from a seed of the Hall apple by John Kinny around 1828 or 1829 in Davidson County, North Carolina. It was named by Dr. William Holt of Davidson College and recorded in 1854. In central Virginia, where it was often called Bonum, it was produced commercially from the late nineteenth century until the beginning of World War II. Due to this variety's high susceptibility to cedar apple rust, all of the red cedars (*Juniperus virginiana*, the host plant of the spores that cause the disease), were removed from orchard sites. A Virginia law at the time of the Magnum Bonum's high commercial production even permitted the fruit grower to remove cedars growing on his neighbor's property.

EXTERIOR DESCRIPTION This medium-sized apple has a roundish-oblate shape. The greenish-yellow background is mostly covered with indistinct red striping and conspicuous white and russet dots.

INTERIOR DESCRIPTION The white flesh is sometimes stained red under the skin. It is tender and juicy with an aromatic, subacid flavor.

TREE CHARACTERISTICS Hardy and productive, the tree begins to bear within two or three years (even on standard rootstock), but growth is moderate. Attention to soil calcium is essential to produce high-quality fruit.

DISEASE RESISTANCE Although it is highly susceptible to cedar apple rust, this superb culinary apple can be produced successfully even with organic spray protection. It does not seem to be severely affected by other major apple diseases.

SEASON OF RIPENING Late summer to early fall

USES Dessert and particularly for pie making

STORAGE QUALITY Poor

Maiden Blush

During the month of August in the Blue Ridge Mountains of Virginia, my grandmother Burford always filled fruit bowls with Maiden Blush apples as soon as they ripened. When they were really mellow, they were sliced and dried. This was a favorite apple for drying—the flesh remains white and bright—and also for making summer cider.

OTHER NAMES Lady Blush, Red Cheek, Vestal. It is sometimes spelled Maidenblush. An Irish apple called Maiden Blush is a distinct variety.

HISTORY Noted in 1817, it appeared in Burlington, New Jersey, and was named by Samuel Allinson. It was described by Coxe in 1817 as "popular in the Philadelphia market."

EXTERIOR DESCRIPTION Fruit is medium to large and very round. The thin, tough, smooth skin is waxen yellow blushed with crimson.

INTERIOR DESCRIPTION The white flesh has a slightly yellow tinge. It is crisp and tender with a sharp acid flavor that mellows when fully ripe.

TREE CHARACTERISTICS The upright-growing tree is vigorous and bears early and annually. It is generally a heavy bearer but some years the crop will be light. The bark is olive colored and the dull, smooth leaves have a slight bluish cast and sharp, regular serrations.

DISEASE RESISTANCE Resistant to cedar apple rust; susceptible to fireblight, apple scab, and apple blotch.

SEASON OF RIPENING Late summer. It ripens over a period of approximately one month.

USES Dessert, drying, and cider

STORAGE QUALITY Poor

McIntosh

THIS CLASSIC New England and Canadian apple has a distinctively tart and spicy taste. Like the Winesap apple, over time it has become known as a category for other similar-tasting apples. Sometimes one will hear the remark, "it has the Mac flavor."

OTHER NAMES None, except cultivar names

HISTORY It was discovered in 1796 by John McIntosh of Ontario, Canada (Dundas County), and was propagated forty years later by his son, Allan McIntosh. It was named in 1870.

EXTERIOR DESCRIPTION This medium to large apple is round and slightly flattened on the ends. It has pale yellow skin which is flushed and striped with a deep bright red and covered with a bloom. Some cultivars are faintly ribbed.

INTERIOR DESCRIPTION The white flesh is sometimes tinged red. It is fine-grained, crisp, and tender with a subacid-to-sweet flavor.

TREE CHARACTERISTICS The vigorous, self-fertile tree sets heavy crops, blooms early, and is a good pollinator for other varieties. New bark is red. The dull, rough, oval leaves are marked with shallow, indistinct serrations.

DISEASE RESISTANCE Moderately resistant to the major diseases

SEASON OF RIPENING Fall

USES Dessert, baking, and cider

STORAGE QUALITY Good

Melba

As a five-year-old in the late 1930s, one of my first orchard chores was picking Melba seeds from the pomace at the cider mill. This was an imperative summer cider variety for our family even though the taste was not of particularly high quality. Rather, it was the seeds that were valued for their tendency to produce grafting rootstock with a vigorous root system and a smooth, straight stem. Once washed and dried, the seeds were planted for rootstock production in the Burford Brothers Nursery.

OTHER NAMES None. There is a sport called Red Melba (or Melred) and a sport called White Melba.

HISTORY This seedling was developed around 1924 at the Canadian Department of Agriculture Research Station in Ottawa, Canada. It came from an open-pollinated McIntosh thought to have been crossed with the Livland (or Lowland) Raspberry apple. In 1927 Melba was awarded the Silver Wilder Medal by the American Pomological Society.

EXTERIOR DESCRIPTION The medium-sized, roundish apple has yellow skin with pinkish stripes and flecks. A white bloom covers the surface.

INTERIOR DESCRIPTION The very white flesh is firm and crisp with a subacid peach-like flavor and an intense aroma.

TREE CHARACTERISTICS This vigorous grower has long, stout reddish shoots. The dull, medium-green leaves are large, oval, and nearly flat with shallow serrations. The tree blooms early and is somewhat self-fertile. It is subject to pre-harvest drop.

DISEASE RESISTANCE Susceptible to apple scab; moderately susceptible to the other major diseases.

SEASON OF RIPENING Midsummer to late summer

USES Baking, frying, and sometimes dessert

STORAGE QUALITY Poor

Melon

ALTHOUGH MELON HAS no commercial potential—it is difficult to grow and usually has a high mortality rate in the fruit tree nursery—the sprightly taste alone makes it worth planting in home orchards. It is claimed that Melon came from the same New York seedling orchard as Early Joe and Northern Spy, but the number of winner varieties produced in that orchard may have been exaggerated.

OTHER NAMES Melon Apple, Melon Norton, Norton's Melon, Norton Watermelon, Watermelon

HISTORY It was known around 1800 and introduced in 1845 in East Bloomfield, New York (Ontario County). It is said to have come from seeds brought from Connecticut by Heman Chapin to plant a seedling orchard, probably for cider making.

EXTERIOR DESCRIPTION Fruit is medium to large and roundish-conical with faint ribbing. It has rich yellow skin covered irregularly with brownish-red dots. The stem cavity often displays some green coloring and russeting.

INTERIOR DESCRIPTION The white flesh is fine-grained, crisp, juicy, and tender with a subacid flavor.

TREE CHARACTERISTICS The medium-sized, moderately vigorous tree grows upright and densely; the treetop requires careful annual pruning to open it to sunlight and air circulation and to prevent its tendency toward biennial bearing. The tree grows very slowly when young but it is early to bear.

DISEASE RESISTANCE Susceptible to apple scab; somewhat susceptible to the other major diseases.

SEASON OF RIPENING Late fall

USES Dessert

STORAGE QUALITY Poor. It loses its flavor and quality quickly in storage.

Melrose

During a discussion about the trite expression "it feels good in the hand," often used to describe the variety Hubbardston Nonesuch, my friend Robert Nitschke pointed out that the same could be said of Melrose. Both apples are the right size and shape to be comfortable when lifted, a characteristic that apple marketers recognize and implement. Next time you are at the supermarket, notice that many varieties are neither heavy or light nor big or small: they feel good in the hand.

OTHER NAMES None. There is a strain called Melrouge. Scottish Melrose is a distinct variety.

HISTORY This cross of Red Delicious and Jonathan was made in 1931 by Dr. Freeman Howlett and introduced in 1944 at the Ohio Agricultural Experiment Station in Wooster. It is the official state apple of Ohio.

EXTERIOR DESCRIPTION Fruit is medium to large in size and variably shaped from oblate to conic (Melrose is larger than Jonathan but often has a similar shape). The greenish-yellow skin is overlaid with red and sometimes russeted in the stem end.

INTERIOR DESCRIPTION The whitish flesh is juicy, firm, and aromatic with a slight acid flavor.

TREE CHARACTERISTICS Growing large even on dwarfing rootstock, this tree is a vigorous annual bearer when thinned. The growth habit is spreading and somewhat willowy; limbs must be opened up to permit sunlight to color the fruit. Peculiarly, the flowers are often petal incomplete.

DISEASE RESISTANCE Susceptible to apple scab; slightly susceptible to powdery mildew.

SEASON OF RIPENING Late fall

USES Dessert and pie making

STORAGE QUALITY Good

Milam

Samuel Clemens (more commonly known as Mark Twain) wrote in *Tom Sawyer*: "Here's a big Milum apple I've been saving for you, Tom, if you was ever found again—now go long to school." Perhaps the writer was influenced by the fact that the Clemens family's heritage dated back to the Milam orchard region of Virginia. The apple's appearance often varies significantly because it was widely distributed by sprouts dug from under the trees. From my experience it is important to rely on its sweet taste to determine identity.

OTHER NAMES Blair, Harrigan, Thomas

HISTORY The place of origin is unknown but it was noted before 1850. It was introduced into the Midwest around that time by the nurseryman Joseph Curtis, who mistakenly identified it as Red Winter Pearmain—a variety with which it is often confused.

EXTERIOR DESCRIPTION Fruit is small to medium and round. The greenish-yellow background is marbled with dull red (which darkens to crimson) and most of the surface is covered with prominent gray spots. Milam is redder in color but otherwise greatly resembles Ralls.

INTERIOR DESCRIPTION The creamy white flesh is coarse, crisp, and juicy with a sweet, subacid flavor.

TREE CHARACTERISTICS Milam has the unique tendency to sprout prolifically from its roots and can be propagated easily this way. The vigorous tree grows upright and spreading with long slender branches. It is dense and brushy like Ralls.

DISEASE RESISTANCE Moderately susceptible to the major diseases

SEASON OF RIPENING Fall

USES Dessert

STORAGE QUALITY Good

Milton

WHEN ANY APPLE variety is as successful as McIntosh, it becomes a stud apple for making new varieties in the "laboratory." This was the raison d'être and the fate of Milton, which had only a single different value, a sprightlier flavor, than its parent, "Mac."

OTHER NAMES Milton Early McIntosh

HISTORY This cross of McIntosh and Yellow Transparent was introduced in 1923 by the New York State Agricultural Experiment Station in Geneva.

EXTERIOR DESCRIPTION The medium-sized apple is round and slightly elongated toward the blossom end, sometimes with an unattractive bulge on one side. It has very pale yellow skin covered with a deep red flush, numerous dots, and a heavy bloom.

INTERIOR DESCRIPTION Flesh is very white, soft, and fine-grained. The flavor is described as being sweet, subacid, and sprightlier than McIntosh.

TREE CHARACTERISTICS The treetop is shaped like an inverted bowl. It has slender branches and dark reddish bark. The dull, oval leaves are a slightly yellowish medium-green color with a pebbly leather surface and sharp serrations.

DISEASE RESISTANCE Resistant to cedar apple rust; moderately susceptible to the other major diseases.

SEASON OF RIPENING Fall

USES Applesauce and dessert

STORAGE QUALITY Fair

Missouri Pippin

STARK BRO'S NURSERY in Missouri was an early adopter of the newly developed railroad system to ship trees to faraway places, but Missouri Pippin did not filter back East. By the middle of the nineteenth century, thousands of new varieties existed with limited demand for wide distribution so nurseries had to be discriminating when choosing which varieties to ship.

OTHER NAMES Missouri Keeper, Missouri Orange, Stone's Eureka

HISTORY First fruited in 1854, Missouri Pippin came from apple seeds planted around 1839 by Brinkley Hornsby on his farm in Kingsville, Missouri (Johnson County). Hornsby referred to it as the "dollar and cents" apple because it was profitable. It was originally marketed as Missouri Keeper; a nursery in St. Louis renamed it Missouri Pippin in 1869.

EXTERIOR DESCRIPTION This is a medium-sized, conical apple with flattened ends and a short stubby stem. The yellow background is partially covered with a reddish blush and streaks, as well as sparse, irregularly spaced brownish lenticels. The stem cavity is russeted over the shoulders of the apple. The thick, tough skin makes it suitable for transport and rough handling at harvest, a time when many apples are damaged.

INTERIOR DESCRIPTION The whitish-yellow flesh is coarse, crunchy, and firm. It is not very juicy.

TREE CHARACTERISTICS The upright-growing tree with slender branches is only moderately vigorous. It begins to bear early but production starts to degrade from over-bearing after about twenty years; thinning will encourage the tree to continue producing medium-sized fruit.

DISEASE RESISTANCE Moderately resistant to the major diseases

SEASON OF RIPENING Late fall

USES All-purpose

STORAGE QUALITY Good

Mollies Delicious

MOLLIES DELICIOUS IS a choice apple for out-of-hand eating. It was the darling of the apple world in the late 1960s and the 1970s due to large size, interesting coloration, distinctively sweet flavor, pleasing aftertaste, and noticeable aromatic quality. It will also keep for a few months in common storage which is unusual for a summer apple. Interest was further enhanced by its comparison to that bully apple, Red Delicious.

OTHER NAMES None. It is often confused with strains of Red Delicious.

HISTORY This cross of Golden Delicious, Gravenstein, Close, and Edgewood was introduced in 1966 by the New Jersey Agricultural Experiment Station in New Brunswick.

EXTERIOR DESCRIPTION Fruit is very large and slightly conical. The greenish-yellow skin is covered with a red blush over more than half the surface.

INTERIOR DESCRIPTION The greenish-white flesh is crisp, juicy, and aromatic with a mildly sweet flavor.

TREE CHARACTERISTICS This vigorous grower is a shy bearer for the first few years but it is expected to produce full annual crops as it ages. It can generally be harvested in a single picking although some regions report that multiple pickings are necessary. The fruit tends to set in clusters; there is little pre-harvest drop.

DISEASE RESISTANCE Susceptible to apple scab and powdery mildew

SEASON OF RIPENING Late summer

USES Applesauce and dessert

STORAGE QUALITY Fair

Monark

A LARGE APPLE with a satisfying lightly tart flavor, Monark is an excellent midsummer variety for the backyard orchard. It ripens when few other summer apples are in the marketplace and it has broad appeal as a single-variety pie maker. It will keep in storage for three or four months but the flavor will degrade the longer it is stored.

OTHER NAMES None. A British apple called Monarch is not related.

HISTORY In the 1960s the University of Arkansas at Fayetteville began to explore apples with some disease resistance, especially to apple scab. Monark was one of the first varieties to be developed and selected.

EXTERIOR DESCRIPTION Fruit is large and round. The greenish-yellow background has some pinkish-red coloring over most of the skin and an even pattern of red stripes. There is little russeting on the skin.

INTERIOR DESCRIPTION Flesh is firm and crisp with a pleasing tartness.

TREE CHARACTERISTICS This vigorous and spreading tree bears crops early and annually.

DISEASE RESISTANCE Good resistance to the major diseases

SEASON OF RIPENING Midsummer

USES Dessert and pie making

STORAGE QUALITY Good

Mother

Visitors to my orchard often headed to sample this variety first because of its distinctive balsamic flavor and an aroma which has been likened to chick wintergreen. Although this apple has American roots it was extensively planted in England after World War II, speculatively to honor the American forces. England's climate and soil type has proven favorable for production of "American Mother," as it is most often called abroad.

OTHER NAMES American Mother, Gardener's Apple, Mother of American, Queen Anne

HISTORY It was discovered on the farm of General Stephen Gardener in Bolton, Massachusetts (Worcester County). This region was a hotbed for emerging classic American varieties likely because it was concentrated with cider seedling orchards. Mother was exhibited at the Massachusetts Horticultural Society meeting in 1844.

EXTERIOR DESCRIPTION This medium-sized apple is long and conical. It has smooth skin that is mottled bright red over a dark yellow background. The color becomes dull after picking in hot and humid summer climates; in cooler regions, it remains bright.

INTERIOR DESCRIPTION The creamy yellow flesh is juicy, sweet, and acidulous with a distinctive flavor.

TREE CHARACTERISTICS The moderately vigorous, late-blooming tree is slow to begin fruiting. It matures into a hardy dependable bearer that tends to overbear if not thinned. A good pollinator like Grimes Golden, Winter Banana, or Ben Davis will increase the yield. Shoots grow particularly straight and the bark has a greenish-olive color. The oval, shiny, dark green leaves are folded and reflexed with sharp, regular serrations.

DISEASE RESISTANCE Somewhat resistant to apple scab and most other apple diseases; somewhat susceptible to fireblight.

SEASON OF RIPENING Late summer to early fall. It usually ripens when few other fall apples are available.

USES Dessert

STORAGE QUALITY Fair

Newtown Pippin

MARCH OR APRIL, just as the last of these apples were coming out of winter storage, was when my father often remarked that we should have just started to eat them: the long storage time imbued the remaining ones with an extraordinary taste that lingered on the tongue. Cider made from the fruit is very clear and considered to be of the highest quality. The Burfords referred to it as "Sunday cider."

OTHER NAMES In New England and the Midwest it is mostly known as Newtown Pippin; on the West Coast it is known as Yellow Newtown Pippin; and in the mid-Atlantic it is known as Albemarle Pippin. It is also known by dozens of other names including Brooke Pippin, Green Newtown Pippin, Mountain Pippin, Virginia Pippin, and Yellow Pippin.

HISTORY It appeared around 1759 on the estate of Gershom Moore in Newtown, Long Island, New York. During the reign of Queen Victoria, it was the only food commodity exempt from crown import tax because the court favored the variety. In the late nineteenth and early twentieth centuries, this apple was revered by the growers on the eastern slopes of the Blue Ridge Mountains in Virginia because shipments to England made them small fortunes.

EXTERIOR DESCRIPTION This variety's appearance (and taste) is influenced to a certain extent by soil and weather conditions. Size and color vary, but it is usually medium to large and solid green (ripening to yellow or greenish yellow) with a reddish blush and a scattering of small russet dots on the surface. Some russeting may be present within and out of the stem cavity. It has a roundish, flattened, angular shape and a short stem.

INTERIOR DESCRIPTION The yellowish flesh is very firm, crisp, juicy, and subacid with a taste that is sometimes described as clean and fresh. The purplish-black seeds are oblong.

TREE CHARACTERISTICS A vigorous, reliable early bearer. Shoots grow medium in length and fairly straight with short internodes. The fruit hangs well on the tree. It has fairly small, oval leaves that are folded and reflexed with irregular serrations; leaves are medium green in color with a bluish cast and occasionally browned edges. The wood of the tree when sawn into lumber is brown and close grained.

DISEASE RESISTANCE Susceptible to apple scab; moderately susceptible to the other major diseases, except for collar rot to which it is moderately resistant.

SEASON OF RIPENING Late fall

USES Dessert, baking, pie making, vinegar, and cider

STORAGE QUALITY Excellent. The apple's optimum flavor will develop after a few months in storage.

Newtown Spitzenburg

THIS APPLE TAKES the first part of its name from the town and the farmer who first discovered it in New York state. It is speculated that "Spitzenburg" was added to market the variety and pass it off as the more desirably flavored Esopus Spitzenburg when in fact the two apples are quite dissimilar.

OTHER NAMES Burlington Spitzenburg, English Spitzenburg, Joe Berry, Kountz, Matchless, Ox Eye. It is also mistakenly called Vandevere.

HISTORY It appeared before 1817 near Newtown, Long Island, New York (where the Newtown Pippin originated as well). It was grown commercially in the Hudson Valley of New York early in the nineteenth century.

EXTERIOR DESCRIPTION The medium-sized apple has a rectangular to convex shape. The greenish-yellow skin is almost entirely covered with a red-orange color and russet dots. The stem length will vary depending on growing location.

INTERIOR DESCRIPTION Creamy-yellow flesh is firm and coarse with a sweet, subacid flavor. The core is small and the sparse seeds are ovate and pointed.

TREE CHARACTERISTICS The vigorously growing tree has especially long branches and dark brown wood with a grayish hue and whitish spots. It is an unreliable cropper that produces a high percentage of small fruit.

DISEASE RESISTANCE Susceptible to the major diseases

SEASON OF RIPENING Fall

USES Dessert and sometimes baking

STORAGE QUALITY Fair

Nickajack

UNLIKE THE VAST majority of apples, for which thousands of seedlings must be grown before one produces a pleasant-tasting fruit, Nickajack will present a good likeness from seed. For this reason Nickajack seeds were widely distributed and were often given a new name when they fruited—hence the apple's many, many synonyms garnered over the years.

OTHER NAMES Aberdeen, Accidental, Alleghany, Berry, Big Hill, Buckman's Red, Carolina, Carolina Spice, Caroline, Chatham, Cheatan, Cheataw, Dahlonega. Edward's Forsythe's Seedling, Gowden, Gowdie, Graham's Red Warrior, Haward, Howard, Hubbard, Jackson Red, Leanham, Missouri Pippin, Missouri Red, Mobbs, Pound, Red Hazel, Red Pippin, Red Warrior, Rickman's Red, Ruckman, Summerour, Treanham, Walb, Wall, Wander, Winter Horse, Winter Rose, Wonder, World's Wonder, and numerous other names.

HISTORY It was originally called Winter Rose and was noted in 1853, but it probably dates back to the late eighteenth century. It came from the area of Nickajack Creek, North Carolina (Macon County).

EXTERIOR DESCRIPTION This medium to large apple has a rectangular to truncate-conic shape. At higher elevations and in cooler regions, the greenish-yellow skin is nearly covered with orange-red or red streaks and it is dotted with prominent brownish lenticels; in warmer regions the skin color is washed-out. A short, stubby stem projects obliquely from an often-furrowed cavity.

INTERIOR DESCRIPTION The noticeably aromatic white flesh has a tinge of green under the skin. It is firm, crisp, and coarse with a subacid to sweet flavor.

TREE CHARACTERISTICS The large tree grows upright and spreading and is a prolific annual bearer. Branches that are three or four years old will have woody knobs or warts of various sizes which, when cut from the branch, are found to contain kernels entirely detached from the regular grain of the wood.

DISEASE RESISTANCE Even with some spray protection the late-summer diseases of sooty blotch and flyspeck can be present. Otherwise, it is moderately resistant to the major diseases. Some years a benign virus causes the leaves to yellow and defoliate but does not affect fruit production.

SEASON OF RIPENING Late fall

USES Dessert

STORAGE QUALITY Good

Nittany

This variety was created as a clonotype of York without the serious problem of corking—the development of large, spongy brown spots in the flesh caused by a boron deficiency. The deep yellow flesh imparts a similar color when processed into products like applesauce, baby food, and frozen apple pies. The flesh also oxidizes very slowly so it is a good choice for salads.

OTHER NAMES None

HISTORY This cross of Golden Delicious and York was developed in 1979 by Penn State University and named for the school's sports mascot, the Nittany Lion.

EXTERIOR DESCRIPTION The medium to large apple is truncate-conical and slightly oblate on the blossom end. Some of the fruit have scarfskin and the skin color varies from dull to bright red depending on the climate in which it grows. Internal wax production as the fruit matures will make the apples feel greasy.

INTERIOR DESCRIPTION Flesh is yellow and firm with a tart to subacid flavor that is similar to York.

TREE CHARACTERISTICS It must be aggressively thinned to prevent biennial bearing. It blooms late in the season which makes it a good pollinator for many other late-blooming and mid-season varieties.

DISEASE RESISTANCE Susceptible to the major diseases

SEASON OF RIPENING Fall

USES Mostly apple butter and applesauce, but also dessert and salads

STORAGE QUALITY Very good

Nodhead

THE NAME NODHEAD is said to have come from Samuel Jewett, a farmer who lived with his wife, Sarah, and their eight children in the vicinity of this apple's origin. Jewett is reported to have habitually nodded his head when walking or talking. In New England it was originally called Jewett's Red but is now popularly known as Nodhead.

OTHER NAMES Jewell's Fine Red, Jewett, Jewett's Red

HISTORY Noted in 1842, it likely originated near Hollis, New Hampshire.

EXTERIOR DESCRIPTION Fruit is medium in size and truncate-conical with a very short stem and tough skin. The yellow background is nearly covered by a deep red flush and stripes and is overspread with a blue bloom.

INTERIOR DESCRIPTION The yellow flesh is fine-grained, juicy, and aromatic with a subacid flavor. Some have described the tenderness of the flesh as melting.

TREE CHARACTERISTICS The tree is a slow grower (especially in the nursery) but it begins to bear early and produces moderate crops. Excellent growing conditions are required for the production of high-quality fruit. It is difficult to grow in the mid-Atlantic.

DISEASE RESISTANCE Moderately resistant to the major diseases

SEASON OF RIPENING Fall

USES Dessert

STORAGE QUALITY Fair

Northern Spy

When my grandfather's brother was in his early nineties he planted a large orchard of Northern Spy, knowing that the trees would not begin to bear for ten years or more. He was thought mad to begin such a venture but he lived past one hundred and sampled the first crop. My grandfather too was quite fond of Northern Spy and planted the trees along the long driveway to his home, exclusively for cider making.

OTHER NAMES Northern Spice, Red Northern Spy, Red Spy. Originally it may have had the name Northern Pie Apple.

HISTORY This apple is thought to have come from seeds that were brought from Connecticut and planted around 1800 near East Bloomfield, New York (Ontario County). The varieties Melon and Early Joe came from the same seedling orchard. Northern Spy has been selected for use in the development of new varieties and in rootstock research.

EXTERIOR DESCRIPTION The apple is large, especially on young trees, and oblate. Color can be quite variable depending on the climate in which the fruit is grown and the season of development—it can even vary on the same tree. Well-colored fruit are clear yellow with bright red tints that are almost scarlet and distinct streaks. The apples bruise easily.

INTERIOR DESCRIPTION The white flesh is very juicy, crisp, tender, and aromatic. It has a sweet, rich, subacid flavor.

TREE CHARACTERISTICS The large hardy tree has an upright, free-growing habit with long, curved branches and dense foliage. Leaves are shiny, smooth, and medium in size; folded, reflexed, and slightly waved with sharp and shallow but indistinct serrations; slow to unfold and displaying prominent principal veins. The tree is noted as slow to begin bearing and tending toward biennial production. The bloom period is late so it escapes late frosts.

DISEASE RESISTANCE Somewhat resistant to fireblight; susceptible to bitter pit and blossom fireblight.

SEASON OF RIPENING Late fall

USES Dessert, pie making, frying, apple butter, cider, and brandy

STORAGE QUALITY Excellent. The apples retain good flavor even after long storage.

Northfield Beauty

THE LOST-AND-FOUND plight of Northfield Beauty, and its eventual return to cultivation, reminds me of other varieties, particularly Ralls, that lived in obscurity until made prominent in the apple world either by association with another variety or because someone took a specific interest in it. For Ralls, this fame came when it was crossed with Red Delicious to make the Fuji; in the case of Northfield Beauty, it was the attention of plant breeder Albert Etter.

OTHER NAMES None

HISTORY It originated in Vermont but the exact date is unknown. When the California plant breeder Albert Etter started his homestead program in the early twentieth century, he grafted around 600 different varieties from scionwood that came from the University of California at Davis, a group which included the obscure Northfield Beauty. In the 1980s the tree was rescued from an abandoned Etter orchard and returned to cultivation.

EXTERIOR DESCRIPTION Fruit is medium to large with a somewhat asymmetrical, blocky shape. The whitish-yellow background is mostly covered by a medium red color with faint red stripes.

INTERIOR DESCRIPTION Flesh is crisp and white with a subacid flavor.

TREE CHARACTERISTICS This heavy annual bearer produces high-quality apples that will hang long on the tree.

DISEASE RESISTANCE Highly resistant to apple scab; moderately susceptible to the other major diseases.

SEASON OF RIPENING Late summer to early fall

USES Baking and dessert

STORAGE QUALITY Good for a summer variety

Northwest Greening

Hardiness, large size, and long storage—coupled with its superiority as a pie apple—make this an entrenched variety for regions with severe cold weather. Northwest Greening is a good substitute in areas where the higher-quality Rhode Island Greening will not survive.

OTHER NAMES Northwestern Greening

HISTORY This cross of Golden Russet and Alexander (from which it gets its hardiness) originated in 1872 in Waupaca County, Wisconsin.

EXTERIOR DESCRIPTION Fruit is medium to large (some will reach 5 inches in diameter) and roundish conical. The thin, tough, smooth, waxy skin is yellowish green, ripening to pale yellow.

INTERIOR DESCRIPTION The greenish-white flesh is coarse and juicy with a mild subacid flavor. Flesh within the core line can be corky because of a short growing season.

TREE CHARACTERISTICS The hardy, vigorous tree grows tall, producing long, slender, straight shoots that are inclined to droop. Leaves are shiny green, medium in size, and ovate with small, regular, shallow serrations. The dark reddish bark has large yellowish-gray lenticels that can be easily felt with the finger. It is a good late-season pollinator.

DISEASE RESISTANCE Moderately resistant to the major diseases

SEASON OF RIPENING Late fall

USES Baking and pie making

STORAGE QUALITY Good. The taste quality improves with a few months storage.

Nova Easygro

GIVE AN APPLE a bad name—even in an attractive skin package—and the consumer will leave it on the shelf and out of the orchard. This was the fate that Nova Easygro suffered as other scab-resistant apples with catchier names such as Liberty and Freedom, as well as the incredibly popular McIntosh, appeared on the market at about the same time.

OTHER NAMES None

HISTORY This cross of Spartan and PRI 565 was introduced in 1971 by the Canadian Department of Agriculture in Nova Scotia.

EXTERIOR DESCRIPTION The large, flattish fruit has a greenish-yellow background with reddish stripes over about 75 percent of the skin.

INTERIOR DESCRIPTION The very white flesh is firm, crisp, and juicy with a sweet taste. It is somewhat tough when first picked but the tenderness improves in storage.

TREE CHARACTERISTICS This moderately productive tree blooms around the same time as McIntosh.

DISEASE RESISTANCE It is susceptible to cedar apple rust but demonstrates good resistance to other diseases, especially apple scab.

SEASON OF RIPENING Late fall

USES Dessert

STORAGE QUALITY Very good

Ohio Nonpareil

THE APPELLATION NONPAREIL, meaning "having no equal," has been applied to towns, almonds, potatoes, plums, and candy—as well as apples. In the apple world "nonsuch" or "nonesuch" are other words employed to call attention to an apple that rises above the rest. However, this was likely a nineteenth-century marketing stratagem as the apple doesn't quite seem to live up to its hyperbolic name.

OTHER NAMES None

HISTORY It appeared before 1850 near Massillon, Ohio (Stark County). It came from a seedling that originated with someone known only as Mr. Meyers.

EXTERIOR DESCRIPTION This large dessert fruit has an oblate and sometimes lopsided shape. The pale yellow skin is washed, marbled, and striped with varying degrees of pink and crimson.

INTERIOR DESCRIPTION The creamy white flesh is fine-grained and very juicy with a mild, aromatic, subacid flavor. It has a small core.

TREE CHARACTERISTICS This vigorous and wide-spreading tree has a number of undesirable characteristics, particularly a slowness to begin bearing.

DISEASE RESISTANCE Moderately resistant to the major diseases

SEASON OF RIPENING Early fall

USES Dessert

STORAGE QUALITY Fair

Oliver

OLIVER WAS A successful variety in the commercial market at the end of the nineteenth and the beginning of the twentieth century when it was bought, trademarked, and renamed "Senator" by Stark Bro's Nursery (the Stark family was prominent in the national Congress at the time). The apple's attractive catalog appearance promoted sales but disappointed many in hotter growing regions where it fails to achieve the brilliant red depicted.

OTHER NAMES All-Over-Red, Oliver's Red, Senator

HISTORY It appeared early in the nineteenth century on the farm of John Oliver, seven miles south of Lincoln, Arkansas (Washington County). It was grafted and distributed in this region by John Holt who called it Oliver's Red; this perhaps became All-Over-Red. Oliver was extensively planted in the South after the Civil War, particularly in the Ozarks of Arkansas.

EXTERIOR DESCRIPTION Fruit is medium to large and oblate. The smooth golden-yellow skin is nearly completely coated with crimson and some darker red streaks. It also has very conspicuous lenticels. The apple becomes waxy in storage which keeps it from shriveling.

INTERIOR DESCRIPTION The juicy yellow flesh is sometimes stained red.

TREE CHARACTERISTICS This is a vigorous, upright-growing tree with long branches.

DISEASE RESISTANCE Moderately resistant to apple scab, powdery mildew, and cedar apple rust; susceptible to fireblight, crown gall, and sunscald when conditions are favorable.

SEASON OF RIPENING Fall

USES Dessert

STORAGE QUALITY Good

Opalescent

WITH ITS SCARLET-STRIPED apples hanging like beautiful ornaments, Opalescent trees were always the showstoppers when I gave late autumn tours through my collection orchard of hundreds of varieties. The variety is very susceptible to fireblight, as well as other apple diseases, but it is worth the effort to cultivate even in the hot and humid South. The apples will still look beautiful despite ratty foliage during seasons of cultural adversity.

OTHER NAMES Hudson's Pride of Michigan

HISTORY In 1880, George Hudson found this seedling while he was digging out oak stumps in Barry County, Michigan, and when it fruited the Opalescent resulted. He sent the tree out for sale with the label "Hudson's Pride of Michigan," but it was renamed and distributed as "Opalescent" by Dayton Star Nursery. It was introduced into the nursery trade in 1899 by McNary & Gaines Nursery of Xenia, Ohio.

EXTERIOR DESCRIPTION This large, conical apple has pale yellow skin that is flushed and striped bright scarlet; the surface is usually evenly dotted with small tan lenticels.

INTERIOR DESCRIPTION The creamy yellow flesh is firm and crisp with a sweet flavor.

TREE CHARACTERISTICS The vigorous, upright-growing tree has long, straight shoots and yellowish or olive bark. The medium green leaves are ovate in shape and distinctly folded, reflexed, and waved with small, regular, and fairly sharp serrations.

DISEASE RESISTANCE Very susceptible to fireblight

SEASON OF RIPENING Late fall

USES Dessert and baking

STORAGE QUALITY Good. It becomes waxy in storage and that prolongs its storage time.

Ortley

CONSIDERABLE CONFUSION OFTEN surrounds the true identity of Ortley. I have found ancient trees of what appear to be Ortley but quite possibly could be Newtown Pippin or Yellow Bellflower. For identification it is important to graft from the old tree and fruit it on new stock for more positive characteristics. When grown in the South, Ortley has a washed-out color and the flavor is not as sprightly.

OTHER NAMES Cleo, Cleopatra (its commercial name in England and Australia), Crane's Pippin, Davis, Detroit of the West, Golden Pippin, Greasy Pippin, Green Bellflower, Hollow Core Pippin, Inman, Jersey Greening, Marrow Pippin, Melting Pippin, Ohio Favorite, Tom Woodward Pippin, Van Dyme, Warren Pippin, White Bellflower, Willow Leaf Pippin, Woodman's Song, Woolman's Long Pippin (its original name), Yellow Pippin

HISTORY The apple was found in the New Jersey orchard of Michael Ortley in the early nineteenth century and described by Coxe in 1817 under the name Woolman's Long Pippin. The "Woolman" in the original name was likely for John Woolman, the Quaker preacher and abolitionist, who came, like Coxe, from Burlington, New Jersey.

EXTERIOR DESCRIPTION The medium to large apple has a tall rectangular shape. The skin is waxy, smooth, thin, and tough. It is mostly yellow with green stripes and occasionally has a slight dull red flush on the sun-exposed side. The stem cavity usually remains green even when ripe.

Some specimens have long stems; on others, stems are short and stubby. Because of uncertainty in identification, and the many sports and cultivars, variability is understandable.

INTERIOR DESCRIPTION The creamy yellow flesh is fine-textured, crisp, and tender with a subacid, sprightly flavor.

TREE CHARACTERISTICS The branches on this moderately vigorous tree often break under the weight of a heavy crop. It has medium-sized, dark green, oval leaves with small, sharp, indistinct serrations. The leaves are somewhat stiff and the wood is brittle.

DISEASE RESISTANCE Susceptible to apple scab; fairly resistant to the other major apple diseases.

SEASON OF RIPENING Fall

USES Dessert, baking, apple butter, and frying

STORAGE QUALITY Good

Palouse

PALOUSE CAME FROM a seed planted on the West Coast during the third wave of seedling orchards in America. The first orchards, on the Eastern seaboard, were the result of seeds brought from Europe and Britain early in the seventeenth century; the second wave of orchards came from seeds collected and planted during the settlements along the Ohio and Mississippi Valleys during the nineteenth century. The genetic diversity with thousands of named varieties was remarkable.

OTHER NAMES None

HISTORY In 1879 it appeared in Whitman County, Washington, from a seed brought from Illinois. Palouse is thought to be a seedling of Tompkins County King.

EXTERIOR DESCRIPTION Fruit is large, ribbed, and oblong to conical; it has a long, slender stem. The bright yellow skin has a crimson blush and evenly spaced darker red stripes on more than half of the surface. A few inconspicuous tan-colored dots are also scattered on the skin.

INTERIOR DESCRIPTION The yellow flesh is crisp, juicy, subacid, and highly aromatic.

TREE CHARACTERISTICS This tree is a heavy bearer; thinning is required to increase fruit size.

DISEASE RESISTANCE Moderately susceptible to the major apple diseases

SEASON OF RIPENING Midsummer

USES Dessert

STORAGE QUALITY Fair

Parmar

My father told me that during and after World War II, many homesteads in the Blue Ridge Mountains of Virginia planted small Parmar orchards specifically for the purpose of producing apple brandy. This variety is also known for making very yellow applesauce with a consistency so thick that a spoon will nearly stand up in it. Parmar apples combined with another variety, like Winesap, make a distinctive apple pie.

OTHER NAMES Parmer, Yellow Flat

HISTORY This eighteenth-century variety likely originated in Virginia and was most often propagated for the specific use of brandy and cider making. Orchards that I now design for artisanal cider production are well represented by Parmar.

EXTERIOR DESCRIPTION The small, oblate apple has dark yellow skin with irregular russet patches over most of the surface.

INTERIOR DESCRIPTION The dense flesh is dark yellow, especially just beneath the skin, and it has a subacid flavor.

TREE CHARACTERISTICS Tree size and vigor are moderate and the brushy growth produces heavy crops annually.

DISEASE RESISTANCE Good resistance to the major diseases

SEASON OF RIPENING Late summer

USES Cider, brandy, applesauce, pie making, and apple butter

STORAGE QUALITY Fair

Peck's Pleasant

THE LIST OF undesirable traits assigned to Peck's Pleasant reads something like this: the tree is short lived, subject to disease, and shy bearing; it is difficult to grow in the nursery and the orchard; the apples will scald unless stored immediately after harvest. But when eaten at its zenith of flavor, all of the apple's shortcomings are forgiven. This remarkable taste was celebrated even by some historically prominent pomologists reputed to give little praise in the realm of apple flavor.

OTHER NAMES Dutch Greening, Peck, Waltz Apple, Watts Apple

HISTORY It originated in Rhode Island around 1832. It is speculated to be a seedling of Calville Blanc d'Hiver and, perhaps, Newtown Pippin.

EXTERIOR DESCRIPTION The medium to large fruit is roundish and flattened with an indistinct furrow on one side. When first harvested, the skin is green with some dark red streaks, but after ripening it becomes clear yellow with a bright blush and gray dots.

INTERIOR DESCRIPTION The yellowish-white flesh is fine-grained, juicy, and firm yet tender. It is very aromatic and the flavor is more tart than sweet. Dark reddish-brown seeds are ovate.

TREE CHARACTERISTICS Upright and spreading with dense foliage, the weak-rooted tree is subject to root rot and canker. The somewhat rigid leaves are medium in size and dark green with small, sharp, indistinct serrations.

DISEASE RESISTANCE Moderately resistant to most major apple diseases.

SEASON OF RIPENING Late fall

USES Mainly dessert but occasionally for baking

STORAGE QUALITY Good. The color will develop but the flavor will degrade in storage.

Pilot

I EMBARKED ON a wild goose chase to find this apple after the death of the Pilot trees located at the Heritage Orchard in Steele's Tavern, Virginia. I first learned that scionwood had been taken from a family farm near the origin site to graft in North Carolina—but a long road trip revealed the grafts did not survive. A few years later, I was heartened to hear that an old timer had a Pilot tree growing in his backyard—until he informed me that the tree had died the year before. Finally, in 2009 I discovered another ancient tree in good bearing condition growing near the site of origin at Three Springs Farm in Nelson County, Virginia. Scionwood was taken and the propagated tree is now available from three nurseries.

OTHER NAMES Virginia Pilot

HISTORY It was known around 1831 and originated on the farm of John Lobban (or Lobbin) at the foot of Pilot Mountain in Nelson County, Virginia. A John Dollins (of Albemarle County, Virginia) sent specimens to the American Pomological Society in 1871 and later propagated the apple. A local story from the owner of the property where Pilot originated tells that it was brought from England and valued for its great keeping quality, but I have found no documentation to support this speculation.

EXTERIOR DESCRIPTION Fruit is medium to large and round (sometimes approaching conical) with a short, slender stalk that projects from a large, deep cavity. The yellow background has red stripes and dots and specks of russet.

INTERIOR DESCRIPTION The yellowish flesh is fine-grained, crisp, and juicy with a mild, subacid flavor. The core is small for a large apple.

TREE CHARACTERISTICS The tree seems to bear at a younger age and has fewer tendencies toward biennial production when grown on size-controlling rootstock. Fruit quality is increased when grown at elevations of 1,000 feet or higher; at lower elevations and in poor soil the fruit is subject to many rots and the tree is light bearing.

DISEASE RESISTANCE Moderately resistant to the major diseases

SEASON OF RIPENING Late fall

USES Dessert, baking, cider, and apple butter

STORAGE QUALITY Excellent. In 1908 it was reported by the USDA that some growers would simply cover the fruit on the ground beneath the tree with straw, and in the spring they would pack the apples in barrels for the market.

Pink Pearl

HEAT AND HUMIDITY can make growing Pink Pearl quite difficult in the mid-Atlantic and the South. Sometimes the interior pink coloration is very faint; I have witnessed seasons when it was completely absent. However, in cooler regions and especially in California, the pink flesh is intensely colored and the waxy skin has a vibrant finish.

OTHER NAMES None

HISTORY It was developed in Eureka, California, and introduced in 1944 by Albert Etter, a California plant breeder noted for his work with strawberries. One of its parents, Surprise, has solid green skin but pink flesh.

EXTERIOR DESCRIPTION It is a medium-sized and irregularly conical apple, shaped somewhat like Yellow Bellflower. The skin is cream and pale green with a light crimson cheek. When the skin is broken, it is aromatic. It bruises easily.

INTERIOR DESCRIPTION The pinkish flesh is fine-grained and crisp. It generally has a good tart-sweet balance, but the flavor will vary with the season and the locale where it is grown.

TREE CHARACTERISTICS The tree grows medium to large and blooms early in the season, displaying crimson pink blossoms. A pollinator will increase fruit set.

DISEASE RESISTANCE Susceptible to apple scab; moderately resistant to the other major diseases.

SEASON OF RIPENING Late summer to early fall

USES Dessert and pink applesauce

STORAGE QUALITY Good

Pink Pearmain

PINK PEARMAIN IS among the dozens of apples with flesh color ranging from faint pinkish to bright red, most of which possess a color gene that can be traced back to a few red-fleshed crabapples. The flavors of this type of apple are as diverse as the colors. Our subjective taste evaluations often assign benchmark flavors of berries, herbs, and other tree fruits; the aftertaste of Pink Pearmain has been described as tart and berry-like.

OTHER NAMES Pink Sparkle. Pink Pearmain is a registered trademark of Greenmantle Nursery.

HISTORY The exact date of origin is not known but it was found in the 1980s by Ram and Marissa Fishman of Greenmantle Nursery in an old orchard in Whale Gulch, California.

EXTERIOR DESCRIPTION The shape of this medium-sized apple is sometimes described as upside down: narrow at the stem end and tapering to wide at the blossom end. The pinkish-yellow background is mottled with rich red.

INTERIOR DESCRIPTION The deep pink flesh is mildly sweet with a tart aftertaste.

TREE CHARACTERISTICS A late-blooming pollinator will increase the yield of this late-blooming tree.

DISEASE RESISTANCE Moderately resistant to the major diseases

SEASON OF RIPENING Fall

USES Dessert, baking, and pink applesauce

STORAGE QUALITY Good

Porter

PORTER IS HISTORICALLY valued as one of the great pie making apples of America and was endorsed as such in early editions of the Fannie Farmer Cookbooks. The quality is very high when cooked and the cut sections hold their shape. Regrettably, it is not as available in the market as it deserves to be.

OTHER NAMES Jennings, Yellow Summer Pearmain

HISTORY It was found around 1800 in Shelburne, Massachusetts.

EXTERIOR DESCRIPTION Fruit is medium to large, oblong to conical, and sometimes ribbed near the crown. The bright, clear yellow skin has a blushed cheek on the sun-exposed side and often develops spots of crimson red.

INTERIOR DESCRIPTION The yellowish-white flesh is fine-grained, crisp, tender, juicy, and subacid in flavor. The brown seeds are large, acute, and pointed.

TREE CHARACTERISTICS The moderately vigorous, early-bearing tree matures into a round-headed shape and tends toward biennial production. Bark is yellowish and the small oval leaves are sharply and regularly serrated.

DISEASE RESISTANCE Moderately resistant to the major diseases

SEASON OF RIPENING Late summer

USES All-purpose, especially baking and pie making

STORAGE QUALITY Fair for a summer apple

Priscilla

WHEN THIS DISEASE-RESISTANT apple was developed in the 1960s, there were few other commercially available apples that ripened in early fall. This period of availability alone gave Priscilla significant consumer appeal but it was ultimately pushed aside as other competing varieties were developed during the following decades.

OTHER NAMES Co-op 4

HISTORY Priscilla was produced in the PRI (Purdue, Rutgers, and University of Illinois) joint breeding program by crossing Starking Delicious as the seed parent and seedling 610-2 as the pollen parent. (Seedling 610-2 was produced in 1961 at the Peninsular Agricultural Research Station in Door County, Wisconsin; it was then planted in the breeding orchard at Purdue University in Lafayette, Indiana, where it first fruited in 1966.) The variety name was chosen to honor Priscilla Hovde, wife of Frederick Boyd Hovde, seventh president of Purdue.

EXTERIOR DESCRIPTION The medium-sized fruit has a slightly oblate shape and smooth, waxy, yellow skin with a red blush over most of the surface.

INTERIOR DESCRIPTION The yellowish flesh is crisp, breaking, and aromatic.

TREE CHARACTERISTICS The tree is moderately spreading and vigorous.

DISEASE RESISTANCE Resistant to apple scab, fireblight, and powdery mildew

SEASON OF RIPENING Early fall. It ripens about two weeks before Red Delicious.

USES Dessert

STORAGE QUALITY Good. It will store for a few months.

Pristine

If forced to choose just three apple trees for the backyard orchard—one each to ripen in summer, fall, and winter—the sweet and splendid Pristine would certainly be counted among my selections. It ripens over a few weeks in the summer, at that time of the year when one is fresh-apple hungry. No apple will be wasted.

OTHER NAMES Co-op 32

HISTORY This variety came from a cross made in 1974 at the Rutgers Fruit and Ornamental Research Extension Center in Cream Ridge, New Jersey. It was first selected in 1982 by E. B. Williams on the Hinsley tract of the Purdue University Horticultural Research Farm in West Lafayette, Indiana.

EXTERIOR DESCRIPTION The medium to large, round apple has smooth, glossy skin without any russeting. It has a pale green-yellow or cream color at harvest, ripening to deep yellow with an orange blush on the sun-exposed side.

INTERIOR DESCRIPTION Pale yellow flesh is crisp and slightly breaking yet melting. It is a medium- to fine-grained apple with a sweet, slightly acid, and spicy full flavor. The flavor is sweeter than another summer-ripening variety, the ubiquitous Lodi.

TREE CHARACTERISTICS This vigorous and spreading tree has wide crotch angles. The branches can break under heavy crop loads so thinning is recommended to improve production. It has some tendency toward biennial bearing. The apples are also subject to bruising and scald.

DISEASE RESISTANCE Highly resistant to apple scab; moderately resistant to fireblight; slightly resistant to cedar apple rust.

SEASON OF RIPENING Summer. It ripens shortly after Lodi.

USES Dessert and applesauce

STORAGE QUALITY Good. It will last for about six weeks in refrigerated storage.

Pumpkin Russet

LARGE, SWEET, RICHLY flavored Pumpkin Russet was *the* baking apple of New England until Rome Beauty arrived on the commercial market. Other apples, like Porter, also had a baking reputation, but this variety was more plentifully planted. The vigorous trees were a fixture in many backyards and the fruit readily available in the kitchen.

OTHER NAMES Flint Russet, Kingsbury Russet, Pumpkin Sweet, Sweet Russet, York Russet

HISTORY It was known in 1832 and it is speculated to have originated somewhere in New England, but the exact location is unknown. In 1845 the pomologist Downing described it under the name Pumpkin Russet for the first time.

EXTERIOR DESCRIPTION Fruit is large and oblate to conical. The greenish-yellow skin is covered with patches of russet and then overlaid with a netting of russet veins and large russet lenticels.

INTERIOR DESCRIPTION The greenish-white flesh is firm, juicy, and sweet.

TREE CHARACTERISTICS A very vigorous grower, the tree becomes roundish and spreading with long, curved branches.

DISEASE RESISTANCE Moderately resistant to the major diseases

SEASON OF RIPENING Fall

USES Dessert, baking, apple butter, and cider

STORAGE QUALITY Good

Pumpkin Sweet

As a child, there always seemed to be a surplus of fallen fruit beneath the Pumpkin Sweet trees. I would get enormous enjoyment from hurling these very large apples (sometimes called Pound Sweet for that reason) into the chicken lot and watching the hens frenetically peck until the fruit disappeared. As with Orange Sweet and Northern Sweet, feeding this variety to livestock was common practice.

OTHER NAMES Lyman's Large Yellow (likely a distinct variety), Pound Sweet, Pound Sweeting, Pumpkin Sweeting, Rhode Island Sweet, Round Sweet, Sweet Pumpkin, Vermont Pumpkin Sweet, Vermont Sweet, Yankee Apple. A strain called McCarty is smaller, yellower, and able to store longer.

HISTORY It was found around 1834 in Manchester, Connecticut. During the American Civil War orchards of Pumpkin Sweet were planted, specifically for the purpose of making apple butter, around Conneaut, Ohio. The butter was shipped in kegs and barrels and sold for ten to twenty-five cents a gallon to the war commissaries of both the northern and southern forces.

EXTERIOR DESCRIPTION This large apple has a rectangular to truncate-conic shape and shallow furrows coming out of the stem cavity and fading into the shoulder of the apple. The marbled greenish-yellow skin is usually flushed brown. Tiny brown lenticels surrounded by whitish halos appear over much of the surface. Scarfskin is also present.

INTERIOR DESCRIPTION The yellow flesh is firm and crisp with a sweet flavor.

TREE CHARACTERISTICS The vigorous, upright-growing tree has a spreading, drooping habit. It is a highly productive biennial bearer but the fruit ripens unevenly and tends to water core. The tree has greenish-yellow bark and waved leaves.

DISEASE RESISTANCE Moderately resistant to the major diseases

SEASON OF RIPENING Fall

USES Apple butter, baking, frying, drying, dessert, and livestock food

STORAGE QUALITY Poor

Rainbow

Since I had never seen a Rainbow apple and scant documentation was available, identification reinforcement was made by an octogenarian who had grown up in the region of West Virginia where the old trees were found. When shown the apple, he immediately said, "Why that's an old Rainbow apple. I haven't seen one since I was a child!"

OTHER NAMES None

HISTORY It is speculated to have come from Missouri although its exact place of origin is unknown. As early as 1898 some Virginia nurseries propagated it to market and in 1900 it was sold by Stark Bro's Nursery. However it disappeared from cultivation for many years until Carlos Manning located the apple in the 1990s and promoted it in the Appalachian region where it was grown many years before.

EXTERIOR DESCRIPTION Fruit is large and conical with a fairly long stem. The rich yellow background is striped and splashed scarlet with an overlay of crimson stripes. Small white dots also cover the skin surface.

INTERIOR DESCRIPTION Flesh is yellow, juicy, crisp, and fine-grained.

TREE CHARACTERISTICS The moderately vigorous tree produces crops annually and can live for a long time.

DISEASE RESISTANCE Moderately resistant to the major diseases

SEASON OF RIPENING Fall

USES Dessert

STORAGE QUALITY Good

Ralls

Along with a number of other American seedling varieties, Ralls was imported by the Japanese to establish an apple-breeding program at the Tohoku Research Station in Aomori, Japan. In the late 1930s, a cross of Ralls and Red Delicious resulted in Fuji, which is now a major commercial variety.

OTHER NAMES Kokko (its name in Japan), Neverfail, Ralls Genet, Ralls Janet, Rockremain, Rock Rimmon, Winter Genneting, and dozens of other names. In China, where it is also widely grown (particularly in the northern provinces), it is called "Glory of the Fatherland." A predominately red apple called Ralls that is in circulation in New England and the upper Midwest is not the original Ralls.

HISTORY It first appeared around 1785 in Amherst County, Virginia. Some people speculate that Thomas Jefferson received the apple from Edmond Genet, the French minister when Jefferson was secretary of state, but I have searched in France and have found no records of the apple. Others hold the view that Jefferson received it directly from Ralls, a local nurseryman whose property was just across the James River from Jefferson's summer home, Poplar Forest.

EXTERIOR DESCRIPTION Fruit is medium in size and roundish-oblate in shape. The greenish-yellow background is flushed, mottled, and streaked with various shades of pink, red, and crimson over at least half of the surface. It also has conspicuous yellow or russet dots and scarfskin may be present on some fruit. The thick stem is sometimes partially covered by a fleshy protuberance within the russeted cavity.

INTERIOR DESCRIPTION The dense, crisp, tender flesh is yellowish with a tinge of green. It has a balanced tart-sweet flavor and exudes a sweet aroma when cut. The seeds are large, brown, and ovate.

TREE CHARACTERISTICS The moderately vigorous tree develops an open framework with considerably twiggy growth (sometimes described as brushy) which makes it difficult to prune. The green oval leaves are folded, reflexed, and slightly waved with sharp, regular, prominent serrations. In thinning, consideration must be made that June drop does not affect this variety. It blooms very late, assuring a crop set and accounting for its central Virginia name of Neverfail.

DISEASE RESISTANCE It is slightly susceptible to apple scab and bitter rot but will still produce good fruit under a low-spray program, particularly on standard rootstock. Blossom fireblight is its major disease problem, but even when severe, the fruit set and production are not affected. The tree seems to have high resistance to collar rot.

SEASON OF RIPENING Fall

USES Dessert, pie making, frying, apple butter, and cider

STORAGE QUALITY Excellent

Ramsdell Sweet

SOME PEOPLE WILL remark on how light in weight Ramsdell Sweet apples feel when picked up, a characteristic that becomes especially obvious when lifting a bushel. On the opposite end of the spectrum are the "heavy in the hand" apples such as Twenty Ounce. This was a popular kitchen orchard variety for its tendency to bear early, producing incredibly sweet fruit to relish.

OTHER NAMES Avery Sweet, English Sweet, Hurlbut, Hurlbut Sweet, Ramsdell, Red Pumpkin Sweet

HISTORY It originated in 1838 in Thompson, Connecticut, and was introduced to the Massachusetts Horticultural Society by the Reverend H. S. Ramsdell. It was renamed with the single name Ramsdell and cataloged by the American Pomological Society in 1862.

EXTERIOR DESCRIPTION This medium to large apple varies in shape from truncate-conic to rectangular. The yellow skin is nearly totally covered with a dark red flush and occasionally with darker stripes. The fruit also has large pale dots over the surface and a blue bloom.

INTERIOR DESCRIPTION The yellowish-white flesh is firm and tender with a very sweet flavor. In storage it becomes mealy and dry and loses its flavor quickly.

TREE CHARACTERISTICS The tree grows particularly upright; it bears early and produces heavy crops annually.

DISEASE RESISTANCE Somewhat susceptible to fireblight in the warmer, humid growing regions; moderately resistant to the other major diseases.

SEASON OF RIPENING Fall

USES Dessert and baking

STORAGE QUALITY Fair. It becomes mealy in storage.

Raven

IT CAN BE a bit startling to watch the bright red juice flow from Raven apples when they are pressed for cider making. The unique color is also reflected in the cider after fermentation just as it is with Surprise and Burford Redflesh apples. Some people report that the apples also make for a high-flavored treat when they are sliced and slowly dried.

OTHER NAMES None

HISTORY The date of origin is not known. It is speculated to have come from New England and has historically been mostly known in New York, but since the 1980s it has been distributed to states in the upper Midwest and the Northwest.

EXTERIOR DESCRIPTION Fruit is small to medium and round with a slightly flattened stem end. The yellow background is mostly hidden by deep red (sometimes nearly black) hues. Prominent yellow irregularly shaped lenticels also appear on the surface. The short stem comes out of a deep cavity that is russeted to the rim. Raven has been compared to the old-fashioned Winesap in appearance.

INTERIOR DESCRIPTION The flesh is reddish and flavorful. This variety is inherently subject to water coring, a condition in which sugar cells become water-soaked and translucent and the flesh takes on a harsh, artificial sweetness.

TREE CHARACTERISTICS It is moderately vigorous and has twiggy growth unless pruned. Fruit size is generally not that important (because the apples are mainly used for making cider) so after initial scaffold training, the tree only needs light annual pruning.

DISEASE RESISTANCE It is susceptible to the major apple diseases, particularly in the South and mid-Atlantic. In these areas Raven is replaced by Virginia (Hewes) Crab which also is an excellent cider maker but does not water core as severely.

SEASON OF RIPENING Late fall to early winter

USES Primarily cider but sometimes for drying

STORAGE QUALITY Very poor, mainly because of water core

Razor Russet

OCCASIONALLY, A LIMB growing on an apple tree will produce a distinct and valuable new variety. This type of naturally occurring limb mutation was first recorded in a 1741 letter to the Swedish botanist Linnaeus when a russeted apple appeared on a green apple–producing tree. Razor Russet, which grew on a Golden Delicious tree, is a modern example of this phenomenon.

OTHER NAMES None

HISTORY It was discovered in 1960 in the Browning Orchard near Wallingford, Kentucky, by the late William Armstrong, a former extension specialist with the University of Kentucky.

EXTERIOR DESCRIPTION Fruit is large, symmetrical, and round to somewhat conical. It has a uniformly golden-brown skin.

INTERIOR DESCRIPTION The coarse yellowish-white flesh has a rich, spicy, sweet-tart flavor.

TREE CHARACTERISTICS This heavy annual bearer grows moderately, developing an open and roundish shape. The habit is similar to Golden Russet trees.

DISEASE RESISTANCE Moderately resistant to the major diseases

SEASON OF RIPENING Fall

USES Dessert, cider, and drying

STORAGE QUALITY Good

Red Butterscotch

APPLE FLAVOR EXPRESSIONS are beginning to approach the complexity of wine tastings. In the hundreds of organized apple tastings I have conducted, rating sheets will always record a new and original flavor—some defy the imagination, but after all, taste is subjective. As evidenced by its name, a hint of butterscotch is often detected by the palates experiencing this apple.

OTHER NAMES None

HISTORY It was first known to me in the upper Midwest. After extensive inquiries, the origin of Red Butterscotch is still unknown.

EXTERIOR DESCRIPTION This small-to medium-sized, conical apple can be a showstopper because of its striking bright appearance. The yellowish-green background is covered by orange and red stripes except for within the stem cavity. The surface is also irregularly patterned with russet dots.

INTERIOR DESCRIPTION The whitish flesh is fine-grained and sweet.

TREE CHARACTERISTICS The moderately vigorous tree is a hardy annual bearer.

DISEASE RESISTANCE Moderately resistant to the major diseases

SEASON OF RIPENING Fall

USES Dessert

STORAGE QUALITY Fair for a fall apple

Redfield

REDFIELD IS KNOWN for producing quite an interesting cider; the reddish color and distinctive flavor is pleasing to eyes and palate alike. This vintage apple resurfaced in the American cider making renaissance as a favorite of Judith and Terry Maloney, early innovators and promoters of artisanal cider at West County Cider in Colrain, Massachusetts.

OTHER NAMES None

HISTORY This cross of Wolf River and Niedzwetzskayana Red Crab was developed in 1938 at the New York State Agricultural Experiment Station in Geneva.

EXTERIOR DESCRIPTION This medium to large apple has an oblate-oblique shape. The smooth, glossy skin varies in color from pink to red.

INTERIOR DESCRIPTION The red flesh is dry, very acidic, and tart.

TREE CHARACTERISTICS The tree is a hardy, vigorous grower in New England, less so in the mid-Atlantic. It is sometimes selected as a focal point for landscape design due to its ornamental reddish-bronze foliage and large deep pink blossoms.

DISEASE RESISTANCE Resistant to the major diseases

SEASON OF RIPENING Fall

USES Primarily cider, but also baking, vinegar, applesauce, jelly, and landscape design

STORAGE QUALITY Fair

Redfree

THIS DISEASE-RESISTANT variety was developed to fill a particular niche in the apple market: a summer apple for eating out of hand with an appearance attractive to consumers. It was not until the later introductions of Gala and Ginger Gold that other summer dessert varieties become available.

OTHER NAMES Co-op 13

HISTORY It was developed in 1981 as part of the program to establish disease-resistant varieties at Purdue University in West Lafayette, Indiana.

EXTERIOR DESCRIPTION The medium-sized, round-oblate apple has smooth, waxy skin. When the tree is grown in cooler climates, the yellow background of the apple will be mostly coated with bright red; more yellow color is exposed when grown in warmer climates. Conspicuous white dots also appear on the surface.

INTERIOR DESCRIPTION Flesh is firm, crisp, and juicy with a well-balanced flavor.

TREE CHARACTERISTICS The tree is vigorous and spreading with wide crotch angles. It bears full crops annually and thinning is usually not necessary. Redfree ripens unevenly, necessitating two or more pickings.

DISEASE RESISTANCE Very resistant to apple scab and cedar apple rust; moderately resistant to fireblight and powdery mildew.

SEASON OF RIPENING Early fall. It ripens approximately six weeks before Red Delicious.

USES Dessert

STORAGE QUALITY Good

Red Limbertwig

OUT OF MORE than forty noted varieties in the Limbertwig apple category, Red Limbertwig has most often been called the original, the oldest, and the common Limbertwig. However, we can only speculate about its origin because there is no known documentation. The history of many, if not most, Limbertwigs is murky and full of considerable confusion.

OTHER NAMES Common Limbertwig, Green Limbertwig, James River Limbertwig, Mountain Limbertwig, Red Jewel

HISTORY The date and place of origin is unknown; some suspect it came from Virginia.

EXTERIOR DESCRIPTION This medium-sized, oblate apple displays the stem-end russeting typical of many Limbertwigs. The rough greenish-yellow skin has a dull red blush on the sun-exposed side. Brownish dots also cover the surface.

INTERIOR DESCRIPTION Flesh is firm and creamy white. It has the classic rich-tasting flavor that one begins to recognize after sampling numerous Limbertwig varieties.

TREE CHARACTERISTICS Like many Limbertwigs, this tree has long branches with moderate drooping. It should be carefully pruned to enhance fruit quality.

DISEASE RESISTANCE Moderately susceptible to the major apple diseases

SEASON OF RIPENING Late fall

USES Dessert, apple butter, jelly, and drying

STORAGE QUALITY Excellent

Red Winter Pearmain

THIS IS THE variety that can be credited with launching the apple career of Carlos Manning after he visited me in central Virginia to learn how to propagate the generations-old Red Winter Pearmain tree that was growing—or rather, dying—on his grandfather's property. Carlos went on to found Manning Nursery in Lester, West Virginia, and has become a respected ambassador for the unique apples of his region.

OTHER NAMES Batchelor, Buncombe, Bunkum, Jackson's Red, Kisby's Red, Powers, Red Fall Pippin, Red Gilliflower, Red Lady Finger, Red Vandevere, Robertson's Pearmain, Southern Fall Pippin, Tinson's Red

HISTORY First described in 1857, this apple came from Buncombe County, North Carolina.

EXTERIOR DESCRIPTION This medium to large fruit varies in shape from rectangular to conic. The smooth yellow skin is almost entirely flushed maroon with indistinct stripes and large light dots.

INTERIOR DESCRIPTION The whitish-yellow flesh is tender and juicy. It has a subacid to slightly sweet flavor and a pronounced aroma.

TREE CHARACTERISTICS This moderately vigorous tree is long-lived and bears crops annually. As with the apple's likely parents, Winesap and Red Limbertwig, proper annual pruning will improve fruit quality. Red Winter Pearmain produces root suckers like Milam (a variety with which is often confused) which accounts for the wide distribution of both varieties during the nineteenth century.

DISEASE RESISTANCE Moderately resistant to the major diseases

SEASON OF RIPENING Fall

USES Dessert, baking, drying, and apple butter

STORAGE QUALITY Fair

Reverend Morgan

THE CYCLING AND bearing of apple trees depends on receiving an adequate number of hours at temperatures below 45 degrees F. Reverend Morgan grows well in warm regions (as well as cooler ones) because it requires only 400 to 500 chill hours whereas most apple trees need at least 800. Unlike the majority of low-chill apples which are associated with mild tastes, this variety has a prominent flavor that does not degrade quickly after harvesting.

OTHER NAMES None

HISTORY This seedling of Granny Smith was developed in 1965 by Reverend Herman T. Morgan of Houston, Texas; the tree first fruited in 1970.

EXTERIOR DESCRIPTION This medium to large apple is round, tapering toward the blossom end. The yellow-green skin is layered with a pinkish-red blush. The stem projects obliquely.

INTERIOR DESCRIPTION The fine-grained, white flesh is rich and complex in flavor.

TREE CHARACTERISTICS The tree is moderately vigorous and bears full crops annually. When grown in Virginia, it loses its leaves earlier than most varieties.

DISEASE RESISTANCE Somewhat resistant to most of the major apple diseases

SEASON OF RIPENING Late summer

USES Dessert and frying

STORAGE QUALITY Fair

Rhode Island Greening

At New England apple events, this classic culinary variety is often brought to me for identification from very old trees. I was once tasked with identifying an apple that was no larger than a big cherry. Even at that size, the prominent white lenticels hinted at the identity and a tiny bite offered sufficient confirmation.

OTHER NAMES Burlington Greening, Ganges, Greening, Green Newtown Pippin, Green Winter Pippin, Jersey Greening, Russine

HISTORY It originated in 1650 in the village of Green's End in Newport (now called Middletown), Rhode Island. It is reported that the tree was grown by a tavern keeper named Green who distributed its cuttings for propagation so generously that the tree died. It was a major commercial variety in nineteenth-century America.

EXTERIOR DESCRIPTION The medium to large apple is round with flattened ends and is ribbed at the eye and on the body. It has yellowish-green skin (which may have a brownish or orange blush) with russeting at the base and some white or pale russet dots on the surface.

INTERIOR DESCRIPTION The greenish-yellow flesh is fine-textured and firm, becoming tender and golden brown when cooked. It has an acid flavor, a small core, and ovate, pointed seeds.

TREE CHARACTERISTICS This triploid should be grown in combination with two different pollen-producing trees. The tree is slow to begin bearing and has a tendency toward biennial bearing but it is vigorous and will live a long time. It has smooth reddish-olive bark with few lenticels. The large, oval, deep green leaves are flat and sharply serrated. Pre-harvest drop is a problem on some soils and in some climates.

DISEASE RESISTANCE Resistant to the major diseases but some damage from blossom and twig blight may occur.

SEASON OF RIPENING Late fall

USES Primarily frying and pie making, also dessert and cider

STORAGE QUALITY Good

Rome Beauty

THIS LATE-BLOOMING VARIETY was a typical planting choice during the Great Depression due to its dependability, good size, and attractive appearance. It also gained a reputation as an excellent baking apple with high flavor and slices that hold their shape when cooked. As the years passed, Rome Beauty supplanted many equally valuable heirloom apples like Porter, Stayman, Wolf River, and York.

OTHER NAMES Foust's Rome Beauty, Gillett's, Phoenix, Roman Beauty, Rome, Royal Red, Starbuck. There are many variously colored strains and cultivars, and a tetraploid sport called Rome Beauty Double Red which is flatter and more brightly colored than the original.

HISTORY In 1816, Putman Nursery sold a number of grafted trees to Joel Gillett of Proctorville, Ohio, which is in the township of Rome. One of these trees had sprouted below the graft union and Gillett gave this unknown variety to his son, Alanson Gillett. It produced large attractive apples which Alanson named "Rome." The original tree washed away in an 1860 flood.

EXTERIOR DESCRIPTION The medium to large apple is uniformly round with a long, thick stem that usually projects at an angle. Skin is fairly smooth, tough, well-colored. The greenish-yellow background is mottled and flushed with bright red, deepening to a solid red on the sun-exposed side, and is conspicuously striped bright carmine.

INTERIOR DESCRIPTION The creamy-yellow flesh is coarse, crisp, and juicy.

TREE CHARACTERISTICS The tree has narrow, upright growth with unusually supple limbs (therefore less often damaged by high winds). The bark is reddish olive in color, and the small, shiny, light green leaves are oval and sharply serrated. Rome Beauty is self-fruitful and blooms late, escaping frosts.

DISEASE RESISTANCE Moderately susceptible to the major apple diseases

SEASON OF RIPENING Fall

USES Baking, drying, and dessert

STORAGE QUALITY Good

Roxbury Russet

THIS APPLE, DATING back to the mid-seventeenth century, is probably the oldest named variety in America. A Roxbury Russet apple can be distinguished from the similar Golden Russet by identifying several trademarks of the former: larger size and distinctly elliptical shape, thicker stem, development of a red tinge on one side, and coarser yellow flesh.

OTHER NAMES Belpre Russet, Boston Russet, Hewe's Russet, Leather Coat, Marietta Russet, Putnam Russet, Shippen's Russet, Sylvan Russet, Warner Russet

HISTORY This variety originated in Roxbury, Massachusetts around 1649 and soon thereafter scionwood was taken to Connecticut for propagation.

EXTERIOR DESCRIPTION Fruit is medium to large and elliptical. The green skin has a bronze tinge and is covered with a brownish-yellow russet; it sometimes develops a reddish blush on the sun-exposed side. A hint of ribbing can occasionally be seen.

INTERIOR DESCRIPTION The coarse greenish-yellow flesh is more sweet than tart when fully ripe. The core is compact and the seeds are usually defective. The juice contains 12.87 percent sugar that ferments to 6 percent alcohol.

TREE CHARACTERISTICS The vigorous, open-spreading tree has a flat top and grows at a slant in the nursery or orchard for the first few years. Because the limb structure becomes brushy, attention to pruning is important. It has reddish-olive bark. The deep green, shiny, oval leaves are folded near the edge, slightly reflexed, and regularly and moderately serrated with a heavy pubescence. Cross pollination will increase crop yield.

DISEASE RESISTANCE Resistant to apple scab and powdery mildew; moderately susceptible to fireblight and cedar apple rust.

SEASON OF RIPENING Fall

USES Dessert, pie making, cider, and drying. The dried apple will retain high flavor but the slices will darken.

STORAGE QUALITY Good

Rusty Coat

I ONCE DID a field planting of seeds from about ten named russet varieties and the fruiting produced ten apples divergent in appearance, some with minimal russeting and a few with very heavy coating. It would have been appropriate for me to call each of them Rusty Coat since this is essentially a generic name for russeted apples.

OTHER NAMES None

HISTORY The date and place of origin is unknown. The name Rusty Coat has been attributed to a number of other known russeted varieties either when the name was forgotten or because it became a generic term for any apple with dominating russet on the skin.

EXTERIOR DESCRIPTION This type of apple presents various degrees of skin coating with different textures of russet. The size and shape also fluctuate.

INTERIOR DESCRIPTION It generally has whitish-yellow flesh that is crisp and dry with a sweet-tart flavor; after long storage, the apple becomes more sweet than tart.

TREE CHARACTERISTICS Tree habit is similar to Roxbury Russet, Pomme Gris, and Golden Russet. It bears full crops and the limbs will be heavy, unless pruned.

DISEASE RESISTANCE Moderately resistant to the major diseases

SEASON OF RIPENING Fall

USES Cider, dessert, and drying

STORAGE QUALITY Good

Scott Winter

THIS SUPREMELY USEFUL, high-quality variety is capable of surviving even in the more severe colder climates where Northern Spy or Rhode Island Greening cannot be grown. In the late nineteenth century it was grown commercially on a small scale in Canada and the upper northern regions of the United States.

OTHER NAMES Scott, Scott's Red Winter, Scott's Winter, Wilcox's Winter

HISTORY It originated in 1864 on the Scott farm in Newport, Vermont. It was brought to notice by Dr. T. H. Hoskins of Newport.

EXTERIOR DESCRIPTION This small to medium apple has a roundish-conic to roundish-oblate shape. Skin is smooth and thin. The light yellow background is covered with bright red and overlaid with darker red mottling and stripes. A short, stubby stem emerges from a cavity lined with green.

INTERIOR DESCRIPTION The whitish flesh is tinged with yellow and is sometimes stained red. It is aromatic, crisp, and very juicy.

TREE CHARACTERISTICS The vigorous, hardy tree grows to be medium in size and begins to bear early. It is limb dense; pruning is necessary to improve fruit quality.

DISEASE RESISTANCE Susceptible to apple scab; moderately resistant to the other major diseases.

SEASON OF RIPENING Late fall

USES Dessert, baking, and pie making

STORAGE QUALITY Good. It retains its acidity in storage which makes it good for cooking.

Shiawassee

SHIAWASSEE IS LIKELY an offspring of Fameuse, also known as Snow Apple, which is one of the very few apples that produces a good likeness from seed. Migrants carried seeds of Fameuse collected from cider mills and planted them in distant places, perhaps including Shiawassee County, Michigan, where this apple was discovered in an orchard in the mid-nineteenth century.

OTHER NAMES Michigan Beauty, Nonsuch, Shiawassee Beauty

HISTORY It was found around 1850 in the orchard of Beebe Truesdell near Vernon, Michigan. It was first called Nonsuch, but after gaining popularity it was promoted by the Michigan State Pomological Society and renamed Shiawassee Beauty.

EXTERIOR DESCRIPTION This medium-sized, round apple has shallow furrows projecting out of the stem cavity. The yellow skin is nearly completely covered with a red flush, streaks of carmine, and evenly spaced white dots.

INTERIOR DESCRIPTION The white flesh is crisp, tender, moderately juicy, and fine-grained with a subacid flavor. It has a strong aroma.

TREE CHARACTERISTICS The moderately vigorous and spreading tree bears full crops annually.

DISEASE RESISTANCE Moderately resistant to the major diseases

SEASON OF RIPENING Fall

USES Dessert and baking

STORAGE QUALITY Good

Shockley

In my orchard, Shockley was a remarkable pollinator for other varieties. The bee population doubled at bloom time and when I walked close to the tree, the pollen scent would take my breath away. My nearby Ribston Pippin trees, which are notoriously difficult to pollinate, always produced full crops.

OTHER NAMES Dixie Sweet Romanite, Horse Bud, Neverfail, Waddel Hall, Waddle Hall. The most notable strains are Cantrell and Grizzle; the latter is the larger of the two and more flattened on the ends.

HISTORY It was exhibited at the 1852 Georgia State Fair by a man named Shockley from Jackson County, Georgia.

EXTERIOR DESCRIPTION Fruit ranges in size from small to large; shape is roundish to conic; and the stem length varies from medium to long. It has very smooth yellowish-green skin flushed light to dark red with reddish stripes on the non-flushed area. Conspicuous yellow dots appear over most of the surface. Little russeting appears on the fruit except for within the stem cavity.

INTERIOR DESCRIPTION The crisp yellowish flesh has a sweet, rich, and slightly vinous flavor.

TREE CHARACTERISTICS It grows vigorously and upright and bears heavy crops annually.

DISEASE RESISTANCE Susceptible to cedar apple rust; somewhat tolerant of the other major apple diseases. Under certain conditions, especially late in the summer, rots can be a problem.

SEASON OF RIPENING Late fall

USES Dessert and jelly

STORAGE QUALITY Excellent. I have had usable Shockley apples from the storage in June.

Sierra Beauty

SIERRA BEAUTY IS one of the few uncommon varieties that always had some commercial potential on the West Coast, but was never widely distributed because it does not grow well in less-hospitable regions. The Sierra Beauty apples I've had occasion to eat when visiting California were spectacular, but my attempts to grow it in Virginia produced disappointing results sans flavor and color.

OTHER NAMES None

HISTORY The seedling first appeared around 1890 on a slope of the Sierra Nevada Mountains in California; some speculate that it was a vestige from miners in the early days of the California Gold Rush. It has held sporadic commercial success over the years. It reemerged around 1920 near Chico, California, and was offered for a while by some regional nurseries before being again lost from commerce. It was rediscovered in 1980 by the Gowan family in their Anderson Valley, California, orchard where it is now grown on a small commercial scale.

EXTERIOR DESCRIPTION This medium to large apple is round and blocky, becoming conical at the base. The thick greenish-yellow skin is netted with russet and has bold red stripes that mature to deep pink or sometimes red patches.

INTERIOR DESCRIPTION The light yellow flesh is firm, crisp, juicy, and fine-textured. Flavor is nicely balanced with a tart finish.

TREE CHARACTERISTICS The upright-growing tree is vigorous and hardy with a tendency toward biennial bearing.

DISEASE RESISTANCE Moderately resistant to the major diseases

SEASON OF RIPENING Late fall

USES Dessert and especially for making preserves and pies. The slices hold their shape when cooked.

STORAGE QUALITY Good. The fruit stores well even without refrigeration.

Skinner's Seedling

The fruiting spurs of Skinner's Seedling are quite fragile so extra caution must be taken during harvest to avoid knocking them off. (Those spurs will be responsible for producing the next year's crop as apple trees bear fruit on two-year-old or older limb growth). This variety also needs a strong pollinator like Golden Delicious or a crabapple for effective fruit set.

OTHER NAMES Santa Clara King, Skinner

HISTORY It originated around 1887 with Judge H. C. Skinner of Coyote Creek, which is east of San Jose, California.

EXTERIOR DESCRIPTION The large to very large apple has a conic, flattened shape that is slightly furrowed coming out of the stem cavity. The yellow background is covered with some red stripes and mottling. Lenticels are creamy white and star-shaped with reddish auras.

INTERIOR DESCRIPTION The yellowish-white flesh is juicy and tender with a sprightly, mild acidic flavor.

TREE CHARACTERISTICS The large, moderately vigorous tree is productive but cross pollination is required to produce good crops.

DISEASE RESISTANCE It is susceptible to the major diseases, especially when grown in hot and humid climates.

SEASON OF RIPENING Late summer

USES Mainly dessert, but also applesauce

STORAGE QUALITY Poor

Smith Cider

In hot and humid climates, fireblight will decimate Smith Cider apple trees, reducing limbs to pruned-back stubs. Such was the case in Virginia, where I struggled for many years to grow this variety before finally giving up. Ironically, I have met a few growers in regions less affected by fireblight who told me that they too had stubbed limbs because the tree would overbear and the weight of the excessive fruit would give the same result.

OTHER NAMES Choice Kentuck, Cider, Cider Apple, Fowler, Fuller, Jackson Winesap, Pennsylvania Cider, Poplar Bluff, Smith's. A sport called Makefield has the same characteristics but is all red in color.

HISTORY It appeared around 1817 in Bucks County, Pennsylvania. During the Revolutionary War, Hessian soldiers who were interned in Pennsylvania after the Battle of Trenton brought grafts of Smith Cider to Frederick County, Virginia.

EXTERIOR DESCRIPTION This round and slightly long apple varies in size from small to large. It has clear pale yellow skin, sometimes with a greenish cast, and is splashed and striped carmine. The surface is covered with whitish or russet dots and it is slightly russeted at the base.

INTERIOR DESCRIPTION White flesh is fine-grained and crisp with a subacid flavor.

TREE CHARACTERISTICS The tree is a spreading, vigorous grower with straggling branches. It bears early and fruits heavily, sometimes overbearing and causing severe limb damage. The young wood on the tree is a rich dark brown. It has a low chill hour requirement.

DISEASE RESISTANCE Susceptible to fireblight and powdery mildew; resistant to the other major diseases.

SEASON OF RIPENING Late fall

USES Cider, dessert, and pie making

Smokehouse

THIS IS PROBABLY the apple that changed my life. On a very hot and humid late August day in 1935 my mother and grandmother went to the orchard to get Smokehouse apples, just ripening, to fry for supper. On arrival at the tree my mother said she must return to the house and ten minutes later I came into the world.

OTHER NAMES English Vandevere, Gibbons Smokehouse, Millcreek, Millcreek Vandevere, Red Vandevere, Smoke House

HISTORY It originated on the farm of William Gibbons near Millcreek, Pennsylvania, and was brought to notice in 1837. It is thought to be a seedling of Vandevere.

EXTERIOR DESCRIPTION This large apple has a rectangular to truncate-conic shape. The greenish-yellow skin is flushed red with carmine stripes; russet dots also appear over much of the surface.

INTERIOR DESCRIPTION The yellowish-white flesh is crisp, tender, and very juicy with a subacid flavor.

TREE CHARACTERISTICS A vigorous grower, this tree is a heavy cropper that requires annual pruning. It develops a dense head that must be thinned for sunlight and air penetration. New growth has reddish bark. Leaves are large, oval, green, sharply serrated, smooth, and shiny.

DISEASE RESISTANCE Resistant to collar rot, cedar apple rust, and fireblight; slightly susceptible to apple scab and powdery mildew.

SEASON OF RIPENING Late summer to early fall. It ripens over three weeks.

USES Pie making, frying, dessert, and cider

STORAGE QUALITY Good for a late summer to early fall apple

Spencer

THIS EYE-CATCHING, markedly sweet apple was kept in cultivation by home orchards even though it was never heavily produced in the commercial market. The nineteenth century, when granulated sugar was not yet readily available, was the heyday of very sweet apples. But by the 1930s demand had turned to tarter tastes and most sweet apples were relegated to the minority. Spencer has the potential to make a small commercial comeback as consumers again demand inclusion of sweet apples in the spectrum.

OTHER NAMES None

HISTORY This cross of McIntosh and Golden Delicious was developed in 1926 at the British Columbia Experimental Station in Summerland and released commercially in 1959. Spencer is sometimes found in orchards in Europe.

EXTERIOR DESCRIPTION Fruit is medium to large, tall, and round to conical. The skin's yellow background is flushed and streaked carmine or orange red.

INTERIOR DESCRIPTION The creamy-white flesh is soft and has a sweet, tangy flavor.

TREE CHARACTERISTICS Spreading and fairly vigorous, the tree is slow to begin bearing but then produces full crops annually.

DISEASE RESISTANCE Moderately resistant to the major diseases

SEASON OF RIPENING Early fall

USES Dessert

STORAGE QUALITY Good for an early fall apple

Spice of Old Virginia

FOR MANY YEARS I took this spicy apple for granted, but even among the hundred or so varieties available in my backyard, it was always enticing and thought provoking. The distinctive sprightliness sets it apart, as well as the allure that it might be centuries old.

OTHER NAMES Spice of Virginia. It is confused with an apple called Virginia Spice that was sold in 1859 by Hopewell Nurseries in Fredericksburg, Virginia. But a comparison of the characteristics of the two apples indicates that they are distinct varieties.

HISTORY The date and place of origin are not known. It is possibly the same as the seventeenth-century apple Olde Towne, but no documentation exists to prove my theory.

EXTERIOR DESCRIPTION This small to medium apple is elongated in shape with a fairly long stem. The light yellow skin is usually fully covered on the sun-exposed side with a medium reddish-orange color and red stripes. Brown dots irregularly cover the skin surface. It is russeted from the stem cavity over the apple shoulders.

INTERIOR DESCRIPTION The yellow flesh is firm, crisp, and juicy with a sprightly, memorable flavor.

TREE CHARACTERISTICS This moderately growing tree produces full crops annually. It has brushy limbs and should be carefully pruned for air circulation and sunlight penetration.

DISEASE RESISTANCE Moderately resistant to the major diseases

SEASON OF RIPENING Late fall

USES Dessert, drying, apple butter, and applesauce

STORAGE QUALITY Good

Spokane Beauty

BIG APPLES CAN be a curse for the orchardist: they have a narrow market niche and, for the most part, a forgettable taste. Spokane Beauty, however, has an acidic, rich, complex flavor, remarkable for an apple that can weigh as much as two pounds. I added it to my running list of best drying apples after noting that two apples filled a drying tray.

OTHER NAMES None

HISTORY It originated around 1859 when Stephen Maxon Sr. migrated westward on the Oregon Trail and settled about six miles west of Walla Walla, Washington. There he planted an orchard with seeds that he had brought with him and one of these seeds produced Spokane Beauty. In 1895 the apple was awarded the top prize at the Spokane Fruit Fair.

EXTERIOR DESCRIPTION The fruit is very large in size and often develops a lopsided shape. The smooth yellow skin is mostly covered with bright red, leaving windows of yellow. Some small brownish dots are scattered on the surface.

INTERIOR DESCRIPTION The very white flesh is crisp and juicy with a memorable flavor.

TREE CHARACTERISTICS This vigorous grower is tip bearing, which means it produces fruit on the ends of branches; the tree must be carefully pruned so as not to cut away the fruiting buds.

DISEASE RESISTANCE Moderately resistant to the major diseases

SEASON OF RIPENING Late fall

USES Dessert, baking, and drying

STORAGE QUALITY Good

Stark

Unless grown under favorable conditions of rich soil and good tree management, Stark's sprightly, vinous taste will be hidden beneath washed-out greenish skin. It was once widely distributed by nurseries but demand waned as consumers began to eat with their eyes instead of their mouths.

OTHER NAMES Robinson, Starke Apple, Winter King, Yeats

HISTORY It likely originated around 1867 on the farm of John Main in Delaware County, Ohio. It was promoted by H. P. McMaster of Leonardsburg, Ohio. It has no relationship to Stark Bro's Nursery.

EXTERIOR DESCRIPTION This large apple has a round-elongated shape. The greenish background is layered with a purplish red and it is covered with a dull waxy bloom.

INTERIOR DESCRIPTION The yellowish flesh is coarse, breaking, juicy, and sprightly. It has a subacid flavor that is also sometimes described as vinous.

TREE CHARACTERISTICS A large, vigorously growing, very productive tree, despite its disease susceptibility. It has dark red bark and dark green oval leaves that are generally flat with sharp, regular, distinct serrations. The midrib often tends to form a reverse curvature.

DISEASE RESISTANCE Very susceptible to fireblight and somewhat susceptible to cedar apple rust; resistant to the other major diseases.

SEASON OF RIPENING Late fall

USES Dessert and apple butter

STORAGE QUALITY Good

Stayman

IT IS TOLD that Joseph Stayman, a country horse and buggy doctor from Leavenworth, Kansas, would eat a Winesap apple at the end of the day and save all of the seeds for planting in the spring. Besides enjoying the apple, it was his motive to find a new variety of merit. In 1866 he made the selection and called it Stayman.

OTHER NAMES None. It is mistakenly called Stayman Winesap, but Stayman came from a seed of the Winesap apple and is a new variety. There are many cultivars and sports.

HISTORY It was discovered by Joseph Stayman and introduced by Stark Bro's Nursery in 1895; by the early 1900s commercial distribution to orchardists had already begun. It was widely planted in the valley of Virginia and along the eastern slopes of the Blue Ridge Mountains.

EXTERIOR DESCRIPTION Fruit is medium to large and round to conical. The greenish-yellow skin is flushed dull red with darker red stripes. Most of the surface is covered with a light russet, except for the more heavily russeted stem cavity. The skin is subject to cracking due to possible environmental conditions which has discouraged commercial production of the variety and led to removal from many orchards.

INTERIOR DESCRIPTION Flesh is white with a greenish-yellow tinge; it is firm, tender, and fine-textured. The subacid flavor is distinctive because of its tart and vinous qualities.

TREE CHARACTERISTICS A triploid, Stayman requires a pollinator and it is a poor pollinator for other varieties. Because it will bloom slightly later than many other varieties, it is suitable for frost-prone areas. The moderately vigorous tree bears early and heavily and the growth is straggly; the long shoots have few lenticels and sometimes have brownish, roughened "rust" at their base. Leaves are average sized, medium green, and broadly oval with coarse, sharp serrations. Interestingly, one-year-old trees grow in the nursery in random slanting directions.

DISEASE RESISTANCE Somewhat resistant to fireblight, apple scab, and cedar apple rust

SEASON OF RIPENING Fall

USES Dessert, pie making, apple butter, frying, applesauce, and cider

STORAGE QUALITY Good. It will scald in storage but the flesh quality won't degrade.

Strawberry Pippin

I'VE HEARD MORE than a few describe Strawberry Pippin as "that sweet and pretty apple." This description of taste and appearance is well stated. It is also a talking apple with a pleasant crunch sound at each bite.

OTHER NAMES Strawberry

HISTORY The date and place of origin is not known. It is speculated that it may have been brought from England. It is known in Nova Scotia.

EXTERIOR DESCRIPTION This medium-sized, round apple has yellow skin that is nearly covered with various light and dark red hues. It can develop a light red blush on the sun-exposed side. Prominent yellowish-brown dots irregularly cover the surface. It has little russeting except for deep within the stem cavity.

INTERIOR DESCRIPTION The white flesh is crisp and juicy with a dominating sweetness.

TREE CHARACTERISTICS The tree is moderately vigorous and upright. Limb spreading will help increase the quality of the fruit by opening the tree to air circulation and sunlight penetration.

DISEASE RESISTANCE Moderately resistant to the major diseases

SEASON OF RIPENING Fall

USES Dessert

STORAGE QUALITY Good

Stump

THE STUMP APPLE from Chili, New York, is difficult to propagate and grow in the nursery, which is why it is now seldom found in orchards despite an enticing sprightly, light acidic flavor. This variety is more suitable for the backyard orchard and, even with its shortcomings, deserves preserving and enjoying.

OTHER NAMES None

HISTORY A number of apple varieties are called Stump, likely from their proximity to an old tree stump. In his book, *Old Southern Apples*, North Carolina apple historian Lee Calhoun includes a comprehensive definition of the three candidates: a variety sold in Kentucky around 1870 and reputed to be a seedling of Newtown Pippin, a variety from Delaware described in 1878, and the apple described here which originated before 1875 on the property of John Prue in Chili, New York.

EXTERIOR DESCRIPTION Fruit is medium in size and round-oblate with a short, stocky stem coming out of a russeted cavity. The skin is pink to dark red on a yellow background and lightly striped with carmine; randomly placed russet dots cover most of the surface. It bruises easily.

INTERIOR DESCRIPTION The whitish flesh is fine-grained, juicy, and aromatic with a light acidic sprightliness.

TREE CHARACTERISTICS Upright growing and moderately vigorous, the tree has long branches with heavy fruiting spurs.

DISEASE RESISTANCE Moderately resistant to the major diseases

SEASON OF RIPENING Fall

USES Dessert

STORAGE QUALITY Fair

Summer Banana

Taste and smell evaluations are subjective and will depend on the individual's sensitivity and imagination. Summer Banana is known to elicit remarks ranging from "this smell is stronger than a banana" to "this has no smell." The aroma tends to be more intense when the apples are grown in warm climates; apples produced in the northern states often have little aroma but are more colorful.

OTHER NAMES None

HISTORY This late nineteenth-century apple originated in Marion County, South Carolina. In 1900, the J. Van Lindley Nursery of Greensboro, North Carolina, trademarked Summer Banana and paid seventy-five dollars for the rights. But by the early 1900s, it had already fallen from favor with dwindling sales in South Carolina and North Carolina, where it was once so popular.

EXTERIOR DESCRIPTION The medium-sized, round apple usually has deep yellow skin blushed with faint red and pink stripes, but the appearance varies depending on growing region. In cooler locations, and especially at higher elevations, the skin is more red and bright; in very hot climates the redness can be minimal. The stem is fairly thick and medium in length.

INTERIOR DESCRIPTION The whitish flesh is fine-grained, crisp, and often aromatic.

DISEASE RESISTANCE Moderately resistant to the major diseases

SEASON OF RIPENING Late summer to early fall

USES Dessert and frying

STORAGE QUALITY Poor

Summer Champion

THIS SOUTHERN VARIETY is highly valued for its ability to be planted in the warmer climates where most varieties will not thrive due to a deficiency of chill hours necessary for proper cycling of the plant. Low-chill varieties like Summer Champion generally have a very mild taste, so this apple's intriguingly delicious flavor is especially cherished.

OTHER NAMES Holland, Kincaid

HISTORY Although some sources claim that it originated in Arkansas, Summer Champion has a well-established Texas origin. It came from the home of J. W. Kincaid of Weatherford, Texas, in 1923. The apple was originally named for Kincaid; it was later changed to Holland for G. A. Holland, a prominent citizen of the same town. The variety was marketed and renamed Summer Champion by Stark Bro's Nursery in 1907.

EXTERIOR DESCRIPTION The medium-sized fruit is round to slightly conical. It has yellow skin that is mostly covered by pink and red stripes.

INTERIOR DESCRIPTION The yellowish flesh is crisp and juicy.

TREE CHARACTERISTICS The tree bears early and produces heavy crops; thinning is necessary for quality fruit.

DISEASE RESISTANCE Susceptible to fireblight; somewhat susceptible to the other major diseases.

SEASON OF RIPENING Midsummer

USES Dessert and applesauce

STORAGE QUALITY Poor

Summer Limbertwig

THE RARE QUALITY of ripening during the summer sets this variety apart from the rest of the Limbertwig apples. The tree is among the "limbertwigiest" of the Limbertwigs and its pronounced weeping willow limbs are obvious in the landscape. It also shares the distinctive taste with the other apples in the group, recognizable upon first bite.

OTHER NAMES Weeping Limbertwig

HISTORY It was known in 1855 and is thought to have originated in the area of Greensboro, North Carolina.

EXTERIOR DESCRIPTION This medium-sized apple has a round-oblate shape. The light yellow skin is overlaid with light red to medium red stripes with a light netting of russet. The stem is medium in length and projects slightly to the side from a shallow, russeted cavity.

INTERIOR DESCRIPTION The tender and juicy white flesh is fine-grained and aromatic.

TREE CHARACTERISTICS This tree produces moderate crops annually.

DISEASE RESISTANCE Moderately resistant to the major diseases

SEASON OF RIPENING Late summer to early fall

USES Dessert, baking, and drying

STORAGE QUALITY Fair for a summer variety

Summer Pearmain

IF YOU COULD have only one apple tree at your back door, Summer Pearmain would be an excellent choice. When first planted, the tree will be slow growing, slender in form, and a challenge to prune, but after a few years it becomes moderately vigorous and productive. And most importantly, once fruiting, it provides two months of ripening apples.

OTHER NAMES American Pearmain, American Summer Pearmain, Early Summer Pearmain, Watkins Early

HISTORY It was known in 1806 and its place of origin is speculated to be New Jersey. It was taken to Japan when trade with that country first opened and can now be found in many modern varieties developed by the Japanese.

EXTERIOR DESCRIPTION Fruit is medium in size and oblong. It is mainly light red in color with some streaks and spots of darker red, as well as areas on the skin in which the yellowish background shows through.

INTERIOR DESCRIPTION The creamy flesh is very tender and juicy, considered by some to have a pear-like melting quality. The flesh will dry out if it becomes overripe, leaving behind minimal taste.

TREE CHARACTERISTICS This weak-growing tree is particularly suitable for trellis training because it has heavily spurred slender branches. It grows to a moderate size with a very round and close head. The tree performs remarkably well on light and sandy soils, which are typically a challenge for most apple varieties.

DISEASE RESISTANCE Somewhat susceptible to the major apple diseases; particularly susceptible to fireblight and cracking fruit.

SEASON OF RIPENING Early summer to midsummer

USES Dessert and cooking

STORAGE QUALITY Poor

Summer Rose

THE POMOLOGIST William Coxe, who seldom praised varieties, wrote in 1817 that Summer Rose excelled in beauty and quality for eating and stewing. This early summer apple competed as a cooking apple with Early Harvest throughout the nineteenth century. But even though it was considered better tasting, Summer Rose was eventually supplanted because of its small fruit size and sparse production.

OTHER NAMES French Reinette, Glass Apple, Harvest Apple, Lippencott's Early, Lodge's Early, Symm's Harvest, Woolman's Early, Woolman's Harvest, Woolman's Striped Harvest

HISTORY It likely came from somewhere in New Jersey and was known in 1806.

EXTERIOR DESCRIPTION Fruit is small to medium in size and oblate. The greenish-yellow skin is flushed orange red, streaked carmine, and scattered with patches of russet dots.

INTERIOR DESCRIPTION The white flesh is fine-textured and tender with a mild flavor.

TREE CHARACTERISTICS The vigorous, spreading tree comes into bearing early, but it grows slowly and under certain conditions can have a weak root system. The apples form in clusters and will often crack as they mature. The late-blooming tree is suitable for frost-prone areas.

DISEASE RESISTANCE Moderately resistant to the major diseases

SEASON OF RIPENING Midsummer (for frying and baking) to late summer (for dessert)

USES Dessert, frying, and baking

STORAGE QUALITY Poor

Sundance

THIS APPLE WAS the result of an early effort to make a variety resistant to apple scab, one of the adversities of the commercial apple world. The gene for scab resistance occurs naturally in the crabapple *Malus floribunda*, and it was the challenge, successfully accomplished, to incorporate this gene into the new variety.

OTHER NAMES None

HISTORY It was developed at the PRI (Purdue, Rutgers, and University of Illinois) apple breeding program at Purdue University in West Lafayette, Indiana. It was introduced in 1964.

EXTERIOR DESCRIPTION The large, round-conic apple has a yellow background with a pink to reddish blush.

INTERIOR DESCRIPTION The cream-colored flesh is firm and crisp with a sprightly, subacid flavor.

TREE CHARACTERISTICS A moderate to heavy cropper, the tree is vigorous and slightly upright growing with a biennial tendency. The fruit hangs well on the tree.

DISEASE RESISTANCE Resistant to apple scab, fireblight, and cedar apple rust; moderately resistant to powdery mildew.

SEASON OF RIPENING Late fall

USES Dessert and pie making. The slices hold their shape when cooked.

STORAGE QUALITY Good

Surprise

THIS APPLE RESIDES among scores of pink- or red-fleshed varieties, ranging from the lighter Pink Pearl to the watermelon-colored Burford Redflesh. Many are tannic tasting but Surprise has a pleasant flavor. I've known collectors in America and abroad who have as many as thirty of these enticing varieties in their orchard. The name begs for this apple to be cut open and flashed at an unsuspecting friend with the exclamation of "surprise!"

OTHER NAMES Yellow Surprise

HISTORY Surprise was first noted in England in 1831 and was brought into the Ohio River Valley by German immigrants around 1840. Trees were sold by nurseries in Virginia and Kentucky until about 1870, when the variety fell from favor mainly because of its small fruit size.

EXTERIOR DESCRIPTION When ripe, this small, round apple has a rich yellow skin with a dull red blotch on the sun-exposed side. A few conspicuous brown dots are scattered over the surface of the fruit. The stem is short and stout and the cavity ribbed.

INTERIOR DESCRIPTION Flesh is juicy and tastes more tart than sweet. In cool regions (especially at higher elevations) the flesh develops a pinkish-red coloring all the way to the core; in warm regions it often has very little redness.

TREE CHARACTERISTICS The slow-growing tree can be brushy unless annually pruned. It is hardy and produces light to medium crops annually.

DISEASE RESISTANCE Moderately resistant to the major diseases

SEASON OF RIPENING Fall

USES Late-season pinkish applesauce and making pies and tarts

STORAGE QUALITY Good

Sutton Beauty

VISITORS TOURING MY collection orchard would always pause before the Sutton Beauty tree when it was laden with fruit. The red and yellow color of the apples would cast a pinkish glow throughout the tree, particularly just after dawn and before twilight. The beauty is anything but understated.

OTHER NAMES Beauty, Morris Red, Steele's Red Winter, Steel's Red, Sutton

HISTORY Likely a seedling of Hubbardston Nonesuch, the apple was found around 1757 by Stephen Waters of Sutton, Massachusetts. It was brought to notice in 1848 through the Worcester County Horticultural Society.

EXTERIOR DESCRIPTION This medium-sized, round apple has glossy, bright red skin striped with carmine over a yellow background. Under-colored fruit have less red in the yellow background and the carmine stripes dominate.

INTERIOR DESCRIPTION The creamy flesh is crisp, fine-grained, juicy, and subacid. It is considered by most palates to be mild in flavor.

TREE CHARACTERISTICS The upright-growing tree bears early and heavily; it is biennial in production. The fruit hangs well on the tree.

DISEASE RESISTANCE Susceptible to fireblight; moderately resistant to other major diseases

SEASON OF RIPENING Fall

USES Dessert and sometimes for baking

STORAGE QUALITY Good. It is important to properly store the apples as soon as they are picked to dispel the heat.

Sweet Sixteen

WHAT HAPPENED TO Sweet Sixteen? Like a young lady of sixteen, this apple had so much going for it: attractive color, interesting flavor, good disease resistance, and tendencies to bloom late and bear early. Yet it never made it near the top of the market ladder. New varieties, like Zestar and Honeycrisp, came along and the promise of Sweet Sixteen was forgotten.

OTHER NAMES MN 1630

HISTORY This cross of Malinda and Northern Spy was made in 1973 and released in 1978 by the University of Minnesota.

EXTERIOR DESCRIPTION The apple is large and conical with slight ribbing. It has red stripes on a greenish-yellow background.

INTERIOR DESCRIPTION The cream-colored flesh is crisp and coarse. Generally, it is sweet with a hint of spice and a slightly tart aftertaste.

TREE CHARACTERISTICS This vigorously growing tree is late blooming and early bearing. It is subject to pre-harvest drop.

DISEASE RESISTANCE Resistant to apple scab and fireblight; moderately resistant to other major diseases.

SEASON OF RIPENING Fall

USES Dessert and sometimes baking

STORAGE QUALITY Good

Sweet Winesap

I LEARNED a valuable fireblight control lesson—the hard way—from Sweet Winesap. For fifteen years I cut out fireblight infection until the tree was a butchered wreck, bearing little fruit and spreading infection. Now I know, however passionate one may be to fruit a variety, the tree should be ripped out and isolated if severely infected at the early-bearing age.

OTHER NAMES Hendrick, Hendrick Sweet, Henry Sweet, Red Sweet Winesap, Red Sweet Wine Sop, Rose Sweet, Sweet Pearmain, Sweet Wine Sap

HISTORY It originated before 1867 somewhere in Pennsylvania, but the exact location is not known.

EXTERIOR DESCRIPTION This medium-sized, round apple has a long, slender stem that emerges from a deep cavity. The pale yellow skin is nearly covered by bright red and carmine stripes.

INTERIOR DESCRIPTION White flesh is firm, fine-textured, crisp, and tender with a sweet flavor.

TREE CHARACTERISTICS This moderately vigorous and upright-spreading tree is slow to begin bearing. As it matures, it tends to overbear and produce undersized fruit.

DISEASE RESISTANCE Susceptible to fireblight; moderately susceptible to other apple diseases.

SEASON OF RIPENING Late fall

USES Dessert and baking

STORAGE QUALITY Fair. The apple retains its crispness and flavor but is subject to storage scald, a browning of the skin that develops when it is removed for use.

Swiss Limbertwig

Henry Morton, the late Limbertwig authority from Gatlinburg, Tennessee, was an enthusiastic proponent of the high-flavored apple butter produced by Swiss Limbertwigs. Although some other Limbertwig varieties are equally aromatic, not all will thicken up as readily when cooked.

OTHER NAMES None

HISTORY It was grown during the nineteenth century in Appalachia by a fascinating community of Swiss settlers in the Cumberland Mountains.

EXTERIOR DESCRIPTION The medium-sized apple is round and slightly oblique in shape. It has a greenish-yellow background overlaid by purplish red and scattered with prominent white dots. A stocky, medium-length stem projects from a cavity overflowing with greenish-brown russeting.

INTERIOR DESCRIPTION The whitish flesh is fine-grained, sweet, and exceptionally crisp.

TREE CHARACTERISTICS The hardy, moderately vigorous tree produces light crops annually. The tree's limbs droop slightly, but not as severely as other Limbertwig varieties.

DISEASE RESISTANCE Moderately resistant to the major diseases

SEASON OF RIPENING Late fall

USES Dessert, cider, and apple butter

STORAGE QUALITY Good

Tenderskin

"Hanging like grapes" is a common response to seeing for the first time a cluster of ripening fruit on a Tenderskin tree. Unless carefully thinned, the crop will break the limbs, but it is worth the time and effort to grow this low-chill variety. I recently ate a delectable Tenderskin apple off a tree that I grafted more than fifty years ago.

OTHER NAMES Tenderine, Tender Peeling, Thinskin. It is debated whether it is the same variety as Melt in the Mouth.

HISTORY It was known in 1858 and originated somewhere in South Carolina. It was pushed out of the market by 1950 when labor costs made it prohibitively expensive to market crops that produced clusters of small fruit.

EXTERIOR DESCRIPTION Fruit is small to medium and rectangular to conical. The yellow skin is blushed, striped a pink-to-red color, and covered with a fairly heavy gray bloom.

INTERIOR DESCRIPTION The yellowish flesh is very tender and juicy with a sprightly subacid flavor. The fruit has a pleasing taste even before it fully matures on the tree.

TREE CHARACTERISTICS The vigorous tree bears clusters of heavy crops annually, even in warmer regions. The young wood is reddish brown, downy, and short-jointed with prominent buds. There is little pre-harvest drop.

DISEASE RESISTANCE Resistant to the major apple diseases

SEASON OF RIPENING Late fall

USES Dessert and cider

STORAGE QUALITY Fair

Tolman Sweet

During the nineteenth century, a time when granulated sugar was seldom available, Tolman Sweet was coveted for the pleasantly intense sweetness of its very dry flesh. The candy-like apple is exceptionally good when baked as well as for making cider since it contains 14.6 percent sugar that ferments to 7 percent alcohol.

OTHER NAMES Brown's Golden Sweet, Talman Sweet, Tolman, Tolman Sweeting (the original name)

HISTORY It was noted in 1822. Some reports say that it came from Massachusetts but others claim that the origin is not known.

EXTERIOR DESCRIPTION This medium-sized apple is rectangular to conical. It has pale yellow skin sometimes with a red blush and lines of russet; often a suture line is obvious. The apple bruises easily.

INTERIOR DESCRIPTION The white flesh is more dry than juicy and has a pronounced sweet flavor.

TREE CHARACTERISTICS The spreading tree has long, drooping branches. It blooms late and yields full crops annually. The dull bluish-green leaves are oval, folded, and distinctly waved; they have regular moderately distinct serrations and a heavy pubescence.

DISEASE RESISTANCE Susceptible to fireblight; moderately susceptible to the other major diseases.

SEASON OF RIPENING Fall

USES Dessert, baking, and cider

STORAGE QUALITY Good

Tompkins County King

In my Virginia orchard this variety always produced big apples on a small tree, no matter the rootstock onto which it was grafted, and was known for setting crops under adverse conditions. The apples will be more intensely colored when grown at higher elevations and in cooler regions; otherwise the color is dull and washed out. Regardless of appearance, the flavor excels.

OTHER NAMES Flat Spitzenburg, King, King Apple, King Apple of America, King of Tompkins County, Toma Red, Tommy Red, Tom's Red, Winter King

HISTORY It is thought to have originated near Washington, New Jersey (Warren County). In 1804 Jacob Wycoff brought the apple (which he called "King") to Tompkins County, New York where it was renamed "King of Tompkins County" around 1855. Another report claims that it originated with Thomas Thacker in Warren County, New Jersey.

EXTERIOR DESCRIPTION This large apple is rectangular to truncate-conic in shape and ribbed at the eye and on the body. The yellow background is flushed pale red with darker red stripes and white or russet dots. The stem cavity is also russeted. The skin has a greasy finish, like Black Twig, especially after storage.

INTERIOR DESCRIPTION The yellow flesh is rather coarse but is crisp and tender. It has a subacid, sweet, and aromatic flavor.

TREE CHARACTERISTICS Vigorous and spreading, the tree grows naturally small and the shiny leaves are highly folded with sharp, closely set serrations. The limbs grow nearly horizontal with many crossing branches. A pollen-sterile triploid, it will not pollinate other trees, but it is partially self-fertile.

DISEASE RESISTANCE Susceptible to fireblight; moderately susceptible to the other major diseases.

SEASON OF RIPENING Mid-fall

USES Dessert, baking, and cider

STORAGE QUALITY Fair. It will lose its flavor rapidly during storage.

Twenty Ounce

Twenty Ounce bespeaks its name due to a physical size and density that makes it feel heavy in the hand. During the second half of the nineteenth century it was often found as a backyard variety in New England, most likely because of its long ripening period. The flavor has occasionally been criticized as tasting of vinegar, but many people find the sourness pleasant.

OTHER NAMES Aurora, Cayuga Red Streak, Coleman, Eighteen Ounce, Governor Seward's, Lima, Morgan's Favorite, Twenty Ounce Apple, Wine, Wine of Connecticut. It is mistakenly called Twenty Ounce Pippin, a green-striped apple of lesser quality which is likely a different variety. There is a red sport called Collamer.

HISTORY It originated around 1844 in New York or Connecticut.

EXTERIOR DESCRIPTION This large to extra-large, round apple has broad red stripes over a greenish background. The smooth skin is roughened by white and russet dots. The skin has a "peened" surface of irregular, small, hammered dents like the Granny Smith apple.

INTERIOR DESCRIPTION Yellowish flesh is moderately tender with a subacid flavor.

TREE CHARACTERISTICS The medium-sized tree is an early bearer and a vigorous grower with slender, somewhat drooping branches. The tree grows very dense so it must be pruned extensively to admit sun and air circulation. It has oval, medium green, shiny leaves with shallow, dull serrations.

DISEASE RESISTANCE Susceptible to spray injury, bitter pit, and fireblight; moderately susceptible to the other diseases.

SEASON OF RIPENING Early to late fall. Its tendency to ripen unevenly over a few weeks makes it suitable for backyard production.

USES Baking, frying, and dessert

STORAGE QUALITY Poor. It will only keep for a short time and is subject to storage scald.

Victoria Limbertwig

A WELL-DEVELOPED SPECIMEN of "Vicky," as some familiarly call it, is often stunning—and the more purplish red it becomes, the more attention it attracts. I have presented at a few apple tastings during which the fruit disappeared before the tasting had even begun. The obvious bulges in pockets bore witness to the hiding places.

OTHER NAMES Harpole, Sweet Limbertwig

HISTORY It was known before 1860 and comes from either Grundy or Warren County, Tennessee. It was promoted by M. M. Harpole of Warren County.

EXTERIOR DESCRIPTION This medium-sized apple has an oblate-conic shape. The yellow skin is mostly covered with a deep red that ripens to purplish red with some darker red stripes. Prominent yellowish-brown dots are irregularly spaced over the entire skin surface.

INTERIOR DESCRIPTION The yellowish flesh is crisp and fine-grained with a sweet flavor.

TREE CHARACTERISTICS There is a slight drooping of the branches but it is not readily noticeable. The tree is vigorous and bears crops annually.

DISEASE RESISTANCE Moderately resistant to the major diseases

SEASON OF RIPENING Fall

USES Dessert

STORAGE QUALITY Good

Vine

This southern variety exhibits exaggerated color—a brighter, more expansive red—when grown in cooler regions. When grown in Virginia, particularly at lower elevations, the apple is mostly yellow skinned but the flavor is still good. It takes its name from the vine-like branches produced by the tree.

OTHER NAMES Vine Apple

HISTORY It originated around 1895 in Patrick County, Virginia. At the end of the nineteenth century this variety was a best seller from the J. Van Lindley Nursery in Greensboro, North Carolina, a leading southern nursery of that time.

EXTERIOR DESCRIPTION This medium-sized, round to conical apple has yellow skin blushed with various degrees of red, depending on the growing season and the location.

INTERIOR DESCRIPTION It has yellow flesh which is juicy and crisp.

TREE CHARACTERISTICS The moderately vigorous, long-lived tree produces thin, sinewy branches.

DISEASE RESISTANCE Moderately susceptible to the major apple diseases

SEASON OF RIPENING Late fall

USES Dessert and drying

STORAGE QUALITY Good

Wagener

When heat is applied to Wagener it melts, or "froths up" as described by a London chef friend, which I've found to be a worthy quality for pie making. When combined with Winesap (or another variety that retains its shape well when cooked) the frothiness of Wagener will coat the whole slices to produce an exemplary apple pie.

OTHER NAMES Wagener Apple, Wagener Price Apple, Wagoner

HISTORY It was found in 1791 near Penn Yan, New York. A man named George Wheeler grew it and then gave it to Abraham Wagener for propagation. The Wagener apple is a parent of Idared and possibly Northern Spy.

EXTERIOR DESCRIPTION This medium-sized apple is irregularly shaped and prominently ribbed at the eye and on the body. The greenish-yellow skin is flushed reddish brown with some pale red striping. A light bloom covers the surface and it is greasy to the touch.

INTERIOR DESCRIPTION The white flesh is very crisp, fine-grained, and tender. Its sweet flavor somewhat resembles Northern Spy.

TREE CHARACTERISTICS The tree bears well and heavily and the fruit will hang long after ripening, but the tree diminishes in vigor as it ages. It is somewhat biennial. The growth is narrow and upright and the bark is a yellowish color. Oval and light green in color, the leaves are pronounced folded and slightly waved with sharp regular serration; they are covered with a heavy pubescence. Thinning is necessary to produce large fruit.

DISEASE RESISTANCE Fair

SEASON OF RIPENING Fall

USES Dessert, apple butter, pie making, applesauce, and cider

STORAGE QUALITY Good. It stores well without shriveling.

Waltana

When promoting an apple with which one has a personal relationship, the descriptions of the merits and value are often exaggerated and do not reflect the true characteristic of the fruit. In the case of Waltana, outsiders agree it is certainly decent, but perhaps not quite as extraordinary as claimed by those for which the apple is named.

OTHER NAMES None

HISTORY Developed in California around 1860, this variety was introduced by Walter Etter, the brother of noted plant breeder Albert Etter. It is named for Walter and his wife, Anna, who were so fond of the variety that they topworked their entire orchard to it. It is likely a seedling of Wagener with Manx Codlin as the pollen parent.

EXTERIOR DESCRIPTION The apple is medium to large in size and variably shaped. The greenish-yellow skin has thin red stripes that become more vividly colored as the fruit ripens.

INTERIOR DESCRIPTION The white flesh is dense and crisp with a subacid flavor that can vary from fruit to fruit.

TREE CHARACTERISTICS The trees are vigorous and produce full crops annually. Waltana requires a long growing season for the fruit to properly mature. In colder regions with short growing seasons it can be harvested before full maturity and will ripen well in storage.

DISEASE RESISTANCE Moderate

SEASON OF RIPENING Late fall

USES Dessert, baking, and cider

STORAGE QUALITY Excellent. Waltana is considered to be among the best winter storage apples.

Washington Strawberry

APPLES WILL SOMETIMES reflect other characteristics of their shape that are not accurate. Washington Strawberry, for example, has the stereotypic strawberry shape and large whitish lenticels representing the strawberry's skin seeds. But the ascribed taste of strawberry comes only from power of suggestion.

OTHER NAMES Juniata, Washington, Washington County Seedling, Washington of Maine

HISTORY It was raised by Joe Whipple in Union Springs, New York. In 1849 he exhibited the apple at the New York State Agricultural Society Fair.

EXTERIOR DESCRIPTION This large apple has a truncate-conic to rectangular shape. The yellow skin has a brownish-orange flush and red blotches and stripes. Prominent russet and white dots cover the skin surface.

INTERIOR DESCRIPTION The white flesh is coarse-textured, soft, and tender with a sprightly slight subacid sweet flavor.

TREE CHARACTERISTICS The early-bearing tree is a weak, wide-spreading grower. The young wood is reddish and the rounded buds are prominent.

DISEASE RESISTANCE Moderately resistant to the major diseases

SEASON OF RIPENING Mid-fall

USES Dessert

STORAGE QUALITY Good for a fall variety

Wealthy

THIS VARIETY WAS the result of one man's tenacity and passion to discover the first apple that would survive the harsh weather of Minnesota. After Peter Gideon relocated in 1853 to Excelsior, Minnesota, he began planting thousands of seeds from his native Illinois, but most of the trees died within a few years or produced little fruit. With his few remaining dollars, Gideon ordered another bushel of seeds from Albert Emerson of Bangor, Maine, and continued his experimentations. From one of these seeds—crossed with a seed from his Cherry Crab tree (noted for its hardiness in Canadian and northern New England climates)—Wealthy was the reward.

OTHER NAMES None. There are a number of strains and sports.

HISTORY Discovered by Peter Gideon in 1868, Wealthy was the earliest apple (besides crabapples) to thrive in Minnesota. Gideon, a member of the Minnesota State Horticultural Society, generously shared his seedlings and soon the apple trees were distributed elsewhere in Minnesota and other similarly cold Midwest locations. Early in the twentieth century, Wealthy became one of the top five apple varieties sold in America.

EXTERIOR DESCRIPTION This medium to large apple has a rectangular to truncate-conic shape. Yellow skin is flushed and striped carmine.

INTERIOR DESCRIPTION The greenish-white flesh has a slight pinkish stain under the skin. It is soft and coarse-textured with a sweet subacid flavor.

TREE CHARACTERISTICS A very hardy tree that bears early (when it is four to six years old even on standard rootstock) and produces full crops biennially with the light year varying in production. Its profuse, long blooming period makes it a good pollinator for other varieties. The tree is upright growing with brittle wood. Heavy June drop occurs yet thinning is still necessary to produce large fruit. The small, oval leaves are medium green in color with a dull-pebbled surface, sometimes with a spiral tip. A standard tree will remain fairly small in size.

DISEASE RESISTANCE Susceptible to apple scab, bitter rot, fireblight, and cedar apple rust in the hot and humid conditions of the South and the mid-Atlantic. It can be grown more successfully in cooler or high elevation regions.

SEASON OF RIPENING Fall

USES Dessert, applesauce, and pie making

STORAGE QUALITY Fair

Western Beauty

I WAS VISITED in 1992 by a man who wanted to learn how to graft. This was Carlos Manning of Lester, West Virginia, a treasure trove region for finding varieties of the past in mountain hollows and on abandoned homesteads. Carlos later established Manning Nursery and was instrumental in preserving Western Beauty, among other valuable regional varieties like Red Winter Pearmain and Rainbow, and making these less-than-common trees available.

OTHER NAMES Beauty of the West, Big Rambo, Grosh, Musgrove's Cooper, Ohio Beauty, Wells

HISTORY It is reported to have been found around 1815 by John Grosh in Marietta, Pennsylvania, but it was not described until 1829 in Ohio.

EXTERIOR DESCRIPTION This medium to large, round to oblate apple greatly resembles Summer Rambo. The yellowish-green background is covered with dull and deep red stripes and dotted with gray lenticels.

INTERIOR DESCRIPTION The greenish-white flesh is mild, tender, and juicy.

TREE CHARACTERISTICS This is a vigorous grower; trees that are fifty or seventy-five years old are occasionally found still producing usable fruit. Newly grafted trees can be easily trained by pruning to begin full production in four or five years.

DISEASE RESISTANCE Moderately resistant to the major diseases

SEASON OF RIPENING Late summer. It ripens after Summer Rambo.

USES Dessert, frying, and baking

STORAGE QUALITY Fair

Westfield Seek-No-Further

I RECALL A tasting I did in the 1980s at Old Sturbridge Village in Massachusetts in which Westfield Seek-No-Further received high accolades. Ten minutes before the tasting, we walked to the tree in the Heritage Orchard and picked the apples. Every apple has its great moment when it is at the zenith of flavor: it was the time for these Westfields.

OTHER NAMES Connecticut Seek-No-Further, Marietta Seek-No-Further, New England Seek-No-Further, Red Seek-No-Further, Red Winter Pearmain, Seek-No-Further, Signifinger, Westfield

HISTORY It was known as early as 1796 in Westfield, Massachusetts, but it likely originated some years before. This is one of the very few apple varieties that the pomologist S. A. Beach, author of *Apples of New York* (1905), rated "good to best."

EXTERIOR DESCRIPTION The medium-sized apple has a conic to truncate-conic shape. It has dull greenish-yellow skin that is flushed orange and covered with carmine stripes and russet dots and patches. Shaded fruit is often irregularly russeted all over with little color showing. A bluish bloom covers the surface.

INTERIOR DESCRIPTION The yellowish-white flesh is crisp, tender, and juicy. It has a highly distinctive aroma and a mildly astringent flavor which contributes to its unique taste.

TREE CHARACTERISTICS The tree is a vigorous grower with straight shoots. The medium-sized, medium-green, ovate leaves have sharp, distinct serrations and are prominently folded and reflexed.

DISEASE RESISTANCE Moderately resistant to the major diseases

SEASON OF RIPENING Fall

USES Dessert, baking, cider, and drying. Dried slices have a pronounced apple flavor.

STORAGE QUALITY Fair

Wheeler's Golden Russet

ROBERT NITSCHKE, the founder of Michigan's Southmeadow Fruit Gardens, introduced me to this variety around 1980. At that time any russet apple was considered "ugly" but we both appreciated the unconventional beauty of this flavorful apple.

OTHER NAMES None

HISTORY The date of origin is unknown. It is a mutation found in the orchard of Sidney Wheeler in Belchertown, Massachusetts.

EXTERIOR DESCRIPTION This large, round apple has slightly flattened ends and yellow background skin that is nearly covered with a fawn russet.

INTERIOR DESCRIPTION The whitish-yellow flesh is crisp and juicy. It has a sprightly, spicy, acid bite.

TREE CHARACTERISTICS It has the characteristic tree habit of the Roxbury Russet with heavy branching that should be pruned annually to produce quality fruit.

DISEASE RESISTANCE Good resistance to the major diseases

SEASON OF RIPENING Fall

USES Dessert, baking, drying, and cider

STORAGE QUALITY Good

Whitney Crab

A STREET IN a nearby Virginia city is lined with a row of these ornamental trees, displaying magnificent pink and white blossoms every spring. For a decade, the unused fruit rotted and fell from the trees but now that home cider makers have discovered the value of blending Whitney Crabs with other varieties, not a single apple rots. I encouraged the urban forester to view the "stolen apples" in terms of enhancing tree health because the rotted apples on the ground promoted diseases and insects.

OTHER NAMES None

HISTORY These crabapples were found in 1869 in Franklin Grove, Illinois.

EXTERIOR DESCRIPTION The round to conical apple is about the size of a golf ball. It has greenish-yellow skin that is blushed and striped with red.

INTERIOR DESCRIPTION Yellow flesh is juicy with a slight astringency. It contains 11.39 percent sugar that will ferment to at least 5 percent alcohol.

TREE CHARACTERISTICS This upright-growing tree begins to bear early and will produce heavy crops even when young.

DISEASE RESISTANCE Good resistance to the major diseases

SEASON OF RIPENING Midsummer

USES Canning, cider, and pickling

STORAGE QUALITY Fair

Wickson Crab

WITH THE EMERGENCE of the new American cider industry, Wickson has become very popular and trees are again being planted. It is considered to be more of a crab than an apple, but it has a high sugar content (up to 25 percent) which gives it an extraordinary sweet taste and potential suitability for cider making.

OTHER NAMES None

HISTORY Wickson Crab is a cross of Newtown Pippin and Esopus Spitzenburg, developed by the California plant breeder Albert Etter and named for his fellow pomologist and friend, E. J. Wickson. It was selected in 1944.

EXTERIOR DESCRIPTION The apple is small (ranging from 1 to 2 inches in diameter) and round with slightly flattened ends. The skin has red stripes on a yellow background.

INTERIOR DESCRIPTION The slightly yellow and dense flesh is very sweet but has a pronounced acidic tang aftertaste.

TREE CHARACTERISTICS This tree is moderately vigorous in the South, less so in the mid-Atlantic, and will bear heavily on first and second year growth. Careful pruning encourages the development of apples that are larger and higher in quality. The fruit will hang in garlands on the tree.

DISEASE RESISTANCE Moderately resistant to the major diseases

SEASON OF RIPENING Fall

USES Dessert, cider, and pickling

STORAGE QUALITY Fair

Williams

Because of its durability, striking good looks, and resistance to fireblight, Williams became a major commercial variety in the nineteenth century. But it was soon supplanted by new varieties that did not share its small fruit size and brushy tree growth—two undesirable characteristics in the modern orchard that demanded full annual crops and easy maintenance.

OTHER NAMES Early, Early Red, Favorite, Favorite Red, Lady's Apple, Queen Red, Southern Queen, Williams Early, Williams Favorite, Williams Red

HISTORY It originated around 1750 on the farm of Captain Benjamin Williams near Roxbury, Massachusetts, where it was known as Queen or Lady's Apple. In 1880 it was brought to the notice of the Massachusetts Horticultural Society and renamed Williams.

EXTERIOR DESCRIPTION Fruit is small to medium in size and conical to oblong. It has a pale yellow background overlaid by a deep red with darker red stripes; russet dots are usually scattered over most of the surface. Because of its firm flesh and tough skin, it is suitable for shipping.

INTERIOR DESCRIPTION The yellowish-white flesh is often tinged pink under the skin. It is coarse, juicy, breaking, and subacid in flavor.

TREE CHARACTERISTICS Without the best culture, the tree is small and slow growing with straggly branches. The narrow oval leaves are medium green in color and coarsely waved. It should be thinned to produce quality fruit.

DISEASE RESISTANCE Highly resistant to fireblight; somewhat susceptible to other apple diseases, especially cedar apple rust.

SEASON OF RIPENING Summer

USES Dessert. It is not suitable for culinary use.

STORAGE QUALITY Fair

Willow Twig

As a child, I remember seeing dying Willow Twig trees (called "snags") with only a few producing branches scattered throughout abandoned apple orchards. Planted copiously in the middle of the nineteenth century, this variety no longer had market value in the 1940s and the dying trees were forced to act as a testament to and only vestige of the once-loved apple.

OTHER NAMES James River, James River Willow, Willow, Willow Leaf. Some claim the variety Missing Link is the same as Willow Twig.

HISTORY It was first noted in an 1845 catalog as possibly originating in Virginia. In 1867 Warder noted that large quantities were grown along the Mississippi River for export, as was Ben Davis which later replaced it. High quantities of these apples were shipped to the coast by way of the James River, a major Virginia river, which is likely the source of a few alternate names.

EXTERIOR DESCRIPTION The medium to large apple is roundish-oblate to conical. It has greenish-yellow skin that is flushed and mottled red, streaked with carmine, and dotted with russet.

INTERIOR DESCRIPTION The greenish-yellow flesh is coarse but very firm and crisp with a subacid flavor.

TREE CHARACTERISTICS The moderately vigorous tree has slender, drooping branches (thus, the name Willow Twig) and yellowish bark. It has oval, medium to light green leaves which are folded and reflexed with sharp, small, and regular serrations.

DISEASE RESISTANCE Somewhat susceptible to the major apple diseases. It has a high rate of mortality which makes it difficult to grow in the nursery.

SEASON OF RIPENING Fall

USES Dessert and cider

STORAGE QUALITY Excellent

Winesap

FOR AN APPLE with such widespread name recognition and prodigious production for more than two hundred years, I am always amazed by how many people bring this fruit to me for identification. Once as a teenager, scooping Winesap apples into sluices of running water at a commercial brandy making business, the workers at the adjoining truck began laughing loudly and pointing at a bloated woodchuck sliding down the sluice toward the grinding mill. It was indeed woodchuck brandy!

OTHER NAMES American Wine Sop, Banana, Hendrick's Sweet, Holland's Red Winter, Potpie, Pot Pie Apple, Red Sweet Wine Sop, Refugee, Royal Red of Kentucky, Texan Red, Winter Winesap. Dozens of strains exist, including a darker sport called Virginia Winesap which was found in 1922 at Garland Orchards in Troutville, Virginia, and marketed by Stark Bro's Nursery.

HISTORY It was known in Virginia during the Colonial period but there is no documentation at this time regarding its place of origin. Winesap was first described as a cider fruit in 1804 by Dr. James Mease in Philadelphia; in 1817 it was illustrated and described by William Coxe in *A View of the Cultivation of Fruit Trees.*

EXTERIOR DESCRIPTION The small to medium, round to oblong apple has deep red or maroon skin with the yellow background showing through on the shaded side. Indistinct flushes and stripes of a darker red and sometimes a netting of russet overlay the lighter red.

INTERIOR DESCRIPTION The yellow flesh is sweet, crisp, and aromatic with a vinous flavor. It has short, ovate, brown seeds.

TREE CHARACTERISTICS A dependable bearer, it produces heavy crops annually. The tree grows very vigorously on standard rootstock, reaching at least 30 feet tall and producing close to 100 bushels in a single season. The dull leaves are small, folded, and oval. The new-growth bark is a dark red with few lenticels. The blossoms of Winesap are pink instead of white like most varieties. Ancient trees can be found in abandoned orchards still bearing small but delectable fruit. The tree is highly adaptable, growing well in New England as well as the mid-Atlantic. Because it blooms a few days after most late varieties it escapes the late frosts and can be planted lower on slopes where frost develops.

DISEASE RESISTANCE Moderately resistant to the major apple diseases

SEASON OF RIPENING Late winter

USES Dessert, cider, apple butter, and pie making

STORAGE QUALITY Very good

Winter Rambo

WHENEVER I PRESENT Winter Rambo at a tasting, someone usually mentions the movie *Rambo*, and indeed, there is a link. David Morrell, the author of *First Blood* (which the movie is based upon), reportedly drew inspiration for the protagonist's name from a bowl of Winter Rambo apples on his table. However, this was not, as claimed even today, the favorite apple of Johnny Appleseed. He rejected grafting—thinking of this cloning as an unnatural act—and chose to plant the seeds of wild and unnamed apples.

OTHER NAMES American Seek-No-Further, Bread and Cheese, Delaware, Domine, Fall Romanite, Rambo

HISTORY Noted in 1804. The place of origin is unknown but it was planted in Delaware, Pennsylvania, and New Jersey. The name is thought to have come from a Swedish family called Rambo who settled in Delaware in the seventeenth century.

EXTERIOR DESCRIPTION This is a medium-sized apple with a rounded-oblate shape. The smooth, pale greenish-yellow skin is toughened by russet dots, mottled with red, and striped carmine. It has a grayish bloom.

INTERIOR DESCRIPTION The white flesh has a greenish-yellow tinge. It is fine-grained, very crisp, juicy, and aromatic.

TREE CHARACTERISTICS This medium-sized tree is moderately vigorous with an upright, spreading, open form. On very old trees the rough bark is particularly attractive in the winter landscape.

DISEASE RESISTANCE Moderately resistant to the major diseases

SEASON OF RIPENING Late fall

USES Dessert, cider, and jelly

STORAGE QUALITY Fair

Winter Sweet Paradise

THE BURFORD FAMILY used this very sweet variety to make a distinctive-flavored apple butter that one either loved or hated. But even those that described the aroma as "skunk smelling" never refused a few jars to take home. In the mountain farming communities of my youth, the best varieties for apple butter making were hotly argued. Some makers would vacillate year after year, swearing the present one was the best and only.

OTHER NAMES Grandmother, Honey Sweet, Paradise Sweet, Paradise Winter, Sweet Paradise, White Robinson, Wine Sweet. In the Blue Ridge Mountains of Virginia, it is called Paradise Sweet as often as Winter Sweet Paradise.

HISTORY It is believed to have originated in 1842 near the town of Paradise in Lancaster County, Pennsylvania.

EXTERIOR DESCRIPTION This large, rectangular apple has green skin with a brownish-red blush; when viewed from a distance on the tree it appears to have red stripes. The surface is usually covered with a whitish scarfskin and prominent yellowish-white russet dots spaced at fairly wide intervals. It has a long stem, projecting obliquely from a slightly russeted cavity.

INTERIOR DESCRIPTION The white flesh is fine-grained and juicy with a sprightly, sweet, subacid flavor. Some find the aroma and taste objectionable.

TREE CHARACTERISTICS The vigorous tree grows upright and bears heavily. It is slow to begin bearing. Annual pruning will improve the fruit quality and size.

DISEASE RESISTANCE Susceptible to bitter pit; somewhat resistant to the other major apple diseases.

SEASON OF RIPENING Fall

USES Dessert, baking, frying, and apple butter

STORAGE QUALITY Good

Wolf River

THIS IS ONE of the very few apple varieties that will produce a likeness from its seeds. Consequently, there are many strains of Wolf River with more variation in appearance than taste. This large uncommon apple remains exceptionally popular in Appalachia and the foothills of Virginia's Blue Ridge Mountains, where it is propagated every year by small nurseries and treasured for drying and baking whole.

OTHER NAMES None

HISTORY It is thought to have originated around 1875 near Fremont, Wisconsin. A man named William Springer moved from Quebec, Canada, to a farm near Wisconsin's Wolf River in 1856. There it is speculated that he bought some Alexander apples—a variety originating in Russia which grew well in harsh environments—and from a seed of these apples Wolf River is said to have come.

EXTERIOR DESCRIPTION Fruit is large to very large, roundish, and ribbed at the eye and on the body. The pale background is nearly covered with bright red flush and red stripes. Russeting appears on the base, russet dots cover most of the surface, and a unique russet marking flows from the stem end to terminate in a jagged line around the top of the apple. The smooth skin becomes greasy in storage.

INTERIOR DESCRIPTION The creamy white flesh is soft, tender, and mealy in texture with a subacid flavor.

TREE CHARACTERISTICS Slow to begin bearing, it is a spreading hardy tree with upright straggly growth. The medium-green oval leaves are folded, waved, and reflexed with irregular distinct serrations. Unlike most apples, this variety must be picked in an immature green stage because the fruit will rot if allowed to get too ripe on the tree.

DISEASE RESISTANCE Susceptible to fireblight and sunscald; moderately resistant to apple scab, cedar apple rust, and powdery mildew.

SEASON OF RIPENING Late summer

USES Dessert, baking, apple butter, and drying

STORAGE QUALITY Poor

Yates

AFTER MY NURSERYMAN friend Jim Lawson of Ball Ground, Georgia, introduced me to Yates in the early 1970s, I promptly added it to my collection of a few hundred American, British, and European apples. Since then, a renewed interest in cider making has been steadily building and the value of Yates has been increasingly recognized by professional cider makers. The apple's chemistry imparts the elements essential to a good cider: tannin, acid, sugar, and aroma.

OTHER NAMES Jates, Red Warrior, Yates Winter

HISTORY It was found around 1844 in Fayette County, Georgia.

EXTERIOR DESCRIPTION A small, oblate to conical apple. It has pale yellow skin that is striped and flushed dark red and covered by small gray dots.

INTERIOR DESCRIPTION The yellowish-white flesh is often stained red just under the skin. It is juicy, tender, spicy, and sweet.

TREE CHARACTERISTICS This vigorous tree bears heavy crops annually and is a good pollinator. It has medium-green oval leaves which are shiny, waved, and sharply serrated. It is necessary to thin the fruit to increase their size.

DISEASE RESISTANCE Moderately resistant to the major diseases

SEASON OF RIPENING Late fall

USES Dessert, apple butter, drying, cider, and pickling

STORAGE QUALITY Excellent

Yellow Bellflower

DURING APPLE TASTINGS, it's common to employ our senses of smell, taste, touch, and sight, but rarely do we get to truly listen to an apple. With Yellow Bellflower, however, the core cavity is so large that the seeds will sometimes rattle when the mature apple is shaken. For this enjoyable attribute, it has earned the alternate name "Baby Rattler."

OTHER NAMES Baby Rattler, Bishop's Pippin of Nova Scotia, Lady Washington, Lincoln Pippin, Sheepnose, Warren Pippin, White Bellflower, White Detroit

HISTORY It appeared before 1817 in the area of Crosswicks near Burlington, New Jersey. Yellow Bellflower is speculated to be a parent of Red Delicious.

EXTERIOR DESCRIPTION Fruit is large to medium and oblong to irregularly conical. It has a lemon-yellow background with a red or red-orange blush on the sun-exposed side. The surface is also scattered with conspicuous white or russet dots. It bruises easily.

INTERIOR DESCRIPTION Cream-colored flesh is crisp, juicy, and tender. It is aromatic with a sweet, subacid flavor. A number of cone-shaped strains are marketed in the nursery trade as Yellow Bellflower, but only one has the intense flavor of the original—all others are imposters.

TREE CHARACTERISTICS The tree grows tall and vigorously with spreading growth. The bark is yellowish in color and the medium to dark green, narrow, oval leaves are slighted folded and reflexed with sharp regular serrations. It tends toward biennial production and will produce in the warmer regions.

DISEASE RESISTANCE Susceptible to apple scab; somewhat susceptible to the other major apple diseases.

SEASON OF RIPENING Late fall

USES Pie making, applesauce, and especially cider (it contains 13.61 percent sugar which ferments to at least 6 percent alcohol). Some time in storage will also improves its use as a dessert fruit.

STORAGE QUALITY Fair

York

My father once had a shipment of York apples rejected by a young, inexperienced government inspector who wrote on the report that all of the apples were lopsided without realizing it was the natural shape of the fruit. York was a major dessert export apple from Virginia to England until around 1930 when consumer tastes changed and demand decreased. It soon evolved into an important processing apple as a solution to the surplus planting.

OTHER NAMES Johnson's Fine Winter (the original name), York Imperial. Numerous strains and cultivars are available such as Commander, Ramey, Red Yorking, and Spur. Cultivars are usually cosmetic enhancements with compromised flavor.

HISTORY It was found and brought to notice around 1830 near York, Pennsylvania. For a number of years, a town resident named Johnson had watched school children digging out leaf-covered apples that were in a remarkable state of preservation in the early spring. After propagation by a local nurseryman, it became known as Johnson's Fine Winter until Charles Downing called it an "imperial keeper" in the 1850s and suggested it be renamed York Imperial, which in time has been shortened to York.

EXTERIOR DESCRIPTION Fruit is medium to large, varying in shape from oblate-oblique to oval-oblong. Most apples are decidedly lopsided although modern strains tend to be more symmetrical. The greenish-yellow background is mostly covered by a light red flush. It also displays carmine stripes, russet dots, and streaks of grayish scarfskin.

INTERIOR DESCRIPTION The yellow flesh is coarse, crisp, and juicy with a sprightly subacid to sweet flavor. It has a small, compact core.

TREE CHARACTERISTICS The tree grows upright and stocky with dark green oval leaves that are shiny and slightly serrated. The period from full bloom to fruit maturity is 175 to 185 days.

DISEASE RESISTANCE Susceptible to cedar apple rust, fireblight, and corking; somewhat resistant to apple scab and powdery mildew.

SEASON OF RIPENING Late fall

USES Dessert, baking, cider, drying, and pie making

STORAGE QUALITY Excellent. The flavor does not degrade during storage time.

Part Two
THE ORCHARD PRIMER

Planning and Designing an Orchard

THE MAIN PURPOSE of orchards in early America was to produce fruit to drink—not fruit to eat. Early settlers brought with them the Old World notion that the water was foul, as it was in the towns and cities of Europe. It was also true that some of the water of the New World was brackish and caused illness and death. Colonists from the Mediterranean region first tried planting vineyards for wine production, but when those failed, colonists from the British Isles and Northern Europe introduced the apple from their food culture for cider production.

Today the orchard can have a single purpose, like cider making, or it can be intended for multiple uses, including dessert, drying, applesauce and butter making, wildlife food, vinegar, and even decoration and landscaping. From the beginning, the planter must define the goals for the orchard by asking questions such as: How will the crops be utilized? What are the taste preferences of those eating the apples? Otherwise time, nursery stock, and money will be wasted.

The scope of the orchard will be determined by its purpose and the land available for planting. An orchard can be one or two trees in the yard or it can be dozens, hundreds, or even thousands of trees with or without intended commercial production. It is critical that the mature size of the apple trees be considered and the potential production quantity determined. The ultimate height and width of the tree will be defined by the type of rootstock selected and the variety grafted. The amount of fruit wanted should dictate the number of trees: starting small is smart.

Besides the size of the available land, goals and uses will also be determined by the physical qualities of the space such as air drainage and compass orientation. When planning, aim for the ideal but with the flexibility that compromises can be made. Sometimes, too, aesthetic values are the primary intention of the orchard and override any practical and scientific parameters.

Location and Layout

Site selection for this permanent planting is an incredibly important decision. Before marking the location of the planting sites, stand where the trees will be planted and observe how the sunlight falls at different times of the day. Ideally, the trees should be located in full sun to maintain healthy, vigorous growth and produce quality high-flavored fruit. A planting slope that gets morning sun is desirable because the sunlight will dry the foliage and reduce fungus growth. Often you can increase the amount of available sunlight by removing trees that shade the planting site. If the location does not receive eight or ten hours of sunlight, look elsewhere.

Whenever possible, site the orchard on an eastern slope to allow for the best air and water drainage. Also remove any woodland or thickets at the base of slopes before planting as they can interrupt air flow and become a haven for

▲ Corner of the orchard and nursery at Thomas Jefferson's Monticello near Charlottesville, Virginia. This orchard was able to be restored because of archeological evidence from modern technology and the details of Jefferson's records.

▶ The modest orchard beyond the kitchen at Point of Honor in Lynchburg, Virginia, provided fruit for the Cabell house built in 1806.

insect and disease infestation. Avoid planting on hot south-facing slopes which will encourage early development and emergence of buds that may then be damaged or killed by freezes or frosts.

Wind direction and velocity should be taken into consideration too. Siting trees just below the crest of a hill is one way to prevent wind damage. You can also anchor young trees on wind-swept slopes by individually staking them or tying the stem and branches to a trellis. Strong winds will not only damage trees (particularly young ones) but will discourage bee and other insect movement during the critical pollination time, thus reducing fruit set.

It is also important to choose a planting slope which has an appropriately accessible incline for watering and maintenance. A slope of 6 or 8 percent is comfortable and safe for use but an incline of 10 percent or greater is dangerous when using equipment. Very steep terrain can only be planted when totally maintained without equipment.

Other factors to consider during site selection are frost patterns, maximum and minimum temperatures, water availability for irrigation, and proximity to neighboring properties and streams when toxic agents are used. Although some aspects of the planting environment can be altered, many, like prevailing wind and temperature, cannot. You may have to compromise by accepting

This small commercial orchard is well-fenced for protection against varmints. As a testament to the change in fruit growing today, orchards of this size are appearing more and more frequently.

less-than-ideal conditions. When in doubt, plant a few trees to test the site before committing to the full orchard.

Layout patterns

An orchard is defined by the placement of trees in a certain pattern. The most common arrangements are square, rectangular, and contour or terrace. The size of the planting will often determine the layout with regard to sufficient space for ultimate tree growth; service rows; bee yard; recreation; and a building for storage, equipment, and activities like apple sales or cider making.

For planting areas where it is comfortable to walk and stand, you can use a square or rectangular design. To make a square layout set a tree at each corner of the four corners, following the spacing recommendations for the rootstock onto which the variety is grafted. For a rectangular design, place trees at unequal distances; trees on dwarf stock, for example, might be placed 9 feet apart with 15 feet between rows. If the land is rugged and steep, use the terrace method by staggering rows to maximize air circulation and sunlight. Placing trees to follow the contours of the hillside will reduce erosion of the soil as well as harmonize aesthetically with the site.

Preparing the Site

The soil at the final selected site should be evaluated before planting, and amended if necessary, to accommodate the place where your apple tree will spend the rest of its life. Soil is composed of minerals, organic matter, pore space, and living organisms (bacteria, nematodes, and fungi). Soil texture is categorized as sand, silt, clay, or some combination thereof; the USDA defines twelve soil texture classifications. The soil's ability to hold moisture and nutrients is dependent upon achieving an ideal textural combination called loam (or a variation such as clay loam or sandy loam). Soil fertility can be changed by applying nutrients, increasing the amount of organic material, as well as adjusting the pH to near 6.5. The best soil for planting is well-drained loam 3 or 4 feet deep.

The most conventional method to determine your soil status is by taking a soil sample before planting and at the same time of year for the next few years. The soil test report you get from an agriculture university or an independent lab will give you guidelines for amending. As the tree advances to the second and third year of leaf production, a leaf analysis taken in July or August can give additional details about the nutrient status of the tree. This, in tandem with the soil test, will prevent over- or under-fertilization and will be cost efficient.

From the results of a soil test dig, incorporate the elements of any soil deficiencies like lime or calcium in the planting area; this should preferably be done the year before planting but if necessary it can be done at planting time. The size of the orchard will also determine how the site is prepared. If your orchard only has a few trees, amending individual planting sites in the designated spaces will do. If it is located in a pasture, cropland, abandoned garden site, or tree-cleared land, you will need to lay out the sites with stakes and remove perennial weeds within a 3- to 6-foot planting zone. In addition to incorporating organic matter, larger orchards can be plowed the previous fall and planted with a grass cover (like Kentucky 31 tall fescue) to make the soil more friable.

Variety Selection

Prior to World War II, there were thousands of small fruit tree nurseries sometimes offering hundreds of common and uncommon apple varieties. As these orchard and farm nurseries dwindled, the mega-nurseries gained control and reduced the number of varieties to a few dozen for reasons of practicality and economic profitability. But now that the landscape has once again become peppered with smaller nurseries offering historic favorites as well as modern varieties—many of which have distinctive flavor and some disease resistance—the prospective fruit grower has more options.

Although the name of an apple can be intriguing, it may not sufficiently satisfy your taste buds—a realization that is especially cruel after dedicating five years to growing the tree! And remember that apple trees will often fruit for fifty years or more. Most apple varieties are adapted to certain climates so local environmental conditions should be considered when deciding what trees to plant. It will be worth a fifty-mile drive to sample some of the lesser-known apples that grow well in your area and talk to local nursery growers and orchardists. Attending apple tastings at historic sites, farmers markets, and specialty grocery stores

It's best to sample a wide spectrum of apple flavors and textures before deciding which varieties to plant.

is also effective in finding less-than-mainstream varieties that are not readily available in the local market. After sampling a dozen or so varieties, you should be able to determine where your preferences lie on the spectrum from very tart to very sweet, complex to singular flavor, and crunchy to melt-in-the-mouth texture. However, I once assembled a multiday, mother-of-all apple tasting with more than one hundred varieties for prospective orchardists. And still, after the last apple was sampled, two tasters exclaimed, "What else do you have?"

Varieties that have resistance to pests and diseases are in demand, particularly by organic growers, due to the increasing concern about toxic chemicals. Many modern apple varieties have been developed for resistance to apple scab, cedar apple rust, powdery mildew, and fireblight, although they are still susceptible to the summer diseases (such as sooty blotch, fly speck, and bitter rot) unless a fungicide spray is applied. Some heirloom apples, including the russets and certain early-ripening varieties, continue to resist the major diseases and produce quality fruit, but just because it is in the category of heirloom or antique does not mean that it is any more resistant or susceptible to pests and diseases than modern mainstream varieties.

Other important considerations beyond taste and disease resistance are the apple's season of ripening and the planned use of the fruit. Generally you will want to select a combination of apples to ripen in the summer, fall, and winter, but the number of trees for each season may be affected by the intended use. For instance, if you plan to make a large amount of applesauce then you should select a higher ratio of summer-ripening apples like Early Harvest and Pristine. If you want to store the majority of your apples, choose more winter-ripening varieties. Late-blooming varieties can be located closer to the bottom of a hill, where frost accumulates. Whether for dessert, cider, drying, applesauce, apple butter, wildlife food, or decoration, the apple's intended use should be determined before planting.

How to taste an apple

I find it mildly irksome to see someone eating an apple while walking down the street, unaware that a body sense event is happening, and perhaps focusing on something else entirely at the time. Ideally, one should select a fruit of known ripeness and take it with a plate and knife to a quiet place. Slice it to mouth-size portions, either all at once or as you eat, and when the slice is in the mouth, concentrate on the mouth feel and the flavor. It may immediately enliven the taste buds or slowly unfold its complexity. Analyze the sugar, tannin, acid, and aroma of what you taste and if it is elusive do not despair: the magic of the taste of a particularly variety may be its elusiveness. If given full attention, the act of eating an apple can become a mind-expanding experience.

Rootstocks

Before size-controlling rootstocks were developed, apple trees were propagated from seeds and root cuttings. But these always produced a full-size apple tree with some varieties growing 30 to 40 feet high. As labor costs (particularly for picking) increased, so did demand for smaller trees that could be more easily managed. Around 1912, researchers at the East Malling Research Station in Kent, England, collected clones in France of the dwarfing apple tree Paradise to serve as the foundation of their cloning research. Rootstocks from this station are designated M (Malling), MM (Malling-Merton), or EMLA (East Malling Long Ashton).

Most of the rootstocks used today are hybrid plants developed to impart desired characteristics to the apple tree. Size-controlling rootstocks dominate market sales with ultimate size described as dwarf, semi-dwarf, or semi-standard; the height ranges from a few feet to 80 percent of standard size. Be very aware that ultimate tree size also depends on the inherent vigor of the variety. Rootstocks are grown by specialty nurseries under strict environmental condition to protect them from virus infection. Most rootstock fruits are generally described as bitter and have no commercial value and must be altered by vegetative propagation to make a useful and marketable apple variety.

Those apple rootstock clones first developed and marketed by the British were followed by hundreds of others that are available from sources worldwide and in the nursery stock marketplace. It is often difficult for the home orchard buyer to determine which rootstock the variety is grafted to, and which rootstock would be most suitable for the variety selected. Field proofing of the rootstock is recommended, as many have not been used long enough to draw conclusions from the limited data. However, some rootstocks from the nursery trade that have proven worthy are described here with recognition of positive and negative characteristics.

MALLING 27 is very dwarfing. The central leader must be staked and permanent irrigation provided. It is reported to be susceptible to fireblight, a highly contagious bacterial disease that can destroy small trees in a few years. It begins to bear in two to three years and produces a tree 3 to 5 feet high.

MALLING 9 is a common rootstock for both commercial and backyard plantings. The central leader must be staked and the tree should be planted on a well-drained site. It is susceptible to fireblight and is also known to develop root burrs (tumor-like spurs usually near the graft union). A number of clones of this rootstock are available in varying degrees of vigor. It begins to bear in two to four years and produces a tree 6 to 8 feet high.

MALLING 26 is more vigorous than Malling 9 and varies in size depending on the variety grafted to it and the soil type. It is susceptible to fireblight and collar rot and it abhors poorly drained sites. Compatibility is an issue with Golden Delicious and Rome; it is also particularly incompatible with some triploids. The tree should be planted so the graft union is no higher than 1 to 2 inches above the soil level, otherwise it will produce root burrs. It begins to bear in three to four years and produces a tree 6 to 10 feet high.

MALLING 7 is a popular semi-dwarf or semi-standard tree that may require early staking, particularly in windswept locations, and does not grow well in heavy clay. It is susceptible to collar rot and may sucker freely. The tree should be planted so the graft union is no higher than 1 or 2 inches above the soil line. It begins to bear in three to five years and produces a tree 12 to 14 feet high.

GENEVA 30 is similar to the Malling 7 rootstock but it is reported to have resistance to fireblight and collar rot and is not as prone to suckering. It is more productive and bears a little earlier than Malling 7 but it has some compatibility issues with certain varieties. Because of the brittle graft union the tree will snap off in high winds; appropriate trellis support will alleviate the graft union failure. It begins to bear in three to four years and produces a tree 12 to 14 feet high.

MALLING-MERTON 106 is a freestanding early-bearing tree that will grow somewhat larger than Malling 7. It should not be planted in poorly drained sites because it is susceptible to collar rot. It begins to bear in three to five years and produces a tree 14 to 18 feet high.

MALLING-MERTON 111 is a very popular and reliable rootstock. It tolerates drier soils and is resistant to wooly apple aphids. When planting the tree, it is critical that the graft union is no higher than 1 or 2 inches above the soil line. It begins to bear in four to six years and produces a tree 12 to 18 feet high.

ANTONOVKA, originating in Russia, is a cold-hardy rootstock suitable for regions that experience winter temperatures below 0 degrees F (trees grafted to non-cold-hardy rootstocks shipped from warmer zones will not survive these severe climates). It is well anchored, adaptable to most soils, and moderately productive. It begins to bear in four to six years and produces a tree 14 to 18 feet high.

SEEDLING is a hardy rootstock from any apple seed and sometimes the resulting young tree is called a pippin. The variety would be unknown. Because of the variable genetic makeup, the resistance or susceptibility to diseases, pests, suckering, and virus infections are not determined. It begins to bear in six to ten years and produces a tree 20 to 40 feet high, the maximum of its genetic code.

Nursery Stock

I recommend purchasing one- or two-year-old barerooted plants (properly dug and lifted and stored at the appropriate time) rather than older potted or burlapped plants which are often less economical as well as less healthy. Most apple tree nursery stock is propagated and distributed by large fruit tree nurseries and is readily available in the planting season from farm stores and large box store retailers or by catalog or internet mail order. But first, look locally at mom-and-pop or family nurseries which will often offer regionally appropriate and diverse selections of modern and antique or heirloom apple trees. It is generally advantageous to form an alliance with these smaller agricultural enterprises because most of the time you will get dependable answers and healthy, vigorous trees. Many nurseries offer workshops on fruit tree management skills like pruning and tree care. Some even have sessions on grafting the apple tree, an opportunity to personally build your own orchard at a much lower cost.

When buying from a retailer, determine at the outset if the seller knows the product. If not, look out for doubts and difficulties ahead. One of the first and significant questions to ask is how big the tree will grow. If that question is answered satisfactorily, then inquire the name of the rootstock. An unhesitating answer means you should proceed. Many larger retailers display potted trees in parking lots. A little apple game I play in the springtime is to hide in the parking lot and watch and listen to prospective buyers. Uninitiated apple tree buyers frequently say "I want this one. It is bigger than the others," pointing to the often over-fertilized gawky plants with small root systems. But these are the obese school children of the plant world. Purchasing a smaller one-year-old apple tree and feeding and pruning it properly will bring the surest reward.

The condition of the plant you are buying must be evaluated as well. It is possible, for example, that it was not watered regularly. This drying out puts stress on the foliage (indicated by the obvious wilt) along with the part of the tree that you cannot see: the root system. This means that even after the leaves recover, you will still have an apple tree whose roots are recovering from damage which is often reflected by production of less quality fruit. Remember that beginning with a healthy tree and maintaining the young plant for the first few years in a state of maximum uninterrupted growth will determine the future structure of the framework that will hang many years of quality apples.

Young trees lined out in nursery rows will grow for one year before being sold and transplanted to the orchard site. With good maintenance the trees will reach 3 to 5 feet in height in nine months.

Planting and Cultural Management

A pruning knife and
sharpening stone with
original finish from
around 1935.

APPLE TREES SHOULD generally be planted in early spring, although in warmer regions trees can also be planted in late fall; the question of planting time is important to investigate locally. When the nursery stock is received, inspect the root system to be certain it is moist and protected from drying. The trunk and any limbs should also be inspected for digging and packing damage. If the tree cannot be planted immediately, store the unopened package or potted tree in a cool place out of direct sunlight. On the day of planting, remove the wrapping and examine the root system; if it is dry, soak it for a few hours before planting. To store nursery stock for more than a few days, choose a protected area, dig a temporary trench deep enough to hold the roots, and "heel it in" by placing the stem of the tree at an angle in the trench and covering the roots with soil. Be sure to water thoroughly and keep the tree moist until replanted.

Planting the Tree

The basic steps for planting an apple tree are illustrated on the following pages by ten-year-old James. Before beginning, beware that the roots must not dry out during planting as just a few minutes of drying wind and sun can severely injure or kill the tree; keep roots in a plastic bag or other protective cover until they are positioned in the hole and ready to be covered with soil. Also avoid using chemical fertilizers at the time of planting which will burn the delicate root system. If the tree is growing on a dwarfing or semi-dwarfing rootstock that requires a support system, it's best to place the stake in the hole at the time of planting because disturbing the soil after growth begins can damage the root system. Lastly, be sure to identify each tree with a "permanent" label (keeping in mind that even lettering from permanent markers will likely begin to become illegible after two years); a map of your orchard is a wise backup record.

Trees have been sited on an eastern slope for air and water drainage and exposure to early morning sun.

DIGGING THE HOLE Using a shovel or auger (or a tree planter for large installations), dig a hole that is large enough to accommodate the nursery stock roots. A one-year-old tree, for example, should have a hole as big as a five-gallon bucket. After digging the hole, separate the sod, topsoil, and subsoil in piles. To prepare for refilling, break up the sod that will be spread on top. Work amendments and well-rotted compost thoroughly into the topsoil and subsoil with a shovel or hoe. This medium will surround the roots of the newly planted tree. Be aware that any synthetic chemical fertilizer will damage roots.

POSITIONING THE TREE Standard trees, grafted or not, should be planted the same depth or just slightly deeper than they were growing in the nursery row. A color difference on the stem will show the soil line. Trees grafted for size control should be planted so that the graft site, a slightly irregular area on the stem, is 3 to 4 inches above ground level. If the graft site is in the ground, the scion will root and a standard-size tree will result.

FILLING THE HOLE AND PLACING THE TREE Return the best soil (the amended topsoil and subsoil) to the bottom of the newly dug planting hole in the shape of a pyramid. Place the tree upright over the pyramid and extend the roots outward and downward over the hill of soil. Two people working together make it easier. If you are planting a burlapped root ball, cut the burlap in a number of places to facilitate root growth passage. Continue backfilling the hole with the best soil available, shaking the plant gently up and down and sideways.

WATERING THE TREE Soak the tree with water when the hole has been filled about two-thirds of the way with soil; then add more soil, leaving a very shallow bowl-shaped ring around the plant to trap water. Following this initial watering, the tree should receive an inch of rainfall per week or the equivalent via irrigation. Stress from drought is devastating to young fruit trees.

GENTLY TAMPING THE SOIL After the roots are covered with several inches of soil, use a flat hoe or your foot to gently tamp it down. This will compress and remove any air pockets, where roots can grow and die, and help provide a solid anchor for the young tree.

THE FULLY PREPARED TREE Depending on tree's specific conditions, it may need to be limed, pruned, limb spread, protected by fencing, and mulched. Apply lime when the soil test indicates the pH is below 6.5. Prune one year old whips back to 30 inches from ground level where the first scaffold limbs will emerge. Older trees with scaffold limbs should be spread as shown to an angle of between 45 and 60 degrees. Then, if the orchard is not fenced, construct a fence at least four feet in diameter and four to six feet high around each tree. At this point the tree should also be mulched to about 6 inches deep to suppress unwanted vegetation and retain moisture. A small circle around the stem should remain uncovered to discourage collar rot and mice or vole infestation.

Caring for the Newly Planted Tree

The first four or five years are a critical time in the life of the apple tree. Proper training of the plant by pruning, irrigation, and nutrition will develop a structure to hang future crops of apples. This is the period in the tree's life to grow wood instead of produce fruit so excessive early bearing must be avoided. All but a few apples to proof the variety must be removed to keep the emphasis on wood production. Proof apples should never be allowed to grow on the main terminal because the weight of the apple will bend and crook the branch. Heavy fruiting during this period also retards growth and affects fruiting in subsequent years. A successful 2 feet of growth per year for four years would make a structure ready to hang the first crop of fruit.

Fertilizing a newly planted and staked tree.

Initial pruning

It is very important to spread the limbs with plastic, wire, or wooden devices so that they grow with wide or open crotches. This will limit the amount of corrective pruning later. Unless the fledgling tree has been scaffold developed in the nursery and the first limbs are 30 inches or more above the ground level with a good crotch angle, the whip should be cut back to 30 inches, the site for the emergence of the first scaffold limb. If suitable branches already exist, head back the central leader about 10 inches above the uppermost scaffold. To prevent a stub, make the cut just above a bud on the windward side of the whip. The wind will keep the new growth in an upright position. Remove any branches below 30 inches and as the plant grows, rub or clip off any new ones that emerge. The energy that will go to the growth of these unwanted limbs will be redirected to permanent branches.

Irrigation

Providing sufficient water is imperative to produce a thriving apple tree, particularly during the first four or five years of growth. If the tree is ever stressed for want of moisture, the recovery period will dramatically affect the time of production, fruit size, yield, and the general health and future growth of the tree. In most regions, the formula of an inch of water per week is appropriate, either delivered by rainfall or irrigation. Use your soil sample to identify the soil type and apply water accordingly; sandy soils demand a greater volume and more frequent application than clay soils.

It is possible to over-irrigate apple trees. If drainage at the planting site is poor, the trees will become water-logged and die. For this reason, limit irrigation to the period when the tree is actively growing; the tree's demand for water decreases from the time of defoliation in the fall until leaf growth begins in the spring. Also remember that the amount of water needed is determined by the size of the tree and the temperature. A semi-dwarf apple tree (12 to 16 feet high), for example, will require ten to twenty gallons of water on a hot summer day. All apple trees grafted to dwarfing rootstock (those which grow to less than 8 feet tall) must be supplied with permanent irrigation because of the weak root system on a dwarf tree.

Nutrition

Fertilizer, be it organic or synthetic, is also vital to the first four or five years of growth. To maximize effectiveness fertilizer should be applied in the spring just before growth begins and then anytime thereafter to the point that any new growth stimulated will have time to mature (harden off) before freezing begins. In the climate of the foothills of Virginia's Blue Ridge Mountains the last application is no later than the Fourth of July.

During World War II the new and convenient granulated nitrogen fertilizer became unavailable because of its use in explosives manufacturing. But many agricultural endeavors including my family's orchard and farm had never stopped using the sustainable substance: manure from the animal houses. I particularly remember the nearly overpowering smell of ammonia from the decomposing chicken manure and the nose-holding sessions of scraping out the nitrogen-rich litter, especially that which heaped under the roost poles, where the chickens spent the night digesting and evacuating thousands of bugs in a salad of newly grown grass. My father had devised a clever and expeditious system involving a number of floor boards with handles which could be unattached and the manure shoveled beneath the house that had been intentionally built on stilts. Safe from the degrading rain, it could, as needed, be put in wheelbarrows or on horse-drawn ground slides and taken to the crop sites. Much of it was always reserved for the new orchard, and the vegetable garden was similarly high on its priority list: there was never enough.

In those low-tech days, plant nutrition was measured—not in the scientific formulae now relied upon to determine growth rate (0-0-0)—but by how much the apple tree grew in a given period. It was expected that once the accurate manure rate had been determined, whether approximated from oral history or experimentation, the tree would grow 12 to 24 inches annually, provided the rains came to activate it. For an apple tree between one and four years old, any less growth demanded another "dose" of fertilizer.

During the first four years of growth, nitrogen is the most vital ingredient for vegetative bud production and limb growth; after the fourth year, nitrogen feeding should be reduced to stimulate development of fruit buds. Phosphorus enables plants to store and transfer energy and promotes root, flower, and fruit development, but this can be difficult to determine by soil analysis; leaf analysis will provide the more dependable guidelines. Potassium improves fruit size, color, and flavor, however, apple trees are very sensitive to applications of potassium and a soil test should indicate its use before application. Other elements to consider in testing, particularly as the tree matures, are sulfur, magnesium, calcium, copper, boron, iron, manganese, and zinc. If analysis indicates deficiencies, chemical application of each element should be made, according to the recommendations from the test, by granular or foliar methods.

Pruning and Thinning the Mature Tree

In most orchards or backyard fruit gardens, no tree exactly fits the textbook training system; the art and science of pruning is learned by applying known techniques and practicing. The science of pruning involves awareness of how light affects the tree's growth and how the structure develops over time. The art lies in pruning a tree so that the balance of growth and productivity is aesthetically pleasing to the observer. Until the pruner has experience, the tendency is to prune too little and too timidly. But if the pruner puts aside fears of making a mistake and concentrates on the purpose, soon experience, along with mistakes, will bring the joy of pruning.

Why prune? Some reasons are obvious: to change the size of the tree and control vigor; open up the density to permit air circulation and sunlight penetration; and renew branches for the development of blossoms (hence, fruit). Other

Long tree life and high-quality abundant fruiting begins with the basics of pruning.

reasons to prune—to distribute the fruiting wood along the tree branch, minimize limb breakage, and encourage production of large, high-quality fruit—are tree management techniques that contribute to orchard wellness. Spray coverage and ease of harvesting are also enhanced by annual pruning. Another big reward for pruning is rejuvenating ancient neglected apple trees to once again become productive fruit bearers.

A fact which must be carefully considered when developing the tree for fruiting is that apples bear fruit on two-year-old and older growth, not the previous season's growth. Avoid being a "snipper" who every year cuts off the tip growth of each branch, consequently eliminating fruiting branches for the next year. Before making the first pruning cut you should be able to differentiate between the types of apple tree buds. Leaf-producing buds (also called vegetative buds) dominate new growth and lay flat against the branch. Fruiting buds are fatter and slightly raised from the branch on stalks; they will begin to form in two or three years on the young tree.

To prune the apple tree the grower must have hand pruners, loppers, and a folding or straight-blade saw, as well as a pole pruner for tall trees. All tools must be kept clean and very sharp. Be sure to select the proper tool to make the cut, depending on the thickness of the branches. The long handles of loppers give more leverage and can be used to prune branches that are about an inch in diameter or slightly larger (roughly the width of the average thumb). Attempts to use hand pruners or loppers on oversized limbs can damage the tools, making them unusable. Use a saw if the limb is larger than a few inches in diameter.

Pruning cuts

An extremely important aspect of tree management is the type of pruning cut made—heading, thinning, or bench—because the cuts of one year will determine how the tree will leaf out and set fruit in future years. The successful pruner will be constantly aware of the type of branch removal made and its consequences.

A heading cut removes only the terminal portion of a shoot, promoting growth of lower buds, as well as terminal buds below the cut. When cuts are made into one-year-old wood, the limb at the cut is invigorated and the headed branch becomes strong and rigid with prolific lateral secondary branching; when cuts are made into two-year-old or older wood, the laterals are less invigorated and the tree is held within its allocated space. A thinning cut removes an entire shoot back to a side shoot and will not invigorate the tree as much as a heading cut. This cut is particularly useful to permit sunlight and air flow into the tree.

A bench cut, the last resort, removes vigorous, upright-growing shoots back to more horizontally growing branches, opening up the center of the tree and spreading the branches outward. Use bench cuts only when necessary to prevent over-productive branching. The use of limb spreaders is an alternative.

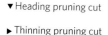
▼ Heading pruning cut

▶ Thinning pruning cut

Training shapes

Free-standing apple trees are generally trained to central leader or modified central leader shape, or occasionally an open center shape. Apple varieties on dwarfing rootstock are trained for imperative support to stakes and wire trellises with numerous design variations; these tree forms demand intense pruning to maximize fruit production and are of greater concern to the commercial grower.

A CENTRAL LEADER is characterized by one main, upright trunk (which is called "the leader") and branches trained around it. Apples and pears, which bear heavy fruit, are often trained to form a central leader. No branch development should be permitted below 3 to 4 feet above ground level to allow for management and air circulation under the tree. The branches can be trained on the leader to be evenly spaced from 4 to 12 inches apart or more, or alternatively, developed in a tiered design. For this adaptation, the first year, three or four branches are selected and should be uniformly spaced around the trunk. In the following years, about 2 feet above the first set of scaffolds, another set is developed until the desired tree height is reached. Maintain open space between limbs and thin secondary branches. As the tree ages, it is possible to switch to a modified central leader.

A MODIFIED CENTRAL LEADER follows the same development as the central leader and is a compromise between the central leader and the open center design. The leader and the scaffold limbs are equally important. When the central leader reaches 8 feet it should be interrupted and four or more evenly spaced scaffolds permitted to grow at this terminus. Modifying the height of the tree will make harvest and general tree management easier.

AN OPEN CENTER is the dominant shape of many stone fruits trees, especially peaches and nectarines, but it can be used for apples that you want to develop maximum color. At the time of planting cut the tree back to 2 to 3 feet above ground level. This will stimulate the development of the top-most buds to form lateral branches. These branches should be 6 to 8 inches apart, evenly spaced around the trunk, and coming out at wide angles. In subsequent years all but the three to five selected scaffolds should be removed as well as any branches that attempt to form a central leader. Limbs are often subject to breaking from heavy fruit loads and thinning is imperative to maintain the shape. The branches should be trained upright to bear the crop weight.

What to remove

Suckers should be removed when small. These buds do not produce quality fruit and a mass of sprouts will develop unless a thinning cut is made.

When you evaluate your apple tree for annual pruning you must be aware of the parts of the tree that you will remove. A good place to start is with suckers, often called water sprouts. These vigorous vegetative shoots are found at the base and in crotches of grafted trees, sometimes growing at right angles to the limbs. Sites of previous pruning cuts will also send out multiple shoots and often must be cut out for a number of years. Suckers have widely spaced buds and are not desirable for propagation except as a last resort. When possible, snip them out when small.

Many types of branches will likely need to be removed. Look for all stubs or broken branches resulting from storm damage, heavy fruit load, and previous improper pruning—these branches may be diseased and should be removed from the orchard. Eliminate crossing branches (which will rub together and injure the bark, inviting insects and diseases); downward-growing branches (which produce few fruit buds and shade and rub more productive scaffold branches); shaded interior branches; and branches with narrow crotches growing more parallel to the main branch. Any competing central leaders should also be removed early in the tree's growth, or, preferably, never allowed to form in the first place.

Although thinning of the fruit is seldom linked to tree pruning, this practice has parallel objectives in terms of enhancing crop production. Thinning will promote optimum growth, improve the fruit quality, increase the tree's vigor, and reduce limb breakage. The objective is to thin the tree so that two apples never touch which can be estimated as the distance between the tips of the thumb and index finger on a spread hand. Fewer large, high-quality apples are more preferable than many small inferior ones so when a very heavy fruit set occurs, you may have to remove as much as three-quarters of the forming apples. This concept is illustrated by an experience my mother once recounted while training a new employee to thin apples on a tree with a very heavy set. The thinner, at the end of the day, proudly announced that the tree was done and asked my mother what tree to do the next day. My mother's response was to thin the same tree again— and pull off just as many apples. Only then, she instructed, would it be just right.

Rejuvenating the Neglected Apple Tree

It takes considerable time, patience, and energy to rejuvenate a long-neglected apple tree, and sometimes, the agonizing decision must be made whether to renovate the tree or remove and replant. Some obvious reasons for removal are if the old tree is diseased or a hazard with falling limbs, or if the tree is a common variety and the fruit is readily available locally. Objectives for renovation include enhancement of the landscape, preservation (for varietal rarity, sentiment, or historical reasons), and the development of a tree for fruit production.

Phases of rejuvenation

After evaluating the tree, you will develop a program to bring the tree back to good health and production over a period of three to five years. The goals of renovation are to control the tree's vigor and size, and to encourage blooming to produce fruit of good quality and size. Since most of the fruiting area of old trees is near the top, the pruning will permit light to penetrate and air to circulate throughout the tree. This will distribute the branches for fruiting throughout the tree, thus lessening limb breakage, increasing spray coverage, and making harvesting easier. For good management, you should avoid massive removal of growth in a single year as that will trigger the tree to produce excess vegetation, only compounding the process.

It will take a long time to repair the tops full of sucker growth on these magnificent ancient Puritan apple trees, but it will be worth the effort.

A good place to begin is by removing any competition for sunlight and nutrients beneath the apple tree, including encroaching species. It is imperative to give the tree breathing room and the maximum sunlight available in order to reduce disease and pest infection. The first phase of pruning—removing dead and diseased limbs, water sprouts, and cross limbs—should take place during the dormant season. Be sure to make these thinning cuts flush with the limb so that you do not leave stubs that can host pests and diseases. The second pruning phase is to bring down the top of the tree, which can be as much as one-quarter of the canopy. Lowering the top will dramatically change the profile of the tree and will be immensely beneficial to the renovation by reducing the potential wind blow over as the tree weakens, and improving accessibility for future management. Conventional pruning must be done each year after the renovation to maintain vigor and production.

Trees fifty years old and older will have extracted most of the natural nutrients from the root zone so extra attention must be given to feeding them. A good method of stimulating adequate new growth is to punch several funnel-shaped holes (at least 6 inches deep) about midway between the drip line and the tree trunk, and fill them with the highest nitrogen-based compost available, like rotted poultry manure or a 20-0-0 synthetic fertilizer. This should be done in the second or third year after pruning. The number of holes should be determined by the size and vigor of the tree; a dozen or more would be a good pilot number on a fifty-year-old tree that is bearing fruit half the normal size with annual growth no more than a few inches.

Weed Control

Along with varmint control, weed control can be a frustrating, overwhelming, and seemingly defeating joy of growing apple trees. It is also controversial, as are most issues that don't have a quick and final answer. These unwanted plants will suck up the nutrients and moisture meant for tree growth, harbor insects and diseases, provide cover and protection from gnawing creatures (like voles), and appear unsightly.

The basic solution is spending long hours physically removing the weeds with your hands and tools, only to be blessed with the rain that brings another crop. The flight from the farm and orchard that began in the late 1940s and early 1950s brought mechanization that—scientifically and politically—revolutionized

Rampant unwanted vegetation under the tree will sap out the nutrients meant for tree growth. Herbicides are the most effective control, but mulching and mowing are also effective practices to suppress weeds.

the farm and orchard cultures of America. Chemicals were available soon after to offer complete eradication.

For those with just a few apple trees, weeds are still one-on-one manageable. But growers with many trees must decide whether to have the necessary human labor or introduce other means of control. Admittedly herbicides, which are carefully formulated to target specific weeds, are the most effective eradication method. However, the combination of mulching and mowing is also a practical solution to suppressing many species of unwanted plants while avoiding chemical agents. Active controls are generally only necessary for the first four years in the life of the apple tree; when the tree begins to bear in the fifth or sixth year, the roots will have penetrated deep enough to not be affected by weed growth.

Pest and Disease Control

Orchard manuals published in 1850 noted just four major pests and diseases to challenge the production of apples. By 1950 forty more were added to the challenge. And since that time—due to global commerce, foreign imports, soil degradation, and the belief that chemicals are the solution—the combat has intensified. Before developing any organic or synthetic chemical based spray program, realize that numerous other measures for pest and disease control can be put in place during the planning and implementation of your orchard, whether it consists of many trees or just a few.

An Integrated Pest Management (IPM) program is a multifaceted method of control based on setting a damage threshold before taking action, identifying and monitoring the pests before using pesticides, preventing pests by the cultural methods of crop rotation, and selecting and planting resistant varieties. Finally, you need to determine the proper control for effectiveness and the degrees of risk. IPM is a major tool for insect control and spray decision making.

As a general rule, the higher the level of pest and disease control, the higher the quality of the apples. But while crops will not be near-perfect unless commercial methods are implemented, less-than-perfect apples can certainly be used to make applesauce, apple butter, dried fruit leather, vinegar, sweet and hard cider, and brandy.

Major apple diseases

Fungal and bacterial diseases can severely damage the apple tree so the grower must be informed and prepared to take action. Above all, it is important to select varieties that are at least moderately resistant to the major apple diseases: apple scab, cedar apple rust, and especially fireblight. Proper pruning of the tree—thinning out branches to permit sunlight and air circulation (so the leaves dry soon after wetting and prevent fungus production)—is another critical practice toward reduction of spray applications. This practice is relevant to combat all the major fungal diseases, along with late-summer diseases like sooty blotch and flyspeck. Some other fungus infections are scab, bitter rot, nectaria twig blight, powdery mildew, cedar apple rust and quince rust. The major apple diseases are described in more detail here.

APPLE SCAB is a fungal disease that defoliates the tree, causes fruit to be misshapen, and affects the stems and twigs. It is the most economically destructive apple disease. The fungus overwinters in infected leaves that have fallen so leaves should be raked and removed from the orchard as a preventive measure. Along with planting scab-resistant varieties, a number of chemicals are available for its suppression.

CEDAR APPLE RUST is a fungal disease occurring east of the Rocky Mountains that defoliates the tree and blemishes the fruit. The trees are infected by spores produced from galls on eastern red cedar trees. When the cedar galls "bloom" (indicated by an orange gelatinous mass) the spores will blow onto the apple tree and infect the leaves, causing small orange spots. Using rust-resistant varieties and removing nearby red cedars will minimize the infection. When planting susceptible varieties you must use a fungicide program with application from tight cluster through first cover spray.

Fireblight—the bane of apple and pear orchards—is very contagious. The infected part should be cut back to healthy tissue, isolated, and removed from the vicinity of the orchard.

FIREBLIGHT is a highly contagious bacterial infection that appears after bloom as blossom blight. In the early stages of infection, the blossoms turn brown or black; the shoot blight phase will come a few weeks after petal fall with the stem tips turning brown or black and bending in the shape of a candy cane. In hot and humid weather, sticky bacterial ooze can be seen on the blighted shoots. The first line of defense against fireblight is to remove infected material; when doing so, be sure to dip the pruners in alcohol between every cut to avoid spreading the disease. I have discovered that collecting the blighted stems and twigs in a black plastic bag and exposing it to the sun for a few weeks will destroy the bacteria so it can then be discarded more comfortably. The chemical approach requires the use of critically timed streptomycin sprays.

Major insect pests

Becoming knowledgeable of the insect pests in the apple orchard is necessary so you can take preventive measures and deal with them when they appear. Possible pests include the European apple sawfly, apple maggots, mites, leaf rollers, aphids, and stinkbugs. The major pests—codling moth, curculio, oriental fruit moth, and San Jose scale—are described here.

CODLING MOTH is capable of producing two or three generations annually. It is a significant pest in the eastern United States but it is even more destructive in the western states. It is the larvae that eat the fruit. Traps with pheromones will not control the codling moth but are an indication of the application time for spraying. The synthetic chemical used to combat codling moth is also used for curculio and apple maggot.

CURCULIO OR PLUM CURCULIO will eat holes through the apple skin to feed on the flesh and the females will leave crescent-shaped marks on the skin when laying eggs. My early orchard schooling for this difficult-to-manage insect came when my father sent me for a bed sheet that we spread under the tree. He instructed me to shake the limbs of the tree above the sheet and as I did, the curculios rained down onto the white cloth. Then, he announced the control method. To the poultry house I went and opened the gate. The flock of hens hopped onto the sheet, devouring every curculio and cocking their heads to ask for another limb shake.

Today toxic sprays are the only total control; no pheromones or dependable monitoring methods are available. However, a bluebird in the apple orchard is more than a romantic notion. If you don't have a flock of chickens to roam the orchard, other large insect predators must be encouraged to become residents. Birds, bats, toads, snakes, lizards, and turtles will reduce varmints both above and below ground.

ORIENTAL FRUIT MOTH was introduced around 1913 from China on a shipment of nursery stock. It was originally considered a major pest of peaches but in more recent times commercial apple production has also been economically affected. The moth produces between three and five generations annually and emerges about the time of apple bloom. The black-headed white larvae enter the fruit of new terminals. Like codling moths, the Oriental fruit moth can be monitored for control by the use of pheromone traps. Also, the parasitic braconid wasp will destroy some of the first two generations.

SAN JOSE SCALE came into California in 1870 on trees imported from China. My grandfather told me that the destruction was rumored to be so severe that it was considered the end of fruit growing in America. Significantly, this was also the beginning of the wholesale manufacture of orchard chemicals that delivered arsenic of lead and DDT across America. Even after the ban, these chemicals were used for insect control in South America and poignantly in Japan, destroying the bee population. Near the beginning of the twentieth century, ladybirds or ladybugs were introduced as method of control; several types of parasitic chalcid wasps have also offered some control in small orchards. Insecticidal sprays can successfully combat overwintering scale, first-flight males, and first-generation crawlers.

Other pests and controls

Deer, squirrels, birds, and other furry varmints above and below ground are a major challenge to the fruit grower. Destruction of the tree and fruit can be diminished by the construction of a mechanical barrier, such as a fence, although breaches should be expected. The fence design and installation must be appropriate for the smaller animals. If you cannot surround the entire orchard with a fence, ring each tree with a fence that is high enough to protect the plant (at least 4 feet tall). After four or five years these individual fences can be recycled to future plantings or shared with a fellow fruit grower. The deer may browse the lower branches but will not destroy the tree. Occasionally, jokingly I will warn the grower not to leave a step ladder in the orchard overnight.

Mechanical exclusion by fence can be augmented by wrapping hardware cloth around the tree trunk. This technique is particularly effective against rodents that can girdle the stem and kill the tree. Opaque coverings should be removed from November to April to inspect for harboring any unwanted insects or their eggs. Another way to discourage pests is to coat the trunk with white latex paint (do not use petroleum-based paint) which may also improve tree health by reflecting the sun and thereby reducing sunscald, a cracking of the bark caused by rapid expansion and contraction.

Netting will discourage birds and some weak-minded squirrels but unless the tree is totally net controlled many varmints will still get to the fruit. Netting is usually made of plastic woven mesh that has openings of various dimensions. Be aware though that netting can also be a hazard to friends of the orchard. Once, a pet black snake named Socrates became entangled and it was only just in the nick of time that I got him out.

Bagging will help improve the fruit finish along with protecting the apple from pests and diseases. The apple should be bagged approximately three weeks after petal fall when fruit is about ¾ of an inch in diameter and should not be removed until a few weeks before harvest. Be aware that apple scab, cedar apple rust, and fireblight will affect the fruit before bagging time and measures to control them must be applied before the apple is bagged. You can use bags designed specifically for the purpose or easily make your own by cutting three-pound paper bags to around 6 inches in length and then cutting a 1½ inch slit on one side into the bag opening. Slide the slit of the bag over the stem, pleat the bag shut, and secure it with a twist tie. About three weeks before harvest remove the bags to allow for some color development.

Harvesting and Storing Apples

So often I am asked, "When do I pick the apples?" and "How do I pick the apples?" There is a temptation to give flippant answers but both are perfectly legitimate questions that I wish would be asked in a pick-your-own operation by those who pull the apple, take a hard look at it and throw it to the ground. If I questioned the wastrel, the reply would be that it didn't look ripe.

The outside appearance of apples is often not an indicator of ripeness or unripeness. The answer is revealed by opening the fruit and examining the color of the seeds. If the seeds are whitish or ivory or undersized, stop picking. When the seeds are mature they will be plump and brown, black, purplish, tan, yellowish, reddish brown, or black, with or without specks and stripes or other markings. If it is the season of that particular variety, cut open another in a few days and see; then, taste.

There is not only variability in each apple that is picked but there is variability in the time that the apple is intentionally removed from the tree. You cannot harvest by the calendar. Growing conditions be it weather, soil, tree condition and health, or unknown factors will make every apple crop different each year. It is ripe for picking when you decide it is ready for immediate eating, processing, or storage for later use. Once the apples are in the kitchen, you can separate the unblemished ones for long storage and use the rest for cooking or processing into apple products such as applesauce. Those that are not used in a few days should be refrigerated properly.

Storage

I have an early orchard memory of piles of apples that looked like giant ant hills beneath the towering trees. These were apples to be stored on site that had been heaped on a bed of straw; later they would be covered with more straw and secured with brush to prevent the straw from blowing away. As the winter season came on, horses pulling low slatted ground slides with wooden runners would take away the apples for either apple butter making or cider pressing. Homesteads also had cellars with dirt floors where the winter apples were stored. They would not freeze and the humidity was high enough to prevent shriveling. Many trips were made down the cellar step to fill a basket woven especially to hold one or two gallons of apples for the evening's festivities.

Apples will store satisfactorily at a temperature around 32 degrees F with about 50 percent humidity; at 40 degrees F the apples will ripen about twice as fast. Relative humidity in modern frost-free refrigerators is low so it is important not to just dump them in the crisper drawer. Good condition can be maintained by putting a small number of apples in a recycled plastic bag, tying the end, cradling the bag in the arm and as it is rotated, punching a dozen or so holes with the thumb. This ensures that a higher humidity is maintained by allowing excess ethylene gas (produced as the apples ripen) to escape while retaining enough moisture to slow down desiccation, the drying out of the apple's water as frequently seen in the wrinkled skin of the Golden Delicious. This bag should be stored in the refrigerator away from the vegetables because escaping ethylene gas will speed their decay and rot. If storing apples in a basement room or an earth floor cellar (you can store around 80 percent of a bushel of apples in one cubic foot of space), the moisture level can be elevated by the use of a humidifier.

There are also commercial cold storages with the apples kept near freezing and with high humidity. Commercial controlled atmosphere (CA) storages reduce the oxygen level and increase the carbon dioxide level. This dramatically slows the ripening process and extends the season of distribution but increases the cost to the consumer.

Some apples are noted keepers for their skin's natural waxing system or for the flavor retained after long storage. But the majority of varieties begin to degrade as soon as stored and effort should be made to consume those apples before any that are known to keep well. However, do not fall victim to selecting only rot spot apples from storage for kitchen use. An old story goes that a child was sent to the cellar to get a pan of apples to bake, with the warning to select only those with rot spots and blemishes. By the next trip the solid ones had developed rot spots, and on and on, so that when the winter was over they had not eaten a single solid apple. Storage in slatted boxes so the apples can breathe will help keep the fruit rot-free.

Propagation

GRAFTING—THE PROCESS TO create an exact reproduction of a plant—has a long and fascinating history. This magical transformation was known in ancient civilizations but the science of it was likely not understood. It was perceived as a mystical act, and the grafter, a manipulator of nature, became an agent of power and authority.

In the first century B.C., Pliny, the Roman naturalist, wrote about the occurrences of natural grafts and described cleft grafting in his *Natural History*. Illustrations of grafting in the third century were depicted in Roman mosaics at Saint-Romain-en-Gal near Vienne, France. Elsewhere in the world, even before the time of Pliny, the early dynasties of China developed sophisticated grafting techniques.

A 1920s-era cleft grafting chisel with a boxwood mallet made in the Burford woodworking shop in the mid-1970s.

From these initial practices of grafting evolved the dynamic world of plant propagation that thrived from the sixteenth century until the middle of the twentieth century. In rural America, children as young as six were taught this great agricultural skill and given a sharp knife to practice. But after World War II this commonplace skill, which had passed from generation to generation, was diminished by the flight from the farm, mechanization and technology, and far-reaching distribution and marketing systems. A generation of fruit tree makers vanished and thousands of varieties disappeared. It was not until the restoration and recreation of orchards at historic sites, and stories resurfaced of the romance of the apple in popular culture, that a demand for uncommon varieties and grafting has once again become vogue.

Grafting Basics

The first question one might ask is: why graft? The simple reason is that apple seeds, when allowed to naturally develop into trees, will not produce the same desirable fruit from which they came. The only way to reproduce a variety is by duplicating or cloning it, which means taking a cutting and grafting it onto another rootstock. Aside from starting a new tree, grafting also facilitates changing the variety on a tree (topworking), putting pollinator limbs on pollen-sterile varieties, producing tree designs (like espaliers), and repairing damaged trees.

The parts required to make an apple tree are a rootstock (a root system) and either a piece of scionwood (scion) or a single bud from a prepared budstick. Rootstocks are usually hybrid plants grown at specialty nurseries (see page 220 for some recommended rootstocks) although it is also possible to use a section of root dug from under an apple tree. The scionwood is a shoot or twig, about ⅜ to ¼ inches in diameter, with buds, that is cut when the tree is dormant. Grafting will only be successful if the scionwood has all vegetative buds, not fruiting buds, so be sure that the scion is cut from the last year of growth (branches that are two years old and older will have both types of buds). A budstick is used for propagating when the weather is warm and must be taken from a tree that is in a state of active growth.

The basic dormant wood grafting process involves cutting the scion section to expose the inactive reproductive cells (cambium) which are then mated to a

▶ A budstick cut during active tree growth to extract a single bud for live wood chip budding.

▼ Rootstocks are most often plants grown at specialty nurseries for making apple trees, but a section of root dug from under an apple tree is also a viable rootstock.

▼▶ Bundles of carefully labeled scionwood to be used for dormant wood grafting with the whip-and-tongue or cleft method.

similar cut on the root system. When the temperature begins to warm, the cambium cells of the two pieces will grow together with the scion buds producing the same fruit as from the tree the buds were taken. In preparation for dormant wood grafting, scionwood is cut during the winter months from the desired variety and stored in a cool but not freezing environment to retard growth until a rootstock is available in late winter or early spring. For live wood grafting, a single bud is extracted from the budstick and then immediately implanted onto another growing plant; because of the higher temperature the cambium cells will immediately begin to reproduce and grow together.

Collecting and storing scionwood

When collecting scionwood try to select bud sections from the middle of the branch. These buds are mature and robust. Sometimes the remaining terminal buds must be used because no others are available. However, some grafters reject these buds because they are succulent and (as the last buds produced from the season) are not always mature. It's important to remember that the young tree will initially grow according to the health and maturity of the grafted buds.

When multiple grafts are planned, the branches should be cut into sticks that are 6, 8, or 12 inches in length for convenience in handling and storage. Leaving two buds on each scion section means you will have enough buds to make two tree grafts. If it is a rare variety or more trees are wanted only one bud can be left, but the risk is that you won't have a backup if it doesn't flourish.

Never collect and use scionwood that is diseased or that has been irreversibly damaged by freezing, drying out, or mechanical crushing. If the scionwood looks healthy but you suspect it to be infected with fireblight or another disease, dip the scions in a solution of one part bleach to nine parts water or rubbing alcohol; allow the material to dry on the bench and then prepare it for storage. This will not eliminate the disease entirely but it will surely lessen the potential for infection.

Be certain to attach a tag or tape onto scionwood sticks or bundles and label each with a permanent ink pen or pencil (pencil markings will not blur out when damp). Place labeled sticks or bundles into a plastic bag and write the variety name on the bag too. Store scionwood above freezing but not over 50 degrees F; your refrigerator should maintain this temperature range. If the scionwood will not be used within a few weeks you can place slightly dampened paper towels in the plastic bag to counteract the moisture that the wood will lose. If you do so, check the wood weekly to make sure it does not become too wet in the bag, causing mold or rot. If droplets of moisture develop you can reverse the bag.

Grafting Tools and Techniques

Along with timing the operation correctly, a successful and pleasurable grafting experience is influenced by the tools used. Most importantly, you will need a knife that is comfortable in your hand. The blade must be thin, 2 to 4 inches long, and sharp as a razor to provide control and a clean cut. A hard-surfaced sharpening stone such as an Arkansas black oil stone or a water stone will, with patience, bring a keen edge. You will also need hand pruners suitable for cutting twigs that are as wide as a pencil; moisture-proof tape (freezer tape works well); and a sealant (grafting seal, wax, glue, or petroleum jelly) to cover all exposed cut surfaces of the graft union where the two parts fit together.

The primary methods of dormant wood propagation are whip-and-tongue grafting and cleft grafting. For cleft grafting, you'll need a few additional tools. If you don't have a grafting chisel for cutting the cleft, a sturdy discarded chef's

Tools for grafting are not specialized and are readily available. From left to right: a sharpening stone, a sharp knife, hand pruners, sealant, and tape.

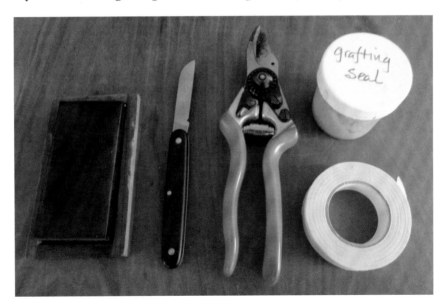

knife with a heavy blade can be substituted. For striking the knife use a wooden mallet or the wooden handle of a hammer; never use a metal hammer that holds the potential to fleck off a metal piece into your eye. A straight screwdriver is needed to permit the insertion of the bud pieces into the cleft.

The main method of live wood propagation is chip budding. An alternate method of live wood propagation called shield budding consists of cutting a "T" slit through the bark at the site selected and inserting a single bud (cut from the variety wanted) beneath the bark so the reproductive cells come together. Today chip budding is the preferred method because it is faster and has a higher success rate.

Dormant wood whip-and-tongue grafting

For this method, you will need a piece of healthy rootstock and a piece of scionwood of approximately the same diameter. This method is known by the alternate name "bench grafting" because the rootstock and scionwood can be brought to a bench to perform the act; or this grafting method can be done outside at the site of the growing plant (in situ) or on a containerized plant.

SHORTENING THE ROOTSTOCK The graft should take place about 2 to 3 inches above the highest roots where there are no buds. Hold the rootstock carefully just above the roots and make a straight or diagonal cut in the selected spot with hand pruners. You can use the top piece of the rootstock to practice your cuts.

MAKING THE WHIP CUT Hold the shortened rootstock with only a few inches of the stem projecting from your hand. Place your knife blade on the stem and set your hands so that you can make a cut that will leave a surface ¾ to 1½ inches long. With the knife firm and comfortable in your hand push the blade through the stem. There will be minimal resistance if the blade is sharp.

MAKING THE TONGUE CUT This second cut will bind the graft and allow for cambium contact. Hold the rootstock with the cut surface facing upward, using your forefinger as support below the new cut. With your other hand, place the knife blade at about one-third the distance from the top of the newly cut surface and at a small angle to bite into the wood. Then pull the knife downward parallel to the back of the stem. The depth of the tongue cut should be at least two-thirds from the tip on the cut surface. The rootstock is now ready for the scion piece.

CUTTING AND SHORTENING THE SCION
Make the same whip and tongue cuts to the scion that you made on the rootstock (I like to call these "mirror cuts"). Be sure to take note of the direction of the buds because they will need to point skyward, away from the rootstock. After making the cuts, use hand pruners to trim the scion to two or three buds; any remaining scionwood should be protected and prepared for storage. Now you are ready to join the two pieces.

JOINING THE PARTS Place the two pieces together, sliding the cut of the scion tongue over the rootstock cut. Work the two slits together carefully. You should be able to slide them down completely. It is imperative that the cambium layers of the two pieces match. If the scion piece is smaller than the rootstock stem, align the pieces along one side of the union site. Any exposed cut area will be covered during the healing process.

WRAPPING THE GRAFT SITE Begin at a point below the root side of the union site and bind the graft with moisture-proof tape. Applying slight pressure, wrap the tape overlapping to a point above the graft union at an upward-spiraling angle. No part of the graft union should be exposed. Cut any surplus tape away and firmly press the tape against the stem.

SEALING THE EXPOSED END CUT Cover the cut tip end of the scion piece with a sealant (grafting seal, wax, glue, or petroleum jelly) to prevent loss of moisture from the new tree. Slide the root system into a plastic bag and secure tightly at the top, or pot up the plant. Let the bagged or potted plant rest for a few weeks in a warm protected place out of direct sun in order to heal and begin growing. Be sure to prepare and attach a label with the variety name and date after completing each graft.

Dormant wood cleft grafting

The objective of cleft grafting is to allow the union of a rootstock limb that is much larger than the scionwood piece. Commercial orchards sometimes use this technique to change the variety of trees that are three or four years old. Cleft grafts are most often performed at the site of the dormant plant before growth begins.

REDUCING THE STEM Select the main stem or scaffold branch of a tree (it should have a diameter in the range of ¾ to 4 inches) and cleanly saw or cut across the stem at a point where it is smooth and free of knots. On a main tree stem, 3 to 5 inches above ground level is appropriate; limbs are more arbitrary and can be from 2 to 12 inches long.

CUTTING THE CLEFT Position a heavy-bladed knife or grafting chisel on the center of the newly exposed cut. Then make a vertical split (cleft) with a wooden mallet or the wooden handle of a hammer as deep as or deeper than the stock diameter to receive the scion piece.

MAKING THE SCION WEDGE CUT Prepare the scionwood piece by making a cut along each side. The cut should be the length of the cleft depth with the outside of the wedge wider than the inside. The wedge cut will concentrate the pressure on the outside at the cambium cell contact point. After making the sloping wedge cuts, reduce the scionwood back to two or three buds above the wedge. If two scion wedges are to be inserted, prepare the second one promptly so it will not dry out.

INSERTING THE SCION Insert the wedge of the grafting tool or wide screwdriver at a right angle into the cleft and turn. This will open the split so you can insert the scion wedge or wedges. Carefully align the cambium layers so that they touch as much as possible.

SEALING THE CUT AREA Cover all exposed surfaces (even the interior of the cleft) with wax or sealant. Be sure that both sides of the cleft are coated as far down as the length of the split. As always, label each graft with the variety name and date. Remember to inspect the coated surfaces regularly and recoat if any cracks develop. If two scions are inserted and both survive, remove the less vigorous of the two when the tree becomes dormant.

Live wood chip budding

This process consists of cutting a single bud from the desired variety near the end of the growing season and implanting it on the stem or limb selected for the site. This budding procedure is usually done in late summer but in the warmer regions of the country it can also be performed in June. In early spring of the following year cut the top just above the top bud to stimulate growth of your new tree.

EXTRACTING THE CHIP Locate a point on your budstick at about ¼ inch below the bud. Then make a cut at a 45 degree angle about ¼ inch through the stock and withdraw the knife. Make another cut to remove the bud by beginning about ½ inch above the bud, moving the knife downward and parallel to the back of the bud. The bud will come free when you intersect with the bottom cut. It will display the green layer of cambium cells near the edge of the bark.

INSERTING CHIP TO STEM Make the same cuts to the stock you are budding at about 4 to 6 inches above the ground. With the bud between your thumb and forefinger match it up with the stock. If the bud is not the same size as the cut, move the bud to one side; it is very important for the cambium cells of the bud and the stem to make contact.

PROTECTING THE BUDDED AREA If you are wrapping the graft with parafilm (as pictured), you can directly cover the buds since they will be able to grow through the material. But if you use another type of binding material (such as budding rubber) you will need to stay clear of the buds. To make a wrap with budding rubber, start with a self-binding loop above the bud followed by three to four wraps, also above the bud. Then move on to below the bud, wrapping two to three times before finishing with a self-binding loop. Remove the wrap after several weeks.

Apple Products

I**N ITS UNALTERED** form, the apple is naturally packaged and one of the most portable major food commodities. But when heat is applied, or when the juice under the skin is extracted, the apple evolves from its natural state into a far-reaching array of products including apple cider, apple butter, apple vinegar, applesauce, dried apples, and apple jelly. This diversity is a testament to the apple's range of expression and transformation.

A hand-cranked cast metal apple peeler from the 1850s.

261

While the popularity of particular apple products has been historically dependent upon region, often reflecting ethnicity and popular culture, it is certainly possible to create any of these in any location, so long as quality fruit and minimal equipment are at hand. Embodying art, science, history, and personal allure, here are four classic ways to transform the apples from the tree.

Apple Cider

The importance of cider in the food culture of America cannot be overemphasized. The first orchards, planted from seeds brought from the Old World to Virginia and Massachusetts early in the seventeenth century, were intended to be exclusively for the production of cider. But with every seed in every apple producing a different apple variety, these orchards became natural laboratories in which, on rare occasion and by genetic randomness, the classic American dessert apple was created.

The intense smell of cider permeated the dirt cellars of farmsteads and the cavernous apple and cider houses of America until the middle of the twentieth century. Unlike harness making, cooperage, or blacksmithing, cider was a dynamic and fluid enterprise—a renewable sale commodity and a universal barter item. For many years, the annual production of cider was consumed and the same or greater sales were expected the following year. But after the enactment of Prohibition in 1919, the flight from rural America after World War II, and the introduction of other beverages—especially the rapid rise of the soft drink industry—cider production and its culture diminished and all but disappeared. Its use for barter, vinegar making, and paying wages and taxes went with it.

As a ten-year-old boy at the end of World War II, I remember cider makers and orchardists lamenting, often in disgust, another major reason for the shambles of the cider industry: the indiscriminate selection of varieties for cider making without regard to the apple's balance of acid, tannin, and sugar. This accusation was especially directed at the popular and overplanted Red Delicious, likely one of the worst varieties that could be used. The surplus production of vile cider made from Red Delicious apples was responsible from turning the next generation away from this natural fruit drink to a beverage manufactured by the soft drink industry. The pride of many cider makers was defiled.

This elegant backyard cider house exemplifies the pride and the importance the new world of cider has engendered.

Happily, in the twenty-first century we are on the threshold of the emergence of a new cider industry that is focused on high-quality regional selection, and diversity from dozens of varieties—not only varieties rescued from our past cider heritage but newly developed modern varieties with cider merit. The selection of varieties is a major agent in producing memorable cider. Few apples alone contain all of the basic elements to make exceptionally tasting cider—sugar, tannin, and acid—so a combination of varieties is typically used. The rare varieties that will singly produce an acceptable and sometimes memorable cider include Roxbury Russet, Golden Russet, Newtown Pippin, and Harrison. You can explore some of my favorite American apples for making cider on page 279, but keep in mind that the particular growing season will determine the quality of flavor and it will vary from year to year. Remember too that the juice of wild or unnamed variety apples also makes good, sometimes very good, cider.

Making cider

Apples for cider making should be harvested when fully ripe and then washed in a bucket, tub, or under running water to remove stick, stones, dirt, and inert objects. The yeasts will come from other sources so don't be concerned about washing it away. Rotten apples should be removed—if you wouldn't eat it, don't put it in your cider to drink—but those with bruises or small rot spots are acceptable. Unless using a commercial press, apples should be chopped into pieces as whole apples do not "bite" as rapidly in the smaller backyard presses.

The next part of the procedure is to grind and press the apples. This can be done in a variety of ways depending on the equipment available. It could be as simple as pounding the apples to release the juice in a large hollowed-out half log, as done in the early seventeenth century in Jamestown, Virginia; as ingenious as repurposing a contraption (think leaf shredder or car jack) instead of buying a conventional apparatus; or as specialized as purchasing automated equipment for hundreds or thousands of dollars. Most beginning cider makers will pursue the middle way of home cider presses. From barns, garages, and farm outbuildings, the cast iron and wooden post relics of the former cider world are being dragged and cleaned and repaired to once again flow with apple juice. The photographs show a mill design popular from the mid-nineteenth century until the

The apples before and after grinding.

The apple pulp is pressed and the juice flows.

mid-twentieth century—the heyday and golden era of cider making in America. That culture has yet to be recaptured but these venerable mills are reappearing and launching a new cider making era.

The objective of grinding or milling is to reduce the apple pieces to about the size of peas or small marbles. If the pieces are too large, all the available juice will not be extracted and the yield will be low; if pieces are too small, they will squeeze through the cloth into the juice. Once the apples have been reduced to pulp, they are ready to be pressed by a plate that lowers from the top of the apparatus with a screw mechanism to give hydraulic pressure. The liquid then flows from the press, capturing the natural yeast from the air and beginning the fermentation process. At this point the liquid can be defined as sweet cider. If the cider is immediately taken from the press and fermentation is interrupted (either by pasteurization or the addition of chemical agents) then you will have apple juice. Only when the yeasts in the cider convert all of the sugar to alcohol does it become hard cider or "real cider," as Ben Watson, cider authority and author of *Cider: Hard and Sweet*, has aptly deemed it. To make real cider with good taste and keeping quality, controlled fermentation is necessary. The process is complex but a number of reference books are available and shops that sell supplies to make cider, beer, and wine often conduct workshops and classes or can usually recommend sources.

If unfermented cider is the goal, simply pour the juice into plastic jugs and consume immediately, freeze for preservation (leaving space in the top of the jug), or pasteurize by heating the capped containers (with about an inch of head room) in a water bath until the temperature reaches 170 degrees F; be sure to maintain this temperature for thirty minutes to destroy any unwanted organisms which would spoil the juice.

The juice-extracted pulp that is left at the end of cider making is known as pomace (or sometimes "cheese" because of its shape) and was traditionally fed to livestock or spread beneath fence rows for weed suppression. A few years later the pomace-strewn rows would profusely sprout apple seedlings which could be dug out in late spring for grafting.

Apple Vinegar

In late summer it was a treat to visit the "pickle room" beneath the laundry house on my grandparents' mountain farm and sample the pickles brining in variously sized stone crocks lined out on the creek gravel floor. My small hand would dive beneath the grape leaves covering the hundreds of curing pickles and draw back a green treat and a vinegar-coated fist. The first act of the childhood pickle-eating ritual was to lick the apple cider vinegar from the hand. How deliciously tart and pleasantly acidic it was, preparing the mouth for the half-brined cucumber to come.

Today, manufactured vinegar would have brought heaves to the body and wild spitting to clear the mouth. The dictum of the Burford vinegar evaluation was "if you cannot swallow and enjoy it, use it for cleaning" and jugs of vinegar were a common fixture in barns and other out buildings. Occasionally, a barrel or stone crock would produce exceptionally good-tasting vinegar and it was set aside for the vinegar cruets and bragged about to the table guests.

Vinegar making is an ancient art and science—the word "vinegar" comes from a French term, *vin aigre*, meaning "soured wine"— consisting of two distinct fermentation processes which must be carefully monitored and controlled. In the first stage, the yeast converts the natural sugar of sweet cider into alcohol; in the second, the acetobacter converts the alcohol into acetic acid. Although the main ingredient of vinegar is acetic acid, acetic acid singly is not vinegar. Vinegar contains vitamins and other compounds, like riboflavin, amino acids, and Vita-min B-1. Above all, vinegar has flavor and is often further enhanced with herbs and spices.

Making apple vinegar

Kitchen countertop or basement work table vinegar can be simply made, but just keep a few things in mind before getting started. The first is that certain variet-ies of apples will produce noteworthy vinegars. My family had two special ones: Horse Apple and Calville Blanc d'Hiver, the classic French dessert apple. If the cider you are using for fermentation has been made with a combination of good cider making varieties (Winesap, Grimes Golden, and Roxbury Russet, among others), then you will likely get a good vinegar. Also note that the environment for vinegar making should be as isolated from cider making as practical to prevent cross contamination of the acetobacter essential to make vinegar.

To begin the fermentation process, insert an air lock (available from wine and beer supplies outlets) into the mouth of a jug of sweet cider. As an alternative to using an air lock, you can place one end of a short section of clear plastic hose about halfway into the jug, seal the opening with duct tape, and place the other end of the hose nearly to the bottom of a glass of water adjacent to the jug. With either air lock or hose in place, nothing will be able to get in and only the fermen-tation bubbles can escape under the water. When the strange gurgling stops (usu-ally within a couple of weeks), this is an indicator that all of the apple's natural sugar has been converted to alcohol.

At this point you can pour the hard cider into a non-corrosive pan, such as glass or stone crockery, and cover it with thin cheesecloth which will exclude dirt but permit oxygen access to the liquid. As the conversion to acetic acid develops, a bacterial slime (the "mother") will form on top of the liquid from the fermenta-tion. The slime is bland tasting and harmless and will be present in all unfiltered vinegars. Commercial vinegar is pasteurized and filtered to make it more appeal-ing to the consumer, but the natural ingredients and integrity of the substance is lost in the processing.

The total time to convert hard cider to vinegar with a 4 to 5 percent acid content will take anywhere from a few weeks to a few months depending on the environment and the condition of the liquid. An ideal liquid temperature (70 to 80 degrees F) will convert the alcohol in the cider to acetic acid at around

1 percent per week; a cooler temperature will take longer but will produce the same product. The old-fashioned technique used by my family to measure the vinegar's acidity was to call in a neighbor farmer—a self-proclaimed expert. He would jab a tasting stick through the bung hole coarsely covered with burlap and into the white oak barrels. After tasting the sample he would pompously assess the state of the vinegar, even assigning an acetic acid percentage without scientific support. If you are seeking a more accurate means of measurement, you can purchase pH test strips that match acidity to color. The desired pH of undiluted apple cider vinegar is typically in the range of 4.25 to 5.00.

The vinegar-making process can be accelerated by saving a pint or quart of the completed vinegar with the "mother" as a starter for the next batch. You can also make a mother by putting some pomace or pome (the apple residue that remains in the cider press after pressing) into a shallow bucket, fermenting it for a few weeks in a warm place out of the sunlight, and then straining the liquid through cheesecloth; the gelatinous mass that remains is the mother.

Apple Butter

Making apple butter, once defined as "apples, a big pot, and lots of patience," was an annual autumn ritual before the first snows fell. Every homestead that had a brass, copper, or iron kettle took part and competition was fierce—sometimes even including neighborhood clashes. The most memorable yelling match I witnessed, between two ladies of the community dressed in pillbox hats and white gloves, took place during a local church fundraiser. It came as no surprise that their argument hinged on the amount of spices to use and when they should be added to the kettle. My mother later described it as "a hair's breadth of becoming a hair pulling," but fortunately the preacher interceded. The two matrons would not speak to each other again for a few weeks, resulting in my teenage realization that adults really do sometimes behave or misbehave as children. And that apple butter making can be a dangerous affair.

In the apple-abundant foothills of the Blue Ridge Mountains of Virginia, families dating back three, four, or five generations always claimed that their particular combination of sweet and tart varieties made the best apple butter.

It is apple butter time. In a fifty-gallon copper kettle the apples will cook throughout the day, a dawn-to-dark operation.

Regardless of the combination, two basic caveats should be heeded: never use Red Delicious and avoid juicy apples which take longer to cook down. Some favorite varieties were Newtown Pippin, Golden Delicious, Grimes Golden, Idared, Jonathan, Stayman, Winesap, York, and, especially in southwestern Virginia, the Limbertwigs. For many years until his death, a friend and fellow Virginian apple enthusiast would send me a homemade jar of apple butter made solely with Limbertwigs. On the lid was a label that read: *Warning: Stand Back When Opening!* Popping the lid would fill the room with a lingering apple aroma, a testament to selection of the proper apple.

Apple butter was traditionally made solely from the sweetest apple variety available with cider to lubricate it during cooking. In order to incorporate tarter varieties for distinctive tastes, boiled cider was used to enhance the sweetness. Making boiled cider is a somewhat arduous process in which cider made from apples with high sugar content (like Grimes Golden or Golden Delicious) is boiled until the volume is reduced to half. Small jars and crocks of boiled cider filled the pantry for use in general cooking and apple butter making until the end of the nineteenth century when this sweetener was abandoned (along with honey) in favor of granulated sugar, and later, gallon cans of applesauce and cinnamon red hots. Recently, the use of boiled cider in apple butter has been making a comeback due to its all-natural qualities and the rediscovery of its intensely sweet apple flavor and aroma.

Kettles, cradles, paddles, and peelers

Designed with a rounded seamless bottom to permit greater exposure to the fire beneath, kettles were historically made from brass. Copper is now the prevalent metal for construction because it is a better conductor of heat. The capacity varies from a few gallons to fifty gallons. Seasoned apple butter makers stressed two major demands about the kettle: cleanliness (before and after use) and security. The cleanliness can be achieved by scouring the kettle with a mixture of vinegar and salt. And on the farm I lived on as a boy the kettles were locked in the smokehouse with the cured meat, although an unsecured one was occasionally stolen to fabricate a brandy still.

A cradle, traditionally crafted from iron or steel in local blacksmith shops, supports the kettle just above its curved bottom and raises it a foot or so above the burning fire. In earlier times, the kettle was suspended by a heavy chain from a sturdy tree limb with the fire built on the ground. There is an art to fire management which involves finding the right balance between flaming and smoldering. A high flaming fire would elicit comments from a visiting neighbor that "the butter is getting close to hell." Certain wood species, like Osage orange wood or sourwood, were favored and bragged to give more heat. Before it became popular for smoking meat on the grill, the wood from old apple trees was also used and known to give intense heat.

Paddles for stirring were made often by the local carpenter. They came in diverse forms but usually had a long handle (up to 16 feet in length, or approximately as long as the kettle was deep) to keep the stirrer away from the heat, smoke, and spitting and spluttering sauce in the kettle; sometimes stirrers with longer handles had a diagonal brace for support. In early American apple culture it was said that only wood should touch the apple, hence the proliferation of wooden shovels, rakes, scoops, double-handled apple barrows, and apple butter paddles and stirrers. The head or foot of these apple butter utensils were often made of durable and food-friendly wood (apple, maple, birch, persimmon, or sassafras) and the handles were made of a lightweight wood like poplar. The bottom of the paddle was rounded to match the shape of the kettle's bottom and it was drilled with four or six holes to accelerate the flow of butter when stirring.

Early in the twentieth century, technological advances came to apple peeling with cast-iron hand-cranked apple peelers. Today peelers are generally available in less sturdy materials with enhancements that will peel, core, and spiral cut the apple. If you plan to use it often, choose the sturdiest peeler you can find in the marketplace; the clamp-on model is more dependable than the suction cup type.

Making apple butter

Prize-winning apple butters are made from the finest fully ripened apples, either singly or in combination, cooked with a proven recipe which has often evolved throughout generations of practice. Although the specific methods of apple butter making are numerous, it can be safely said that one must always start with the apples. For a twenty-five gallons batch, you will need approximately seven bushels of washed apples, as well as about fifty pounds of white sugar and about ten pounds of brown sugar. Most of the apple preparation (cutting out the rots, removing the stems, and peeling and quartering the apples) should be done the day before the making. Unless the prepared apples will be used immediately, put them in a plastic trash bag and store it in a cool place until you are ready to dump the apples in the kettle.

The tradition of adding pennies to the bottom of the kettle before the ingredients has a few variations and explanations. Some recommended adding a solitary penny to generate friction as it was paddled around while others felt a handful of the coins better served the same purpose. A more mystical justification for adding pennies was to give back to the kettle the copper lost by the paddle scraping. For this reason it's worth noting that pennies produced prior to 1983 were 95 percent copper, but those produced after are 97.5 percent zinc with only a thin copper coating.

With pennies added or not, the kettle should be filled about two-thirds of way with the prepared apples and covered with either water or sweet cider or a combination of the two. Some makers wait until the kettle is filled before starting the fire and beginning to stir, but veteran makers will risk the early stick in order to have the fire going and some water and cider heating in the kettle before adding the apples. Paddle movement will face resistance at the beginning so a short-handled paddle is sometimes used just until the chunks soften. As the apples break up, continue to add more apples to the kettle. You can control the consistency by adding water or cider if the sauce becomes too thick. Just use caution because adding too much liquid will extend the cooking time.

In teaching new stirrers one must be dictatorial and threatening. Exclamations to be repeated over and over include "the paddle is never still," "keep it moving," and also "let it burn and you will dump it for all to see." Some makers choose to give unwavering instructions on how the paddle should move through the kettle (for instance: twice around left and once through the middle, then twice around right and once through the middle). My family subscribed to a freer pattern and told new stir apprentices only to be creative and cover the kettle bottom. This omission of specific instructions was horrifying to certain neighbors.

The time to start adding the sugar, little by little, is when the apple butter begins to thicken. The total cooking time varies but usually all of the sugar should be added after about six hours, and after eight hours all of the apples should be incorporated. If you are using boiled cider, add it about an hour before the estimated completion. Hot apple butter tastes sweeter than cold apple butter so if it tastes too sweet when hot, then it may be just right for those that prefer sweet apple butter; those with a tart palate should add sugar judiciously and taste more frequently.

The spices should be added near the very end of cooking since excessive heat will change and degrade the flavor of cinnamon and cloves. You can test the apple butter for doneness before adding the spices by putting a tablespoon on a plate and noting if it "weeps." If no rim water forms around the dollop, it is ready for the spices; if a rim of water forms, continue cooking. Another indicator of doneness is color. This will vary depending on the varieties used, but generally speaking, the redder the better. At this point you are likely tired from the long day, but a few more minutes of cooking can make a remarkable difference in quality and taste. Remember: patience is an absolute necessity for the successful apple butter maker.

The exact amount of cinnamon and clove spices depends on personal preference and the flavor of the apples. A twenty-five gallon batch, for example, might require as much as a cup of cinnamon, but it's a good idea to add half that amount, taste, and then add more if desired. Mix the cinnamon before it goes in the kettle with an equal amount of granulated sugar. Red hots, the cinnamon-flavored candy, are often added to enhance the cinnamon flavor and augment the reddish color. Cloves will affect the flavor more than cinnamon so it's advisable to start small (perhaps a quarter cup) and then taste. If you are using liquid spices, follow the directions very carefully. After spices are added, continue to cook for about ten or fifteen minutes to disperse thoroughly.

The methods of apple butter storage have shifted throughout time. Until the late nineteenth century American coopers made small white oak barrels of a few gallons capacity to store and ship apple butter. Then, until the middle of the twentieth century, hot apple butter was stored in three- to five-gallon stone crocks sealed over with beeswax or paraffin. Nowadays apple butter is typically ladled into canning jars and lidded. If the butter is very hot the jars will likely seal automatically; place jars that do not seal into a hot water bath for ten minutes or so to get that long-awaited popping sound. Any unsealed apple butter can be refrigerated and eaten first.

Dried Apples

Thousands of years ago, pieces of fruit were inadvertently left in the sun and later discovered to be edible and tasty in their dehydrated state. Although advances in technology eventually brought more convenient methods—kitchen stove oven drying and a specialized contraption called a dehydrator—solar drying is still a viable, if time consuming, option.

The tin-roofed chicken houses on the farm of my youth were built on a slope with the roost pole and door on the low side: these were the drying roofs for peaches, apples, and pears. An occasional hen attempting to have a feast of drying fruit had to be shooed off the short flat-stepped ladder which had been built to reach the roof. During the hot days of late August and into late September I was responsible for putting out the many hardware cloth trays of fruit when the sun was up, covering them with cheesecloth, and taking them in at sunset. At the end of each day, once inside and protected, the thousands of slices had to be turned. The most nerve-wracking aspect was anticipating storms that suddenly appeared in the mountains, as the quick transfer of trays that followed was a precarious act for short arms and short legs.

Although I do recall exclamations of dire consequences for failure to perform the chore, my greater motivation was the daily reward of a single slice of apple. After the ceremonial consumption, I reported my evaluations on the state of dryness to a mealtime audience. It certainly raised my self-esteem.

Apples are dried not only to preserve them from decay but also to experience the distinct flavor that each variety expresses. Dried apple slices consumed as is or rehydrated by soaking in a liquid (and then eaten raw or cooked in a recipe) express a broad taste spectrum. I have known tasters to like the dried apple but not a fresh slice of the same and vice versa. Exceptional varieties for drying that I have known since childhood include Black Gilliflower, Ben Davis, Maiden Blush, Stayman, Winesap, and Winter Banana—but any apple can be dried and by sampling you will find a few favorites of your own. Note that juicier apples will require a longer drying time, but don't disregard an apple just because of this factor. Like fresh apples, the choice should be determined by the taste after the moisture is removed. The same is true of the ultimate color of the slices. A dark hue has no bearing on how delicious it will taste: eat with the mouth and not the eyes.

Drying your own

Along with far superior flavor, a price comparison with commercially produced dried apples will prove that drying your own is a real bargain. With practice you will learn how many apples it takes to fill your drying trays, but in general about ten pounds of apples makes about four cups of dried apple pieces.

The apples should be washed regardless of whether you plan to leave the skin on or peel them. Do not assume that the skin is clean just because the apples have never been sprayed because "air dirt" accumulated on the skin can contaminate the peeled flesh and give the slices an off taste. You can peel apples with a knife or use an apple peeler (which will also core and spiral slice). When cutting apples, be aware that moisture will evaporate faster from thinner slices and thick slices tend to remain chewier. Any thickness from $1/8$ to $1/4$ inch will dry in a reasonable amount of time. When using an apple peeler, cut the spirals into flat slices before spreading the prepared apple slices, not touching, onto the pan, screen, or tray.

If you are using a dehydrator, set the temperature to around 150 degrees for the first two or three hours and then reduce it to 130 degrees until the slices are soft and pliable with no moisture in the center. The time to completely remove the moisture in the slices varies depending on the apparatus design, the amount the slices are turned, the apple variety, and especially the thickness of the slices, but it will generally take between three and five hours. In the stove oven, set the temperature to around 140 degrees and keep the door ajar. A stove ventilator fan will expel extra moisture as it is extracted from the slices. It should take six to twelve hours to dry the apples in a stove oven; be sure to turn the slices every three or four hours.

For solar or sun drying, lay out the slices not touching on screens (perforated to permit bottom-drying exposure) and cover with a thin fabric such as cheese-cloth to keep debris and insects off the slices. Black muslin cloth (available from upholstery shops which use it for dust covers under chair seats) also works well, protecting the apples while simultaneously absorbing heat. The drying process typically takes two to four days when the sun is at full brightness and tempera-tures are in the nineties. Turn the slices every two to four hours during the first day of drying and after that at least every four hours until there is no moisture in the center of the slices. Trays should be brought inside at sunset and returned to their drying position around middle morning.

Test slices for dryness by filling a clear container with some slices and secur-ing the lid tightly. If moisture accumulates inside the jar after a few days, dry the slices further. After drying, let the slices condition for about a week before pack-aging them in tightly sealed bags or airtight containers. Dried apples will store for a number of years properly bagged and kept on a cool and dark shelf, but I rec-ommend freezing slices if you do not plan to use them within six to nine months, otherwise they will begin to discolor (unless they have been treated with ascorbic acid) and the flavor will also begin to slowly degrade.

Before making pies, cakes, cookies, and cobblers with dried apple slices, you'll need to put moisture back into the flesh by soaking the slices until they are saturated. I often use cider, fresh or fermented, from the bottles always nearby on the kitchen counter. Other fruit juices can also be used although the flavor will be altered. Occasionally, I have tried apple brandy with remarkably pleasing results. When making cakes and cookies you can snip the slices into small pieces to lessen the saturation time. Rehydration methods besides soaking include steaming the slices for a short time before use (best for cakes and cookies) or boiling the slices in water or cider. When boiling, use one cup of liquid to one cup of fruit for the right consistency. Do not add any sugar during the rehydration as this will block absorption of water.

RECOMMENDED USES OF APPLE VARIETIES

BIBLIOGRAPHY

HELPFUL CONVERSIONS

PHOTOGRAPHY CREDITS

ACKNOWLEDGMENTS

INDEX

Recommended Uses of Apple Varieties

FROM THE VAST ocean of available heirloom and modern varieties, those listed here were selected from personal experience and recipes inherited over my more than three-quarters of a century in the apple world. With taste tweaking and adventure in mind, I encourage embracing change and fluidity. Those you discover and prefer can be added to your own list and you are welcome to plunge some on my list to the bottom as unworthy. That is the joy and prerogative of taste.

For any apple dish you can combine the inherent characteristics of apple varieties for nuances of flavor. This should be particularly noted when baking pies or making cider; for a better balance of acid, sugar, tannin, and flavor combine two or more varieties.

APPLE BUTTER VARIETIES	APPLESAUCE VARIETIES	BAKING VARIETIES
Grimes Golden	Bailey Sweet	Buckingham
Hoover	Cameo	Idared
Idared	Early Harvest	Johnson's Fine Winter
Parmar	Fallawater	Jonathan
Pumpkin Sweet	Idared	King David
Red Limbertwig	Jonathan	Newtown Pippin
Stayman	Lodi	Porter
Swiss Limbertwig	Milton	Rome Beauty
Wagener	Mollies Delicious	Wolf River
Winesap	Parmar	York
Winter Sweet Paradise	Pink Pearl	
Wolf River	Wagener	
Yates	Wealthy	
	Yellow Bellflower	

CIDER VARIETIES

Arkansas Black

Baldwin

Ben Davis

Black Oxford

Black Twig

Burford Redflesh

Chestnut Crab

Empire

Esopus Spitzenburg

Fall Russet

Fall Wine

Golden Delicious

Golden Russet

Goldrush

Grimes Golden

Harrison

Honey Cider

Honeycrisp

Hyslop

Idared

Jonagold

Jonathan

King David

Liberty

Macoun

McIntosh

Newtown Pippin

Northern Spy

Parmar

Ralls

Raven

Razor Russet

Redfield

Roxbury Russet

Smith Cider

Smokehouse

Stayman

Tompkins County King

Whitney Crab

Wickson Crab

Winesap

Yates

York

DESSERT VARIETIES WITH DISTINCTIVE FLAVOR

Black Twig

Cole's Quince

Esopus Spitzenburg

Granite Beauty

Hawaii

King David

Mother

Newtown Pippin

Red Limbertwig

Spice of Old Virginia

Stayman

Westfield Seek-No-Further

Wickson Crab

Winesap

DRYING VARIETIES

Ben Davis

Benham

Black Gilliflower

Black Oxford

Cauley

Goldrush

Keener Seedling

Maiden Blush

Raven

Rome Beauty

Spice of Old Virginia

Spokane Beauty

Vine

Westfield Seek-No-Further

Wolf River

Yates

York

FRYING VARIETIES

Benham

Early Harvest

Grimes Golden

Kinnaird's Choice

Northern Spy

Rhode Island Greening

Smokehouse

Stayman

Summer Banana

PICKLING VARIETIES

Chestnut Crab

Hyslop Crab

Whitney Crab

Wickson Crab

Yates

PIE MAKING VARIETIES

Arkansas Black

Baldwin

Cameo

Ginger Gold

Golden Delicious

Golden Russet

Goldrush

Green Pippin

Idared

Jonathan

Magnum Bonum

Melrose

Newtown Pippin

Northern Spy

Northwest Greening

Porter

Ralls

Rhode Island Greening

Roxbury Russet

Smokehouse

Stayman

Wealthy

Winesap

Yellow Bellflower

York

VINEGAR MAKING VARIETIES

Horse

Newtown Pippin

Redfield

ORNAMENTAL VARIETIES

Burford Redflesh

Chestnut Crab

Hoople's Antique Gold

Hyslop Crabapple

Redfield

Whitney Crab

LONG COMMON STORAGE VARIETIES

Arkansas Black

Ben Davis

Bentley

Bethel

Black Oxford

Black Twig

Cannon Pearmain

Honeycrisp

Goldrush

Keener Seedling

Keepsake

Kentucky Limbertwig

Newtown Pippin

Northern Spy

Pilot

Red Limbertwig

Shockley

Waltana

Willow Twig

Winesap

York

LOW-CHILL VARIETIES FOR WARM REGIONS

Buckingham

Ginger Gold

Hoover

Reverend Morgan

Smith Cider

Summer Champion

Tenderskin

Yellow Bellflower

LATE-BLOOMING VARIETIES FOR FROST ZONES

Gano

Gilpin

Ingram

Kinnaird's Choice

Macoun

Northern Spy

Ralls

Rome Beauty

Tolman Sweet

Winesap

Bibliography

Alwood, William Bradford. 1901. *Orchard Studies* Bulletin No. 130. Blacksburg, VA: Virginia Agricultural Experiment Station.

Alwood, William Bradford. 1903. *A Study of Cider Making in France, Germany, and England with Comments and Comparisons on American Work.* Washington DC: Government Printing Office.

Alwood, William Bradford, R. J. Davidson, and W. A. P. Moncure. 1904. *The Chemical Composition of Apples and Cider.* USDA, Bureau of Chemistry, Bulletin no. 88. Washington DC: Government Printing Office.

Bailey, L. H. 1922. *The Apple-Tree.* New York: Macmillan.

Beach, S. A. 1905. *The Apples of New York*, vol. 1 and 2. Albany, NY: J. B. Lyon Company, Printers.

Burford, Tom. 1960-1991 Journal. *Apples: A Catalog of International Varieties.* Privately printed.

Burford, Tom and Ed Fackler. 2001. *Fruit Grafters Handbook.* Lynchburg, VA: The Design Group.

Calhoun, Creighton Lee. 2010. *Old Southern Apples: A Comprehensive History and Description of Varieties for Collectors, Growers, and Fruit Enthusiasts.* White River Junction, VT: Chelsea Green Publishing.

Cole, S. W. 1849. *The American Fruit Book.* Boston, MA: John P. Jewett; New York: C. M. Saxton.

Coxe, William. 1817. *A View of the Cultivation of Fruit Trees.* Philadelphia: M. Carey and son.

Downing, Andrew Jackson. *Fruits and Fruit Trees of America: Or, the Culture, Propagation, and Management, in the Garden and Orchard, of Fruit Trees Generally.* Multiple editions, 1845–1900. New York: J. Wiley.

Hanson, Beth, ed. 2005. *The Best Apples to Buy and Grow (Brooklyn Botanic Garden All-Region Guide)*. Printed by Science Press, a division of Mack Printing Group.

Hatch, Peter J. 1998. *The Fruits and Fruit Trees of Monticello*. Charlottesville: The University Press of Virginia.

Hovey, Charles Mason. 1852. *The Fruits of America*. New York: D. Appleton & Co.

Kenrick, William. 1842. *The New American Orchardist*. Boston: Otis, Broaders, and Company.

Manhart, Warren. 1995. *Apples for the Twenty-First Century*. Portland, OR: North American Tree Co.

Phillips, Michael. 1998. *The Apple-Grower: A Guide for the Organic Orchardist*. White River Junction, VT: Chelsea Green Publishing.

Pliny the Elder. 1855. *The Natural History*. Translated by John Bostock and H.T. Riley. London: Taylor and Francis.

Watson, Ben. 2009. *Cider, Hard and Sweet: History, Traditions, and Making Your Own*. Woodstock, VT: The Countryman Press.

Yepsen, Roger B. 1994. *Apples*. New York: W. W. Norton.

Helpful Conversions

INCHES	CM
¼	0.6
½	1.3
¾	1.9
1	2.5
2	5.1
3	7.6
4	10
5	13
6	15
7	18
8	20
9	23
10	25

FEET	M
1	0.3
2	0.6
3	0.9
4	1.2
5	1.5
6	1.8
7	2.1
8	2.4
9	2.7
10	3
20	6
30	9
40	12
50	15
100	30
1,000	300

TEMPERATURES

$$°C = \tfrac{5}{9} \times (°F - 32)$$

Photography Credits

All photos by the Design Group unless otherwise noted below.

Shauna James Ahern: page 219.

Tom Burford: pages 215, 216, 226, 233, 234, 235, 237, 251 (bottom left and right), 253, 263, 265, 269.

Giorgio Fochesato/iStock: pages 210–211.

James Henderson: pages 251 (top), 254, 255, 256, 257, 258, 259, 264.

John Hoskins: pages 223, 227, 228, 229, 240, 242.

Marci Hunt LeBrun: pages 2, 6, 224, 248, 260.

Shawn Linehan: pages 5, 14–15, 212, 276–277.

Kim Raff: page 8.

Ben Watson: pages 11, 239.

Acknowledgments

THE DESIGN GROUP of Lynchburg, Virginia—with my friend Nancy Blackwell Marion, the founder and principal, and Blanks Blankinship, the photographer—skillfully captured the look of "real" apples. They were also patient with the logistics of delivering fruit collected throughout North America. Photographers Shauna James Ahern, James Henderson, John Hoskins, Marci Hunt LeBrun, Shawn Linehan, Kim Raff, and Ben Watson collectively helped make this book a visual treat.

Thank you to those who generously provided apples for photographing: Cindy and Tim Ward of Eastman's Antique Apples in Wheeler, Michigan; Ben Watson, friend and fellow explorer, who rambled New England apple country to collect at-risk varieties of merit; and Carlos and Mavis Manning, rescuers and propagators of many "misplaced" apples varieties in West Virginia.

My friend Roger Swain whispered (and surely sometimes yelled) in certain ears that "Tom Burford is getting old and needs to do this now." Thanks a lot, Roger; I really needed the literary kick. At Timber Press, Juree Sondker set the guidelines for bringing forth this book, and editor Mollie Firestone maintained unwavering warmth and professionalism.

To the apple pioneers of the twentieth century who laid the path toward the new apple culture in America, we owe recognition and gratitude. Some that I personally knew were Robert Nitschke of Michigan's Southmeadow Fruit Gardens; Henry Morton of Tennessee, the savior of many Limbertwigs; and my fellow Virginian, Professor Elwood Fisher of Harrisonburg, who once astounded the apple world with his backyard collection. To the hundreds of unnamed others who contributed to this book—I will always be appreciative. As you read, you will discover that you are a part of it.

Above all, I would like to recognize the countless participants in my workshops, seminars, and lectures throughout the last five decades. So many have embraced the art and science of grafting, the satisfaction in bringing a new crop to the cellar, and the delight of sharing the harvest.

Index

Bold page numbers indicate main apple entries.